THE ONES THAT GOT AWAY?

Memorable Murder Acquittals

David Beckett

Published by Sigma Leisure – an imprint of
Sigma Press, 1 South Oak Lane, Wilmslow, Cheshire SK9 6AR, England.

British Library Cataloguing in Publication Data
A CIP record for this book is available from the British Library.

ISBN: 1-85058-466-4

Typesetting and Design by: Sigma Press, Wilmslow, Cheshire.

Printed by: MFP Design & Print

Cover illustration: The Agency, Wilmslow

Preface

Have some people really got away with murder? Clearly, in cases where the killer was never apprehended, the answer is yes. Does it happen in some cases where the defendant is found not guilty by the jury and set free? What about convicted murderers, albeit very few in number, who have been tried by jury, found guilty, sentenced, and then have had their convictions set aside by the Court of Criminal Appeal?

Recent well-publicized cases in the 1980s and 1990s have shown, in the clarity of the glare of the media, that miscarriages of justice do occur. They have been remitted later by the release of prisoners who lost their liberty and suffered unfairly and unnecessarily. Before the abolition of the death penalty in 1965, such judicial mistakes have, for the unfortunate defendant, proved quite literally and irreversibly fatal. The hangings in the 1950s of Timothy John Evans and of Derek Bentley, and the 1962 execution of James Hanratty now appear, with the benefit of hindsight, to have become riddled with doubt and controversy. There exists grave suspicion that these three man may have been, through mistakes and failures in the judicial system, to put it bluntly, judicially murdered.

But what about cases where justice has failed in the opposite direction? Have guilty men and women been set free? This is quite another matter, one which forms the theme of this book. We have to be most cautious before we declare that a murderer has escaped scot free from the consequences of his or her crime. Only the twelve trial jurors will every really know how they came to reach a 'not guilty' verdict. Nevertheless, we can try, in retrospect, to put ourselves in the jury's shoes.

The duty of the jury is to listen to the evidence placed before them in court, to the arguments for and against the defendant expressed by prosecution and defence counsel. After guidance from the judge in his summing-up, they assemble in a room and decide the fate of the prisoner. Until 1957, the jury's collective decision in a murder case, if it were a verdict of 'guilty', would result in the accused being automatically sentenced to death.

Assuming that murderers have been set free without punishment, why should this happen at all? The answer rests partly upon the nature of the evidence presented to the jury. In the vast majority of cases, no-one witnesses the murderous act. Murder is usually a private event, witnessed by the murderer and his victim only. There is rarely any direct eye-witness evidence against the defendant. More often than not, the evidence is totally circumstantial. They jury has the task, sometimes simple, but more usually difficult and baffling, of unravelling the threads of a whole tapestry of incidents, statements, sightings, forensic findings and medical matters, woven together in an intricate design by counsel for the prosecution in an attempt to prove his case.

But what constitutes proof in a court of law? Legal proof is defined in a rather special way. It is not absolute scientific proof, because it cannot be repeatedly tested. After all, an acquittal case is heard once only. The degree of proof which the prosecution is obliged to supply in order to establish guilt is illustrated by the remarks of Mr Justice Glyn-Jones, trial judge in the 1953 proceedings against Louisa Merrifield for the murder of Mrs Ricketts in a Blackpool bungalow. In his final remarks to the jury, defence counsel J.V. Nahum made an unusual and crucial slip. Mr Nahum said:

"This is a case resting wholly on circumstantial evidence. The prosecution have failed to prove a case with the correct standard of proof, an accuracy of mathematics. There are loopholes everywhere."

The judge wasted no time in correcting the defence counsel's error:

"Are you suggesting," the judge asked, "that there is a duty on a prosecution to prove the case with mathematical accuracy? I really must express my surprise that learned counsel should make such a statement."

After a brief exchange with the judge, Mr Nahum corrected himself: "It has to be beyond a reasonable doubt, and I suggest that standard has not been achieved by the prosecution."

Reasonable doubt. What is 'reasonable' doubt in a trial? The real answer and the answer which explains why juries return seemingly controversial verdicts, is that it is the jurors themselves who decide what is reasonable doubt and what is not. They may listen to the guidance and direction provided by the judge in his summing up, but, as any judge will freely admit, a jury is entitled to ignore the judge's remarks, and the speeches of the prosecution and defence counsel too, and should they wish, they can disregard these completely when making their decision. In the words of an old Yorkshire saying, 'there's nought as queer as folk'. It is not the judge that decides guilt, but the twelve jurors.

Now we can see that, on occasions, even when all available evidence has been brought out for and against the accused, and when every possible avenue has been explored by both prosecution and defence, the fate of a defendant rests, in the final analysis, with the hearts and minds of the twelve individuals sworn in as jurors at the start of proceedings. If a jury decide that there is a reasonable doubt about the guilt of a defendant, then, in law, they are bound to give the accused the benefit of that doubt and find him not guilty. But the jury itself is the sole arbiter of 'reasonableness'.

The cases recalled in this book involve the release to freedom of alleged murderers. They are surrounded by varying degrees of controversy. The reader is invited to make up his or her own mind about whether or not justice really did falter in favour of the accused.

There has to be a final word of caution here. One may hold the opinion that an acquittal is riddled with doubt. However, although a verdict of not guilty is not a verdict of 'innocent', an individual cleared of a murder charge has every legal, and indeed, moral right to lay claim to complete freedom from guilt. That right is sacrosanct. In spite of numerous reforms over a long period, the judicial process in English Law, devised and developed by human agency, no matter how carefully it may have been honed towards perfection, is, like human nature itself, essentially flawed. However, is it those very imperfections of the law and of humanity which, it is hoped, make the stories in this book interesting and entertaining to the reader.

Contents

Chapter 1

The Peasenhall Case

The year 1901 saw the death, on January 22nd, of Queen Victoria. A new "Edwardian" era began with the accession to the throne of her second child and eldest son who became King Edward the Seventh. During that year, Marconi, at St John's, Newfoundland, received the very first transatlantic radio signal, transmitted to him from Poldhu in Cornwall. On April 24th was issued the first edition of the *Daily Express* newspaper. In the June of 1901 there came the tragic news of the sinking of the passenger liner *Lusitania* off the Canadian coast. In September, an outbreak of deadly smallpox spread across the British Isles.

In 1901 also, in the tiny Suffolk village of Peasenhall, north of Ipswich, near the old town of Saxmundham, William George Gardiner was living in a double-fronted cottage on the main street of the village. Gardiner, in his forties, was a well-built man of rather swarthy appearance with jet black hair, a moustache and very dark eyes. Married with six children, Gardiner worked as a foreman carpenter at the Peasenhall Drill Works, a factory making farm machinery.

William Gardiner was a very religious man. A member of the Primitive Methodist Chapel at nearby Sibton, he was treasurer, choir master and superintendent of the Sunday School. By 1901, William and his wife had lived in the village of Peasenhall for twelve years. Their eldest child was thirteen and they had four-year-old twins. It would appear that Gardiner had the credentials of a hard-working, well-respected family man. At the time our story begins, however, Gardiner's standing in the village was becoming more than a little tarnished. The context of the darkening of Gardiner's reputation concerned his alleged interest in a young woman by the name of Rose Harsent.

Rose was a popular village girl, much admired by the young men of the district. She was 22 and, as yet, unmarried. She was employed as a general servant in the household of Deacon William Crisp and his wife Georgina at Providence House, a sizable gabled building with a walled garden, standing in the main street. Rose lived in at Providence House. Her bedroom was on the top floor, connected to the kitchen by a flight of steps. William Gardiner and his family lived just across the roadway from Providence House, in a small cottage.

On the evening of Wednesday, May 1st 1901, at about 7.30pm, 20-year-old George Wright was walking with his dog along Rendham Road in Peasenhall. Ahead of him, Wright saw Rose Harsent coming towards him down Rendham Hill. When she reached the foot of the hill, Rose turned off the road and walked through a gateway leading to an old thatched building set back from the main road, opposite the Drill Works. It was known locally as the Doctor's Chapel. As George Wright was to describe later, after he had passed the chapel gate, he met William Gardiner on the road. Wright did not know Gardiner by sight alone. As befitted his surname, George Wright worked in the Drill Works as a wheel-wright. Gardiner was his foreman there. When the two men met that evening, Gardiner made a fuss of Wright's dog. He asked Wright how long he had kept it. When the men parted company, Gardiner gestured to the darkening clouds and said that it looked as if it might rain before long.

True to William Gardiner's prediction, within a minute or so, a sharp rain shower started to moisten the sandy surface of the unmade roadway and spatter noisily on the leafy hedgerows. Being in no hurry to get back to his lodgings, George Wright sheltered with his dog under a convenient tree. Some minutes later, as Wright was gazing back up the Rendham Road, he caught sight of William Gardiner again. Just as Rose Harsent had done earlier, Gardiner walked through the gate of the Doctor's Chapel. As he saw Gardiner disappear from view, George Wright became curious as to just what Rose and Gardiner might be doing together in the same little building at that time of day. As he made his way home with his dog, Wright began to reflect upon what he had seen.

When he arrived back at his lodgings, Wright mentioned the matter to his young co-lodger, Alphonso Skinner, a fitter at the works. The two men decided they would go back together and try to find out what was going on in the Doctor's Chapel. Little did Wright and Skinner imagine that, as they set off on their errand that evening, they would become embroiled in not simply a tasty morsel of village gossip, but what was eventually to amount to a full scale infamous scandal, an alleged sexual liaison between William Gardiner, respected family man, a pillar of Sibton chapel, and pretty little Rose

Harsent, one of his choristers and a former pupil at his Sunday School.

* * * * *

When embarrassing rumours reached William Gardiner's ears, he wrote a letter to Rose Harsent and gave it to her 14-year-old brother to deliver.

The letter read:

> "Dear Rose – I was very much surprised to hear that there is some scandal going around about you and me going into the Doctor's Chapel for immoral purposes, so that I shall put it into other hands at once. I have found out who it was that started it. Wright and Skinner say they saw us there, but I shall summons them for defamation of character unless they withdraw what they have said and give a written apology. I shall see Bob tonight and we will come and see you together if possible. I shall at the same time see your father and tell him."

On the 8th of May, a week after the alleged impropriety in the Doctor's Chapel, Gardiner summoned Wright and Skinner to his office at the works. He dared them to repeat the story they had been circulating about him. They said they were telling the truth about him and had heard what had occurred in the building that night. Gardiner told Wright and Skinner that they had made the whole thing up out of "old stuff". In other words, their allegations amounted to nothing more than discarded rubbish. Gardiner demanded a written apology, or else he would go further and issue them with a writ for slander. When Gardiner threatened legal action, George Wright spoke up against his foreman, making his own attitude crystal clear. He said to Gardiner, "I only have what I stand up in. I don't care what you do, for I know we tell the truth and I am not ashamed to own it."

Events now spiralled. On Saturday, May 11th, an inquiry was due to be held into the allegations at Sibton Methodist Chapel, under the chairmanship of the superintendent minister John Guy. In the meantime, on the morning before the meeting, Gardiner penned another letter to Rose:

> "Dear Rose – I have broken the news to Mrs. Gardiner this morning. She is awfully upset but she says she knows it is wrong for I was home from half-past nine o'clock so I could not possibly be with you an hour so she won't believe anything about it. I have asked Mr. Burgess to ask those

two chaps to come to chapel tonight and have it out there, however they stand by such a tale.

I don't know but I don't think God will forsake me now and if we put our trust in Him it will end right, but it is awfully hard work to have to face people when they are all suspicious of you, but by God's help whether they believe me or not I shall try and live it down and prove by my future conduct that it is all false."

Discounting legal action, Gardiner ended the letter with a chivalrous flourish:

"I only wish I could take it to court but I don't see a shadow of a chance to get the case as I don't think you would be strong enough to face a trial. Trusting that God will direct us and make the way clear, I remain, yours in trouble, W. Gardiner."

The inquiry meeting at Sibton chapel brought Gardiner and Rose Harsent face to face with their accusers. Gardiner's version of events was that on May 1st, in the evening, he had visited the Drill Works to feed and groom a horse he had been using that day to haul a waggon. On emerging from the works gate, he saw Rose Harsent down the road, standing by the Doctor's Chapel gate. He said that she called him over and asked him if he would lock the chapel door for her now that she had finished cleaning the building. The door, he said, was stuck, so he slammed it shut and locked it. Gardiner said he then walked along the road with the girl, talking, he said, about the choice of hymns for the forthcoming anniversary service at Sibton chapel. Rose herself would be singing as a member of the choir.

When it came time for Wright and Skinner to speak, instead of confessing to a rather malicious prank, they stuck, as they said they would, to their guns. The twenty or so chapel members who had turned out that evening were no doubt spellbound by what they heard next.

Wright and Skinner said that they had listened outside the chapel and had heard the sound of a woman's laughter, a lot of "rustling about", and the gasping sounds of a female voice crying "Oh! Oh!" several times. At one point, they heard the woman say, "Did you notice me reading my Bible last Sunday?" To this, a man replied, in a voice they recognised as belonging to Gardiner, "What were you reading about?"

"I was reading about like what we have been doing here tonight. I'll tell you where it is – the 38th chapter of Genesis."

The female voice continued for a while in a lower tone, whereupon the two men heard Gardiner say, "It won't be noticed."

"I shall be out tomorrow night at nine o'clock," said the girl. "You must let me go now."

Here the men made a discreet exit from the scene. Skinner said he hung around for a while and saw a woman come out from the chapel onto Rendham Road. It was Rose. She went to Providence House. Gardiner then came through the gate, tiptoed across to the other side of the road and went away. Skinner said he followed Gardiner up the road and eventually overtook him, but neither he nor Gardiner spoke to each other.

The meeting of inquiry lasted some three hours, although no doubt part of that time was devoted to hymns and prayers. Mr. Guy, who had visited Rose's father and heard her deny the accusations in front of Mr. Harsent, decided that the inquiry had proved inconclusive and advised that the whole matter should be dropped and, if possible, forgotten by all concerned. Gardiner declared that he would immediately resign all his positions and duties in the chapel. He would put himself forward for re-election in a month's time. (In the event, he was reinstated.)

* * * * *

Within a few days of the inquiry, it became clear that William Gardiner had not yet abandoned the idea of taking the initiative against his young accusers. On May 15th, a letter was sent to Wright and to Skinner by a Saxmundham solicitor:

> "Sir – Mr. William Gardiner of Peasenhall has consulted me with reference to certain slanderous statements which he alleges you have uttered and circulated concerning him and a young woman. I have to inform you that unless you tend my client an ample written apology within seven days from this date, legal process will be forthwith commenced against you, without further notice to yourself."

As it turned out, Gardiner took the matter no further, although no apology, neither written nor verbal, did he receive. The affair of the choirmaster and the lady chorister was laid, for the time being at least, to comparative rest. The climate of debate and rumour seemed to have cooled.

* * * * *

Eleven months later, the Gardiner controversy was re-kindled. On

April 14th 1902, Henry Rouse, aged 73, a Sibton labourer and a lay preacher at the Methodist chapel, sent a long letter to Mr. Guy. He complained about William Gardiner's behaviour. Rouse said that one night in the February of 1902, as he was walking home, he met Gardiner and Rose Harsent on the road. It was about 8.45pm and it was dark. According to Rouse, he bade the couple goodnight, but, he said, he received no answer. The following Sunday, Henry Rouse tapped Gardiner on the shoulder as he was coming out of the chapel after the service. "I want to speak to you, if you please," said Rouse to Gardiner. Walking together a little way up the road, Henry Rouse took it upon himself to serve Gardiner with an admonishment:

"I am somewhat surprised that you should continue to walk about with that girl," said Rouse. "There is so much talk. It will do the chapel a great deal of harm you know."

According to Rouse, Gardiner asked him if he had said anything about it, to which Rouse replied, "No. I have not even told my wife."

Gardiner is then reputed to have said, "If you don't say anything about it, it shall never occur again."

This was only one of the complaints against Gardiner. In his letter to John Guy, Rouse said that in late February he was preaching a sermon in the chapel when he noticed that Gardiner was lounging in a pew with his feet resting in Rose Harsent's lap. He had intended to tell one of them – which one he did not say – to leave, but being unwilling to expose the erring couple in public, Rouse simply paused for a moment or two, before resuming his oratorical flow.

Besides writing to Mr. Guy, old Henry Rouse dictated a letter to Gardiner himself, castigating him for his choice of seating position in the chapel pews, accusing Gardiner of fuelling the flames of ungodly rumour. Instead of putting a signature to his letter, Henry Rouse sent it to Gardiner anonymously. This is the text of Rouse's cautionary letter:

> "Mr. G. – I write to warn you of your conduct with that girl Rose, as I find when she comes into the chapel she must place herself next to you, which keeps the people's minds still in the belief that you are a guilty man, and in that case you will drive many from the chapel, and those who would join the cause are kept away through it. I do not wish you to leave God's house, but there must be a difference before God's cause can prosper, which I hope you will see to be right, as people cannot hear when the enemy of souls brings this before them. I write to you as one who loves

your soul, and I hope you will have her sit in some other place, and remove such feeling which for your sake she will do."

On receipt of Rouse's letter of complaint, John Guy again took Gardiner to task about Rose. Gardiner told Guy that although the old man's allegations about his actions in chapel were quite untrue, he did admit he had been indiscreet in continuing to be seen in her company. He promised he would steer well clear of her in future. He said he had become the innocent victim of village gossip. He again offered to resign from the chapel, but Guy told him that resignation would not be necessary. As for Rose, Guy spoke to her, this time in the presence of her mother. Again she denied any improper associations with Gardiner.

Rose Harsent may have been innocent of any affair with William Gardiner, but by the spring of 1902 it was safe to say that she had been connected with a lover. As was soon to become common knowledge in the district, she was several months pregnant by Easter of that year. Mrs. Crisp tackled her about being "in the family way", but Rose said it was untrue. In most people's minds, the chief candidate for the father of Rose's offspring was, unsurprisingly in view of what had already happened, none other than William George Gardiner of Peasenhall.

* * * * *

On the hot sultry evening of Saturday, May 31st 1902, Peasenhall was visited by a series of violent thunderstorms. Earlier that afternoon, soon after 3pm, postman Fred Brewer delivered a letter to Providence House. Contained in a buff-coloured envelope and addressed to Rose Harsent, the letter read,

> "Dear R – I will try to see you tonight at 12 o'clock at your place if you put a light in your window at 10 o'clock for about 10 minutes then you can take it out again. Don't have a light in your room at 12 as I will come round the back."

This letter was unsigned.

Shortly after 10pm that evening, with thunder rumbling around in the distance and flickering sheets of lightning occasionally illuminating the night sky, Mrs. Crisp said goodnight to Rose Harsent in the kitchen of Providence House and went to bed. At about five past ten, Henry Burgess, William Gardiner's next-door neighbour, saw Gardiner standing at his own front door, watching the storm. Burgess went outside to join him. When the two men parted company about ten minutes later, Henry Burgess, just before he turned to go back indoors, looked up at Providence House. In the top window of the house, standing out against the blackening night sky, there shone a distinct yellow light.

Inside Providence House, William and Georgina Crisp had a rather disturbed night. The storm continued periodically into the early hours. The gale force winds which it generated lashed against the big house. Woken up by the raging of the storm, Mrs. Crisp went downstairs to check that all the windows were shut. When she was satisfied that they were secure, Mrs. Crisp closed the door connecting the dining room to the kitchen. Convinced that all was now as it should be, she rejoined her husband upstairs.

But this was not quite all for the Crisps that night. Some time later, the couple were awakened by a thud, as if someone had fallen, followed by the sound of a woman screaming. Georgina wanted to go downstairs to investigate, but William persuaded her to stay put. After all, it was probably that girl Rose, frightened by the storm. She would have to get used to it, they decided. Turning over, they went to sleep.

By 4am the thunderstorm had abated. About 8am on the morning of Sunday, June 1st, Rose Harsent's father, who worked as a carter for the Drill Works, took Rose's clean laundry and some of her new clothes over to Providence House. He usually called on Rose early on Sunday morning and, to avoid disturbing Mr. and Mrs. Crisp, he used to enter the house by the back way. On this particular morning, Mr. Harsent arrived at the house to find that the back door had been left ajar. As he approached the door, he noticed a pungent smell of paraffin.

When he entered the kitchen, William Harsent found his daughter lying flat on her back on the floor in her nightdress and stockings. She was lying at the foot of the little staircase which led up to her room. Her upper body was drenched with blood. A pool of blood had formed around her head and body. Part of her nightdress had burnt away, leaving the right side of her body charred black. On the floor near her body was an oil lamp, its glass top detached from its canister. Shards of glass littered the floor. There could be no doubt that Rose was dead. Her throat had been cut, her windpipe completely severed. Mr. Harsent covered his daughter's body with a hearth-rug, then, without bothering to rouse Mr. and Mrs. Crisp, he ran to the police office as quickly as his legs would carry him.

* * * * *

When Police Constable Eli Nunn arrived at the murder scene, he noticed that Rose's body lay with her head near the stairs and feet pointing towards the kitchen door. The left side of her body rested against the kitchen wall. Beneath her head was a copy of the *East Anglian Daily News*, dated May 30th. To the left of the body lay a candlestick with a burnt-out candle. The stairs door was open. One of the metal brackets supporting a shelf over the door had been broken. Against the fireplace, Nunn found a broken medicine bottle with its cork still in place. The bottle smelled as it if had contained paraffin. It bore a label that read, "2 or 3 teaspoon. A sixth part to be taken every few hours – Mrs. Gardiner's children."

During a search of Rose Harsent's bedroom, the police discovered the letter in the buff envelope which had been delivered to her on the afternoon before her death. On the day after the killing, Superintendent George Staunton showed this letter to Gardiner and asked him if he had written it. Staunton believed that the person who sent the letter, after arranging to meet Rose at Providence House at midnight on the Saturday, had entered the house by the back kitchen door, left open for him by Rose herself. Then, possibly after some kind of dispute or argument, he killed her as she stood holding her candlestick night-light at the foot of her stairs.

"Did you write this letter?" said Staunton to Gardiner. "No, I did not write it," he replied. Staunton opened one of Gardiner's notebooks and showed him the handwriting in it. "You admit this is in your writing, do you not?" "Yes, I wrote that but I did not write the letter." "The writing is the same though, is it not, Mr. Gardiner?" "No," said Gardiner. "There is a similarity, but it is not my writing." Pointing to the buff envelope, the kind of envelope which is still used for business letters, Staunton asked Gardiner, "They use this sort of envelope in the Drill Works, do they not?" "I don't know," replied Gardiner. "I don't use them."

Asked where he was after 10 o'clock on the Saturday night, Gardiner said that at about 11pm he went with his wife to visit a Mrs. Dickenson who kept an ironmongery shop next door to his own cottage. He said that he and his wife stayed at Mrs. Dickenson's house until about 1.30am. He said he left his wife there and went into his own house and to bed, where he slept until after 8am on the Sunday morning.

When Staunton had his talk with Gardiner, the superintendent knew something that Gardiner probably did not know. At about 5am on the Sunday morning, some 3 hours before the discovery of Rose Harsent's body, a gamekeeper called James Morris was walking along the main street. Morris said he noticed a set of foot prints leading across the carriageway. According to Morris, the footprints started at Gardiner's cottage door and went across the road to the gate of Providence House. The gamekeeper, who might have been expected to know about such matters because of his duties in catching poachers, told Supt. Staunton that these curious footprints had been made by a pair of rubber-soled shoes. Knowing that Gardiner owned a pair of shoes fitting that description, believing that Gardiner had indeed sent the letter of assignation to Rose, and being already familiar with the long-standing rumours that Gardiner and Rose were more than just friends, Staunton arrested Gardiner and charged him with Rose's murder. Now a prisoner, Gardiner was taken to Saxmundham and put into a police cell. After a hearing before magistrates at Saxmundham, he was committed for trial at the next Suffolk Assizes at Ipswich.

* * * * *

After spending five months on remand in Ipswich Prison, William Gardiner stood trial for the murder of Rose Harsent in the November of 1902. By now, the conflict between the British Army and the forces of Boer settlers in South Africa, which had been in progress since 1899, was at an end. In fact, on the very night that Rose Harsent lost her life in Providence House at Peasenhall, the Boer War was ended by the signing of the Treaty of Vereeniging, under which Transvaal and the Orange Free State agreed to accept British sovereignty within South Africa.

At William Gardiner's November trial, when it came his turn to give evidence in his own defence, Gardiner made an extremely favourable impression upon the jury. The *East Anglian Daily Times* described the scene:

> "The accused went from the dock into the witness box, and, after stroking his raven-black moustache and beard for a moment or two in a rather nervous way, he pulled himself together, standing somewhat unsteadily, with one hand resting on the ledge in front of him

> – often raising it to emphasize his statements – and the other held close to his side. He spoke in a clear voice, raising it occasionally at the request of counsel so that the jury might hear. The quietude of his demeanour was the subject of general amazement. He gave his answers without hesitation and was never flustered."

The judge, Mr. Justice Grantham, summed up against Gardiner. The jury retired to consider their verdict. It was now 4.15pm on the 4th day of the trial. In those days the judge was unable to accept anything less than a unanimous verdict from the jury. Every jury member had to be of one mind as to the defendant's guilt. At 6.30pm the twelve returned to court. Their foreman told the judge that they were unable to agree a verdict. After a further two hours of deliberation, the jury returned to court again at 8.40pm. They were still in disagreement. Mr. Justice Grantham asked if any juror wished to ask him a question about the evidence. One juryman said he did not wish to ask a question and, possibly because he was the only dissenting juror, said, "I have not made up my mind not to agree if I was convinced the prisoner was guilty, but I have heard nothing to convince me that he is guilty."

At this statement from the juror, a burst of applause broke out. It was quickly silenced by a few raps of Mr. Justice Grantham's gavel. Accepting that there had been a mistrial owing to disagreement among the jury, the judge discharged the jury and brought an end to the proceedings. Gardiner was taken back to his prison cell to await a second trial.

* * * * *

Gardiner's second trial opened at Ipswich on Wednesday, January 21st 1903, before Mr. Justice Lawrance. The Crown's case against Gardiner was led by Henry Dickens K.C., son of the novelist Charles Dickens. Mr. Ernest Wild handled the presentation of Gardiner's defence.

The evidence at the second trial was the same as that in the first one. The first prosecution witnesses were George Wright and Alphonso Skinner. They told the court about how they had overheard Gardiner and Rose in the Doctor's Chapel, how Gardiner threatened them with legal action for what he called "slanderous statements", the interview in Gardiner's office, and the receipt of solicitor's letters. In cross-examination, Mr. Wild attempted to show that Wright may have held a grudge against Gardiner for reprimanding him for slipshod work at the factory. Wright admitted that Gardiner had, indeed, reprimanded him, but that he did so on June 25th, some eight weeks after the Doctor's Chapel incident. Wright said that Gardiner had never found fault with his work before that. Wild attempted to darken Wright's character by suggesting that he and Skinner had gone to eavesdrop at the Doctor's Chapel, not through mere curiosity, but in a spirit of unhealthy prurience.

He asked Wright, "You thought you were going to hear something indecent?"

"Yes," replied Wright.

"Did you young men go along that hedge expecting to hear something indecent?"

A ripple of amusement travelled through the public gallery when Wright replied, "We did not expect to hear a sermon."

Alphonso Skinner's evidence tallied with George Wright's. Skinner said he saw both Gardiner and Rose come out of the chapel. First out was Rose. She went to Providence House. A few minutes later came Gardiner, tiptoeing out into Rendham Road in what must have been a bizarre and comical manner. Skinner told the jury how he and Wright had later gone to the Doctor's Chapel with Harry Burgess and the policeman Eli Nunn. They pointed out exactly where they had stood. It was on the path, behind the hedge running along the side of the building. In cross-examination, Skinner was unshakable. There seemed little doubt that he and Wright were telling the truth.

Superintendent Minister John Guy gave an account of the Sibton chapel inquiry and described how, in May 1901, Gardiner had promised Guy he would stay clear of Rose and also, as Guy put it, "to be careful in his relations with young people." In cross-examination, Mr. Guy said that Gardiner had offered to resign; he had not been asked to resign from the chapel.

The next witness on the first day of the trial was old Henry Rouse. His evidence about the unseemly behaviour of Gardiner with Rose helped the Crown to establish that the couple had a close relationship, close enough perhaps for the jury to believe that it was Gardiner who had made Rose pregnant. Wild's cross-examination of Rouse, however, cast great doubt upon the reliability of the old man's evidence. Wild established that the lay preacher's own character was far from perfect, and not at all what it might have been in view of his position in chapel society. Questioned by Wild, Rouse said that when he lived at Wrentham, he was himself involved in a scandal. He was accused of having an affair with a woman called Mrs. Gooch. While the scandal was at its height, Rouse had his barn burned down. Rouse told the police that a 13-year-old boy had done it, but the magistrate dismissed the charge and set the boy free because of a lack of evidence. Rouse was no stranger to the Assize Court. When he was living at Brampton he gave evidence in a murder case involving the death of a woman called Edna Carter. He accused a man called Snelling of running a brothel, an allegation that was never substantiated.

Having shown a depth of relationship between Gardiner and Rose, prosecuting counsel Henry Dickens now sought to show the jury that Gardiner had arranged for a tryst with Rose at Providence House on the night of the murder. Rose's young brother, Harry, testified that he had often acted as a go-between, delivering letters from Gardiner to his sister. He also said that he used to deliver the *East Anglian Daily Times* to Gardiner at his office in the works. A copy of this newspaper had been found beneath Rose's dead body. In cross-examination, Wild got Harry to say that this paper was read all over Suffolk, thereby prompting the jury to disregard the presence of the paper at the scene of the crime.

Henry Brewer, the postman, was asked to look at the anonymous letter of assignation delivered to Rose on the afternoon of her death. After examining the buff-coloured envelope and its postmark, Brewer said the letter must have been posted at Peasenhall between 6.30pm on Friday, May 30th and 10.55am on the morning of Saturday, May 31st. Brewer also said that this was not the first such letter he had delivered to Providence House. There had been, he said, "three or four others."

Next to go into the witness box was Rose Harsent's mistress at Providence House, Mrs. Georgina Crisp. Mrs. Crisp described how, between 1am and 2am on the night of the storm, she heard a thud, followed about a minute later by "a moaning scream." She said she wanted to go down to investigate, but her husband would not let her. Deacon Crisp was, surprisingly, not called to give evidence. Mrs. Crisp did not take kindly to being cross-examined by Mr. Wild. Parts of her account of the events of the night did not tally with what she had said at the coroner's inquest. As Mr. Wild questioned Mrs. Crisp, an element of farce crept into the proceedings. It is not customary for witnesses to refer to counsel by their names. However, Mrs. Crisp insisted on beginning her answers with the phrase, "Well, Mr. Wild...." Ernest Wild repeatedly objected to such a personal approach from Mrs. Crisp, but she persisted. This altercation, combined with Mrs. Crisp's outrage at having her honesty called into question, created a lively ending to the first day's proceedings. Eventually, Mrs. Crisp sought refuge in the judge. She said to Mr. Justice Lawrance,

"My Lord, Mr. Wild and Mr. Leighton (defence solicitor) came to my house yesterday three weeks." Turning to Mr. Wild, she said, "I have given you every opportunity to come to my house, and I do not know why you should doubt my word."

* * * * *

The second day of the second trial started with evidence from Harry Burgess, a bricklayer who lived next door to Gardiner. Burgess verified that he had seen a light in Rose's window at about 10.05pm on the fateful night. The prosecution would claim that this was a signal to Gardiner, in response to his letter of assignation.

Mrs. Rosanna Dickenson was Gardiner's other next-door neighbour. She said that on the night of the murder, Mrs. Gardiner came into her house between 11pm and 11.30pm. Gardiner himself, according to Mrs. Dickenson, arrived between 11.35pm and midnight. She said Gardiner and his wife left her house together at 1.30am.

James Morris testified about how he discovered the incriminating footprints leading from Gardiner's cottage to the gate of Providence House. The sighting of the footprints, said Morris, was at about 5am on the Sunday. He said he knew nothing of Rose's death until just before noon.

A villager named Herbert Stammers told the court how, at about 7.30am on the Sunday morning, he saw Gardiner going towards the wash-house at the back of his cottage. Some minutes later, he saw Gardiner again. It was clear that a large fire had been lit, so great were the puffs of smoke coming out of the chimney. The fire in the wash-house was much larger, said Stammers, than he had ever seen burning there before. Was this, perhaps, a fire to burn Gardiner's bloodstained clothing? The prosecution would suggest that was just what it was.

The afternoon of the second day was devoted to evidence from the police, in the persons of P.C. Nunn and Superintendent Staunton, and from medical men. Dr. Ryder Richardson, who carried out the post-mortem, described the condition of Rose Harsent's body. Dr. Richardson said there was a long wound in the chest, caused by the upward thrust of a sharp-pointed blade. The girl's throat had been slashed across by two distinct cuts, inflicted with such force that the windpipe was severed. There was a bruise on the girl's right cheek, together with a small cut. Numerous semi-circular defence cuts could be seen on her hands. She had also sustained knife wounds in her chin and jaw. The doctor also said that her wounds could have been caused by a knife belonging to Gardiner, exhibited in court. At the time of her death, Rose was six months pregnant.

Superintendent Staunton read out a signed statement which Gardiner made after he was arrested. It is noticeable that the time he said he spent at Mrs. Dickenson's house did not correspond with what Mrs. Dickenson herself said in the witness box. In the police statement, Gardiner said,

"On Saturday I drove to Kelsale at 2.30pm. I got home about 9.30pm, had my supper, and stayed at the front door because of the storm." The statement continued, "We went to Mrs. Dickenson's about 11.00pm. I left Mrs. Dickenson's with my wife at about 1.30am, went to bed, and did not go out until 8.30am next morning."

Mrs. Dickenson said that Mrs. Gardiner arrived first, followed some time later by Gardiner himself.

The first doctor at the scene on the Sunday morning was Dr. Charles Lacy. He gave his opinion that, from the degree of rigor mortis in the body, death had occurred at least four hours previously, that is, before about 5am. He was unable to give an exact time of death, but, in reply to Mr. Dickens, the doctor said it could have been eight hours previously, at about 1.00am.

The prosecution called a handwriting expert, a Thomas Gurrin, operating from Holborn Viaduct in London. Gurrin said he had given evidence in hundreds of court cases and had seventeen years experience in the comparison of handwriting. In Gurrin's opinion, the letter in the buff envelope was written by Gardiner. He pointed out the excessive use of capital letters.

Proceedings on the second day were concluded by evidence from a young man, a shop assistant called Frederick Davis. Quite why the Crown decided to call this witness is questionable, since his evidence did little towards proving Gardiner's guilt. It may have been introduced to blacken Rose Harsent's character. Questioned by Mr. Dickens, Davis admitted that he had written several obscene letters and verses and sent them to Rose. He said she asked him to write them for her. This was around the September of 1901. Davis also said he lent Rose a medical book. According to Davis, "all the lads in the village knew of them." Davis's evidence completed the second day of the trial, and Mr. Dickens declared the prosecution case closed.

* * * * *

On the Friday morning, January 23rd 1903, Ernest Wild stood up to open the case for the defence. In his opening remarks to the jury, Mr. Wild began by questioning the truth of Wright and Skinner's evidence. Why should Gardiner and Rose choose the chapel, within 200 yards of the girl's house, with "louts" hanging about? Mr. Wild said he would call two qualified surveyors to prove that Wright and Skinner could have heard nothing from outside the chapel. Henry Rouse, said Mr. Wild, did not appear at the committal hearing. This was the first time anyone had heard of the alleged "indecency" which Rouse said he saw while preaching. Would Gardiner have been so foolish as to behave in such a way?

Mr. Wild dismissed the idea of Gardiner having visited Rose on the murder night. He said, "If Gardiner indeed made the appointment for twelve, he could hardly have bothered going back from his wife's bed at 2am when there was only one and a half hours to daylight." (Clocks were then permanently set to Greenwich Mean Time all the year round). "Rose would hardly have waited for him. It would have been unsafe anyway by then." Concerning Mrs. Crisp's evidence, Mr. Wild said, "At first Mrs. Crisp said she heard a thud and a scream between 1am and 2am and then changed her mind and said "it was dark"." "Why," asked Mr. Wild, "was Mr. Crisp kept out of the witness box?" As to the appointment letter, Mr. Wild said it was clearly not Gardiner's letter because "it was a letter of a better-educated man."

Mr. Wild then called his first witness in Gardiner's defence. This was Mrs. Gardiner. It was to be expected that she would give evidence in support of her husband and provide him with an alibi, but, if she was telling the truth, Mrs. Gardiner found it a dreadful ordeal to do so. Eventually, she had to be carried out of the witness box in a state of collapse and played no further part in the day's proceedings.

Mrs. Gardiner testified that Rose Harsent used to visit her house quite often, both before and after the eruption of the scandal. As to her own movements on the night of the killing, Mrs. Gardiner said that she went to bed as the church clock was striking 2am. At 2.20am, she said she got up and took a few sips of brandy to cure a bout of indigestion. During the night, her four-year-old twins woke up. Mrs. Gardiner said she got them back to sleep by putting one of her other children in bed with them. She said her husband slept through the night. She herself woke, "after the clock had struck 5am." She said she and Gardiner finally got up between 8am and 8.30am, during which period she lit the wash-house fire to boil water. Gardiner, she said, took the children to Sunday School at 9.30am. Later, as she was going to chapel, Mrs. Gardiner met Mrs. Dickenson, who told her that Rose had committed suicide. At lunchtime, when Mrs. Gardiner told her husband about Rose's death, he said to her, "I can't think what induced the poor girl to do such a thing as that." He was not, she said, upset by the news.

When she was asked about the arrival of the police at the Gardiner cottage on the Monday morning, Mrs. Gardiner was unable to reply to Mr. Wild's question. She seemed to be on the point of collapse. Defence counsel, Ernest Wild, handed her a bottle of smelling salts and, after a few moments sniffing the ammonia fumes, Mrs. Gardiner felt able to continue her testimony.

Mrs. Gardiner said that the police called on her three times in one day. Three officers called – Staunton, Nunn and another constable. Superintendent Staunton showed her the assignation letter. Mrs. Gardiner said she had not written it and that she did not think her husband had either. Staunton asked her what she knew about the medicine bottle found near Rose's body. It had originally contained medicine for her children. Mrs. Gardiner told him that she had once given Rose a bottle containing camphorated oil for curing a cold and neuralgia pain in her face. A pair of rubber shoes belonging to Gardiner was found in a box among a jumble of odds and ends. She said her husband had not worn those particular shoes for a very long time. The police took away from the house all Gardiner's clothes.

Just before 2pm, Mr. Justice Lawrance adjourned the proceedings for lunch. Mrs. Gardiner fainted in the witness box. Gardiner wept. After lunch, Mrs. Gardiner was in no condition to give evidence and so Mr. Wild called Gardiner into the box to give evidence in his own defence.

* * * * *

Gardiner's version of events at the Doctor's Chapel on the evening of

May 1st 1901 was that he spent no time with Rose inside the building. He said he had simply helped the girl to close the chapel door by slamming it shut and locking it with a key. Gardiner said that he threatened Wright and Skinner with legal action because they were spreading lies about him.

Gardiner denied that Henry Rouse had ever spoken to him about his conduct with Rose. He said he knew nothing about Rouse and nothing about any incident in the Sibton chapel which might have caused Rouse to rebuke him. He said he had written some letters to Rose and that she had written a letter to him about chapel matters. Gardiner said he wrote to her twice in 1901, but never in 1902. He said he had not sent her a letter through the post and had never used buff envelopes.

Gardiner denied any knowledge of a light in Rose's window. He said he was unaware that it could be seen from the roadway in front of his house. Not only did Gardiner say that Wright and Skinner's evidence was false, he also said that Rouse was telling lies and that Herbert Stammers's evidence about the large early-morning fire in his wash-house was also untrue.

The prosecution had a powerful piece of evidence against Gardiner in the form of a clasp knife found in his cottage. Gardiner admitted that the knife did belong to him. Although no blood was found on any items of Gardiner's clothing, nor on his rubber-soled shoes, there were some bloodstains on the clasp knife, on the inside of the handle. In evidence, Gardiner explained that he used his knife to skin and disembowel rabbits before cutting the animals ready for cooking. He called this process "hulking". This was how blood would have got on to the knife's handle, said Gardiner.

William Gardiner's evidence about his movements on the night of the killing matched the evidence his wife had given. He said he had followed a few minutes behind his wife to Mrs. Dickenson's, after he had seen to the children. He said he and his wife went to bed at about 2am, slept through the night and stayed in the bedroom until 8am.

In cross-examination by Mr. Dickens, Gardiner appeared calm and composed, responding to Dickens's questions without hesitation and in a confident style. His excellent comportment in the witness box could not have failed to impress the jury.

Towards the end of the third day, Mr. Wild called James Fairbank, a secretary of the Norfolk and Norwich Savings Bank, part of whose duties was to detect forged cheques. Fairbank said that in his opinion, Gardiner could not have written the assignation letter.

Mr. Wild called defence solicitor Arthur Leighton into the box. Leighton said he had carried out experiments in the Doctor's Chapel which showed that Wright and Skinner could not have heard any conversation from where they stood outside. Two surveyors, a Mr. Corder and a Mr. Permenter, said they had examined the building and were satisfied that anyone standing on the side path could not have heard anything. The day ended with evidence from several members of Sibton Chapel. Each said that they were present at the inquiry in May 1901 and believed then that Wright and Skinner were lying.

* * * * *

On the fourth morning of the trial, it was reported that Mrs. Gardiner, who had not yet undergone cross-examination, was in a hysterical condition. The previous afternoon, after being carried from the witness box, she had been put to lie down on a table in the witnesses' waiting room. When the news of Mrs. Gardiner's morning indisposition was announced, Mr. Wild said, "She shall be brought here, ill or well. Send a doctor to her at once." When Mrs Gardiner did eventually arrive to resume her evidence, she seemed to have recovered. She withstood Mr. Dickens's cross-examination in fine fashion. Mr. Wild then closed the case for the defence.

When Mr. Wild rose to make his final speech to the jury on behalf of Gardiner, he must have realised that the Crown had made out a powerful case against his client. As Wild pointed out, however, it was equally easy to construct a case against young Davis, the shop assistant who had written letters and verses to Rose. Although Mr. Wild said the defence admitted that Davis was unconnected with the crime, how simple it would be to accuse Davis who was, like Gardiner, an innocent man. Concerning the prosecution's claim that the letter in the buff envelope had been posted to Rose by Gardiner, if he were the murderer, he would never have written such a letter. By writing it, Gardiner would, said Mr. Wild, "forge a weapon to hang himself." Mr. Wild here ignored the possibility that Gardiner may have had, at the time of writing the letter, no idea at all of harming Rose. Only when he arrived at Providence House may he have formed a harmful intention.

Mr. Wild said that the letter of assignation was obviously written by a stranger to the district. Why else would the sender have addressed the envelope to "Peasenhall, Saxmundham" when any local person would have known that the two places were entirely separate? Moreover, claimed Mr. Wild, Gardiner would never have made an appointment for midnight because "he would have to be in his bed with his wife at that time." Gardiner would, claimed Wild, "have had to leave his wife, commit the murder and return without her missing him."

Wild touched on a very weak part of the defence case when he said that Gardiner could only have killed Rose that night if his wife knew about his movements. As Wild put it, "He could have committed the murder only if his wife knew of the murder and she is not on trial."

Gardiner's alibi was weak, because no definite time could be fixed for the murder. According to Mrs. Dickenson, Mrs. Gardiner came to her house between 11pm and 11.30pm, followed by Gardiner himself "between 11.45pm and midnight." If Mrs. Dickenson's timings are accepted, then Gardiner was away from his wife for at least fifteen minutes, and perhaps for as long as a whole hour. Did he have enough time to pop across the street to meet Rose? Gardiner said in his statement to the police that he went with his wife to visit Mrs. Dickenson. His words were, "We went into Mrs. Dickenson's at about 11 o'clock." In his trial evidence, however, Gardiner said he followed along after his wife "after seeing to the children." It was to have been expected that Mrs. Gardiner would have been more than willing to support her husband at the trial. What weight would the jury give to her evidence, punctuated as it was by fainting fits and attacks of hysteria?

At the end of his speech to the jury, Mr. Wild said of Gardiner, "He is a man who has gone through very much. I do not put it to you in the way of sympathy, but there must have been something holding him up. I think I can say it of him with reverence and absolute meaning in every word, 'The Eternal God is my refuge and underneath are the everlasting arms'."

After Mr. Dickens had delivered his final address for the Crown, Mr. Justice Lawrance began his summing up to the jury. The judge opened his remarks by outlining the difference between direct and circumstantial evidence.

He said that a body of circumstantial evidence was generally more reliable than some kinds of direct evidence. Mr. Justice Lawrance emphasized that in this case the evidence against the defendant was wholly circumstantial. He advised the jury to ask themselves the question, "Was Wright and Skinner's evidence a lie?" He said that if Wright and Skinner were telling the truth, "here is a man who knew the girl was six months enceinte and had immoral connection with her for a considerable time and who, whether he was the father or not, was pretty sure to have the credit of being the father." Advising the jury on the concept of "reasonable doubt", the judge said to the jury, "The doubt in a case of this kind must be fair and reasonable, and not a trivial doubt, such as the speculative ingenuity of counsel might suggest. You have been told by counsel that you must have a moral certainty. The only certainty you could have about anything would be in regard to something you had seen with your own eyes. The question you have to consider is whether the conclusion to which you are conducted by the evidence, is such as you would come to with any degree of certainty in important affairs of your own. That is the certainty you ought to have in a case of this kind."

The jury retired at 5pm. They returned at 7.12pm. When the twelve jurors had taken their seats, the Clerk of Assize asked their foreman,

"Are you agreed upon your verdict?"

"No, sir," replied the foreman.

The judge said, "You are not agreed. Is there a chance of your agreeing?"

"No, sir."

"None whatever?"

"I am afraid not."

William Gardiner's second trial, like his first, had ended in stalemate. Five days later, a writ of "nolle prosequi" was issued by the Treasury. This enabled the Crown to drop all charges against Gardiner.

On January 29th 1903, William Gardiner was released from Ipswich Prison. No-one else was ever charged in connection with the death of Rose Harsent.

Chapter 2

The Merrett Case

By 1926 Mrs. Bertha Merrett had experienced a varied and eventful life. She was born in 1871 at Birkdale near Southport, the youngest daughter of William Henry Milner, a wine and spirits merchant in Manchester. On a sea voyage to Egypt, Bertha Milner met an electrical engineer named John Alfred Merrett. He was on his way to New Zealand, where the couple were later married. On August 17th 1908 at Levin, North Island, Bertha Merrett gave birth to a son. They named him John Donald. He was to be their only child.

It is out of the complex relationship between Mrs. Merrett and her son Donald that our tragic story has its origins. Perhaps because Bertha Merrett was 37 years old when she bore Donald, he may have been the child she had always longed for and may sometimes have believed she would never have. For whatever reasons, Bertha doted on the child, showering him with love and affection, devoting herself unstintingly to his well-being and welfare.

Mr. Merrett's business obligations compelled him to move, with Bertha and Donald, from New Zealand to St. Petersburg in Tsarist Russia. It was here that the Merretts' marriage began to collapse. The harsh Russian winter proved too much for Bertha. Claiming that the climate did not suit Donald, she took him with her to Switzerland. He was placed in the charge of a governess. It was in Switzerland that mother and son spent the years of the First World War, safe from the full force of the conflict, but becoming increasingly aware of its dreadful consequences. During the war years, Mrs. Merrett worked as a nurse, looking after wounded British army officers who had been discharged from the Kaiser's prisoner-of-war camps.

At the end of the war, still estranged from her husband, Mrs. Merrett travelled with her son back to New Zealand. They settled in Oamaru, South Island. In 1923, when Donald was 16, Mrs. Merrett returned to England. She rented a cottage near Reading, while Donald, who was now hopefully destined for a career in the diplomatic service, attended school at Malvern College.

In the latter part of 1925, young Donald Merrett, now 17, was offered a place at Edinburgh University. In January 1926, so that she could live with her son while he was pursuing his studies, Bertha Merrett took rooms at 7 Mayfield Road in Edinburgh. After three weeks there, they moved into a boarding house in Palmerston Place. Eventually, Mrs. Merrett managed to secure the tenancy of an apartment at 31 Buckingham Terrace, a converted West End mansion divided into three dwellings. Their first floor accommodation consisted of a sitting room and a small bedroom at the front, and a larger bedroom, kitchen and bathroom at the rear. After paying four months' rent in advance, Mrs. Merrett and young Donald moved into their new abode on March 10th 1926.

Bertha Merrett's devotion to Donald had not waned over the years. In fact, now that he had grown into a young man, she was more than ever dedicated to his happiness and success. Having paid the tuition fees for his Bachelor of Arts studies at the University, Mrs. Merrett gave her son a weekly allowance of ten shillings. Each day, Donald set off in the morning with his books, returning home in the evening.

Bertha came to believe that her son was studying too much. He would go to bed early and lock his bedroom door. She would often hear Donald's footfalls as he paced up and down in his bedroom in the early hours.

Although Mrs. Merrett did not know it, her son was deceiving her. For some time now, since early February 1926, Donald had been neglecting his studies. In fact, by the time they moved into Buckingham Terrace, Donald had, for some four weeks, not been attending the university at all. Instead, he had been wandering about the city at his leisure. At night, he left the apartment in secret, making use of a rope lowered from his bedroom window. He had told his mother the rope was there as a safety device, to prevent him from falling into the street. He was, he said, afflicted with episodes of sleep-walking. What Mrs. Merrett made of this outlandish arrangement is not known, but the rope was allowed to remain in position.

Donald Merrett had formed some kind of attachment to a young lady dancing instructor at the Dunedin Palace in Picardy Place. On March 6th Merrett bought a second-hand A.J.S. motorcycle from a dealer in Greenside Place. In the afternoons and evenings he would hire the services of dancer Betty Christie and drive her, on the pillion, out into the countryside.

Booking Miss Christie out of the dance academy would cost

Donald fifteen shillings for an afternoon of her company, a pound in the early evening, and thirty shillings for a late-night outing.

On his ten-shillings allowance from his mother, Merrett managed to purchase two jade and opal rings costing £4 5s. One of the rings he gave to his friend Betty, as a keepsake. On February 13th, while living at Palmerston Place, Merrett went into Hardy Brothers' gun shop on Princes Street and bought an automatic pistol with fifty rounds of ammunition. After a visit to the police, he was issued with a firearms certificate. He told the police he wanted to go into the Braids to shoot rabbits.

A month after seventeen-year-old Donald Merrett equipped himself with the pistol, a letter was sent to Mrs. Merrett from the Clydesdale Bank. The letter informed her that her account was overdrawn to the tune of twenty-two pounds, a sum in the region of a thousand pounds in 1990s value. Three days later, the bank sent a similar letter, quoting the overdraft figure as £6 11s 3d. The first letter arrived on March 15th. The second was delivered to Mrs. Merrett at Buckingham Terrace on the morning of Wednesday, March 17th – a day that, both for Bertha Merrett and for her son Donald, would be like no other.

* * * * *

The exact train of events which occurred at 31 Buckingham Terrace, Edinburgh on March 17th 1926 has never been fully established. In the apartment that Wednesday morning, apart from Mrs. Merrett and her son Donald, was a 28-year-old woman named Henrietta Sutherland. Mrs. Sutherland, who was then living apart from her husband, had been hired by Mrs. Merrett to work as a maidservant. She worked each morning for three hours, cleaning the apartment and preparing a midday meal.

That morning, Henrietta, who liked to be called "Rita", arrived at Buckingham Terrace at 9am. She was later to give two differing accounts of what happened that morning. It is upon the first of these two accounts that the next part of our story is based.

At about 9.40am, as Rita was working in the kitchen at the rear of the apartment, Mrs. Merrett and Donald were in the front sitting room. Mrs. Merrett was seated at an oval gateleg table, facing the door. She was writing. Behind her was a bureau, its drop-leaf surface lowered, revealing a number of pigeon-hole compartments. When Rita left the sitting room, Donald was sitting in a recess on the opposite side of the room. He was either reading a book or sorting through some of his books before setting out for the university or, presumably, in some entirely different direction. The door of the sitting room had been left wide open.

Rita Sutherland collected a bucket of coal from the cellar in the hallway and went into the kitchen to make a fire. As she was arranging lumps of coal on top of kindling wood, Rita heard a loud explosion, followed quickly by a piercing scream and the heavy thudding sound of a falling body. The sounds seemed to come from the sitting room. The next thing Rita remembered was the sound of Donald Merrett's boots coming towards her along the hallway. The tumbling sound of falling books preceded Donald's arrival in the kitchen. As he stood looking at her, Donald said, "Rita, my mother has shot herself." He looked as if he were about to burst into tears.

As she had been working at Buckingham Terrace for only a week, Rita Sutherland knew very little about Mrs. Merrett's personal affairs. Consequently, she was completely at a loss to hazard a guess as to why she should have shot herself. All Rita could say to Donald was, "She seemed quite all right this morning, sir."

Donald told Rita his mother had received a letter from the bank that morning and that she was terribly worried about "money matters". He also said that he had been wasting his mother's money. She had quarrelled with him about it. He thought she was worried over that.

In the sitting room, Mrs. Merrett lay between the table and the bureau, bleeding from a wound in her right ear. Her chair had been overturned. A pistol lay front right on the bureau. Using the telephone in the hallway, Donald rang for the police.

When Donald returned from the phone, he asked Rita if she would help him to lift his mother onto a sofa. Rita replied, "I think we had best leave her, sir." Merrett, apparently in a shocked condition, and perhaps believing his mother to be dead, said "Let's go out. I cannot stand to look at it any longer." They went down to the street door. A minute or two later, the police arrived with an ambulance. Mrs. Merrett was not dead. She was taken to Edinburgh Royal Infirmary and put into a locked ward reserved for dangerous and suicidal patients.

At the infirmary, Mrs. Merrett was admitted to Ward 3 in the care of Dr. Roy Holcombe. At about noon, she regained consciousness.

After washing blood from her head with a swab, Dr. Holcombe could see an entry wound in Mrs. Merrett's skull. It was just behind her left ear. The hole was extremely small, about the size of a narrow pencil, but well-defined. Apart from a slight reddish discoloration, the surrounding skin was unmarked. Dr. Holcombe saw no blackening, which he might well have expected to see if there had been any powder burns from the pistol.

On the Wednesday afternoon, Mrs. Merrett slept. That evening, she awoke, complaining of a severe pain in her ear. Since, by attempting to kill herself, Mrs. Merrett had committed a crime, the infirmary maintained a policy of silence as far as discussing any details with Mrs. Merrett of what had happened to her. When she asked what was causing the pain, Dr. Holcombe told her "You have had a little accident, Mrs. Merrett."

The following evening, on the 18th, the ward sister, Elizabeth Grant, together with Nurse Innes, was changing Mrs. Merrett's bed linen. "What has happened to me?" asked Mrs. Merrett. "It's extraordinary," she said. Sworn to secrecy, Sister Grant said she did not know what had happened. The Sister did know a pistol shot had been heard. "Wasn't there a pistol there?" asked the Sister. "No, was there?" asked Mrs. Merrett, in apparent surprise. "Donald was standing beside me," she said. "He was waiting to post the letter."

At 7pm that evening, Sister Grant reported the conversation to Dr. Holcombe. Before Mrs. Merrett was admitted to Ward 3, Sister Grant had asked Donald what had happened to his mother. He said that he found his mother "shot in the face." She had, he said, been "quite normal that morning and the night before." Donald had explained to the Sister about his mother being worried about money. The Sister was puzzled and a little disturbed by the situation but, because she was experienced enough to know that patients involved in accidents very often could not remember anything about what had happened to them, she was not at that time unduly alarmed.

Briefed by Sister Grant, Dr. Holcombe came to Ward 3 and spoke to Mrs. Merrett. She asked him, "What did the X-ray show? Can I see an ear specialist?" Brushing aside her questions, Dr. Holcombe said, "Now, Mrs. Merrett, how did this accident happen?" "Well," said Mrs. Merrett, "I was sitting down writing letters and my son Donald was standing beside me. I said to him, 'Go away, Donald, and don't annoy me'. The next thing I heard a kind of explosion. I don't remember any more."

The Edinburgh police appeared to accept at face value that Mrs. Merrett had tried to kill herself. They did not inquire into any other scenario. If Mrs. Merrett had not shot herself, the alternative hypothesis was that Donald had shot her. This possibility, if, in fact, it occurred to the authorities, was passed over. As a result, no sick-bed statement was taken from Mrs. Merrett, neither was there any formal interview with Donald Merrett.

On the day after his conversation with Mrs. Merrett, Dr. Holcombe, beginning to suspect that foul play might have been involved, reported the matter to the police. On that day also, Dr. Holcombe asked Donald to explain what had happened. He said that he was over in the corner of the sitting room when he heard a shot and saw his mother falling to the ground, a revolver falling from her hand.

Although they did not realise it at the time, the police had already received two entirely different versions of the shooting incident from Rita Sutherland. Rita's first version was given to Constable Thomas Middlemiss when he arrived first at the apartment with Constable David Izatt. Rita told Middlemiss that she was in the kitchen when she heard the gunshot, and that Donald came into the kitchen to tell her what had happened. The second version, Rita gave to Detective Inspector Fleming when he arrived at 10am that morning. She told Fleming she was in the kitchen, heard a shot, and rushed into the hall-way from where, she said, she looked into the sitting room in time to see Mrs. Merrett falling from her chair, a pistol dropping from her grasp. It appeared that Fleming had accepted Rita's second version and had either ignored, or been unaware of, what she had told Middlemiss.

* * * * *

On Friday, March 19th, two days after the shooting, Mrs. Merrett received a visit from a close friend, a Mrs. Bertha Hill. At his mother's request, Donald had sent a telegram to Mrs. Hill. She had made the long journey from her home in Brighton. If Mrs. Hill expected to find her friend full of remorse and regret for what she had done to herself, this was not what she found when she spoke to Mrs. Merrett.

"Why am I here? What has happened to me?" asked Mrs. Merrett.

"You have had a fall," explained Mrs. Hill.

"But my left side is injured."

"Yes, you have had a fall on this side and it has injured your leg."

"No, I have not had a fall," said Mrs. Merrett. "I was writing a letter."

"To whom, Bertha?"

"To Mrs. Anderson, and a pistol went off under my ear."

"How could it?" asked Mrs. Hill. "Did you see the pistol?"

"No."

"Did you handle one?"

"No."

"Was there one there?"

"No."

Not wishing to press the matter further or to excite her friend, Mrs. Hill handed Mrs. Merrett a drink of water and moved away from her bedside.

Mrs. Hill sent a telegram to Mrs. Merrett's sister, Alice Penn. She lived in Chichester, but was then holidaying in the South of France. Mrs. Penn and her husband arrived in Edinburgh on March 24th and saw Mrs. Merrett that morning.

Mrs. Penn could not accept that her sister had tried to kill herself. She believed that such an act was not in Bertha's nature. Nothing she heard that day caused Mrs. Penn to change her opinion. Mrs. Merrett told Mrs. Penn that she may have had a fall, but she wasn't sure about it. She again said that she was writing a letter when "an explosion went off" in her ear. Mrs. Merrett then asked an extraordinary and sinister question, "Did Donald not do it? He is such a naughty boy!" Such a question probably showed that Mrs. Merrett was still unaware that she had actually been injured by the bullet fired from the gun.

Two days later, on March 26th, the Penns paid a second visit, this time accompanied by Donald. Dr. Holcombe explained to them that the prospects for Mrs. Merrett's recovery were far from good. As the bullet had lodged itself in her brain, the surgeons were unable to remove it safely. In reality, said Dr. Holcombe, there was no serious hope at all that Mrs. Merrett would survive very long. Hearing this news, Mrs. Penn became very distressed. In Sister Grant's room at the infirmary, Mrs. Penn decided to tackle Donald. "Donald," she said, "didn't you do it?" "No," said Donald, "I didn't do it. It must have been an accident."

As they left the infirmary, Alice and Walter Penn, in spite of their suspicions, decided to try to accept that the whole affair had, indeed, been a tragic accident. Nevertheless, it was very difficult for them to accept the idea completely.

When Mr. and Mrs. Penn and Donald arrived back at the apartment, they tried to reconstruct the accident. From their experiments they came to the conclusion that Mrs. Merrett might have unknowingly taken the pistol, with some papers, out of the drawer of the bureau and discharged the gun accidentally. In spite of what Donald had first told her, for Mrs. Penn suicide was not a possible motive.

Mrs. Merrett's health began to fail. On the night of Thursday, March 25th she was in a delirious condition. Next day she babbled away incoherently. On Saturday, March 27th, Mrs. Merrett lapsed into a coma. She lingered until the following Thursday, April 1st, at about 1am, when she died.

* * * * *

Just what had Donald Merrett been up to in the two weeks his mother was in hospital? On the day his mother was shot, he went to the Dunedin Palace and at 2pm "booked out" Betty Christie for the day. He took her on his motorcycle to Queensferry, where they had tea. Donald told Betty that his mother had shot herself, perhaps by accident. When they got back to the apartment at Buckingham Terrace, they were joined by a man friend of Betty by the name of Scott. Donald told him what had happened to his mother, saying it occurred when the maid was in the kitchen. Betty and the two men then went to the infirmary.

When Donald learned that his mother was conscious, he warned Betty and Scott not to tell her she had been shot. Before he left the infirmary, Donald told Sister Grant that she could find him, if need be, until 1am at the Dunedin Palace. He then booked into a room in the County Hotel, next to the Caley Picture House in Lothian Road.

Donald Merrett made no attempt to get in touch with any of his mother's Edinburgh friends. He did not meet Mrs. Hill when she arrived at Waverley Station on the 19th. She had to make her way to the Royal Infirmary alone at 6am, in order to discover where Donald could be found. After breakfast in his hotel, he took Mrs. Hill to see his mother, promising to return to meet her at lunchtime. Mrs. Hill waited until 2pm and telephoned the hotel, but all in vain. Finally, Donald looked in on her at 6.30pm, promising to see her on to the night express to King's Cross. He failed to turn up.

On the following Monday, Donald ordered a new H.A.D. racing motorcycle from Rossleigh Motors for £139, giving his A.J.S. for £30 in part-exchange.

On Tuesday, March 30th, two days before Mrs. Merrett's death, and nearly a fortnight after she was shot, the Edinburgh authorities showed some outward signs of activity. On that day, Mr. Penn, who was now living with his wife, and with Donald, at the apartment, telephoned Detective Inspector Fleming. Mr. Penn told him he had found a spent cartridge case in the sitting room. It was lying about a foot from the side of the bay window, some eight feet from where Mrs. Merrett had been sitting. When he arrived at the apartment, Fleming formally cautioned Donald and took a statement from him. This was the first time the police had interviewed him. This is part of Donald Merrett's signed statement,

"About noon on Saturday, March 12th, I had the pistol and loaded it with six cartridges. One was in the breech, with the safety catch on. I was going to the Braids to shoot rabbits. I wanted to take it on the Sunday morning, but my mother took it away from me and put it in the small drawer in the writing bureau. I think I told my mother to be careful, that it was loaded. I never saw the pistol again."

Merrett's statement continued, "On the morning of the 17th I saw an envelope addressed to Mrs. Anderson of 64 Murray Place, *Edinburgh*. Mrs. Anderson actually lived in Perth. I pointed out the mistake. My mother said, 'Go away, you worry me.' I went to the other side of the room to get my books, when I heard a report and saw my mother fall. She fell on her left side and the revolver was lying beside her right hand."

Donald then said, "I saw the maid in the hall and said to her, 'My mother has hurt herself.' I telephoned for the police."

Donald also said he lifted the pistol off the floor and put it on the corner of the bureau. He tried to lift his mother, but could not. All this, he said, was before he had seen the maid. He said he had destroyed the unfinished letter, seen by Fleming on the 17th, because there were blood marks on it. However, Fleming had noticed no blood on the letter.

Tackled again by Fleming, Rita Sutherland now said she was in the kitchen when Mrs. Merrett was shot and fell, and was not standing in the hall-way watching her fall.

After Mrs. Merrett's death, Mr. and Mrs. Penn, Donald and Rita stayed on in the apartment. In a medical report, Harvey Littlejohn, Professor of Forensic Medicine at Edinburgh University, stated that he was unable to say how Mrs. Merrett came to be shot. He said that, "there was nothing to indicate the distance at which the discharge of the weapon took place." The position of the wound was, "consistent with suicide, although an accident cannot wholly be excluded." Meanwhile, Donald went down to London with a taxi-driver friend and two girls. Some ten days later, he turned up at the Edinburgh apartment saying he was broke and had "walked back" from London. Soon afterwards, the university sacked him for absenteeism. Donald lived in the Ramsay Students' Lodge until the end of the summer term, after which he enjoyed a yachting holiday on the Clyde.

Mrs. Merrett willed money to her son, but the legacy was to be kept in the hands of the Public Trustee until he reached the age of 25. Believing that Donald may have avoided his studies because of some kind of derangement, the Trustee had him mentally examined. He was declared sound in body and perfectly sane. In August of 1926, Donald was sent to live at a vicarage in High Wycombe, both to get away from Edinburgh and to have private tuition with a view to going up to Oxford.

The police were slow-moving. On June 3rd, believing that Donald had withdrawn money from his mother's accounts by forging her cheques, he was taken to the police office and told to copy out Mrs. Merrett's signature for the purpose of comparison. Following a prolonged investigation, Merrett was taken into police custody on December 3rd and charged with uttering forged cheques to the value of £457 13s 6d.

After ballistic tests by Professor Littlejohn and Professor John Glaister, and a second medical report from Littlejohn, which now said that Mrs. Merrett's bullet wound could not have been self-inflicted, the forgery charge against Merrett was supplemented, on January 14th, by one for the murder of his mother. He was committed to stand trial at the Edinburgh High Court. Had the cheque forgeries not come to light, it is more than likely that Merrett would never have been tried for murder. It was almost as if he had been accused of killing his mother as an afterthought on the part of the authorities, a situation which was to weaken seriously the case against him. The fact that the murder charge was made some ten months after the event meant that witnesses' memories would be dimmed and numerous salient facts might be forgotten.

* * * * *

The trial began at Edinburgh on Tuesday, February 1st 1927, before the Lord Justice-Clerk, Lord Alness. The prosecution of Merrett was in the hands of Lord Advocate William Watson and Lord Kinross. Defence counsel were Craigie Aitchison K.C. and MacGregor Mitchell K.C. . An unusual feature was that Merrett would be tried on two charges at once – for forgery and for murder. It was not a case of trying him on the more serious charge first. The jury, fifteen strong under Scottish Law, consisted of six men and nine women. They would have to consider a verdict on each charge. From such an arrangement one can deduce that the Crown was not fully confident of getting a conviction for murder. As well as "guilty" and "not guilty" verdicts, that of "not proven" was also available to the jury.

In his opening address for the Crown, William Watson outlined the Merretts' domestic situation as it stood on the morning of the shooting, Wednesday, March 17th. Mrs. Merrett had written to the Midland Bank to ask for a new cheque book, but it had seemingly not been sent to her. On March 12th she dictated a letter to Donald asking why the bank had not sent the book. Mr. Watson said that Donald, having intercepted the Midland cheque book, wrote a post card to the bank, cancelling his mother's letter and saying that the book had now been found. A letter from the Clydesdale Bank, indicating an overdraft of £22, arrived on Monday, March 15th. Mr. Watson said that Donald paid this off on the Tuesday, using a forged Midland cheque, but because of a late clearance of one of his earlier cheques, a second Clydesdale overdraft letter, for £6 10s, arrived at the apartment on the Wednesday morning. It was this embarrassing letter that lay open on Mrs. Merrett's bureau. Mr. Watson told the jury he would call forensic, medical and other evidence to show that Mrs. Merrett did not shoot herself, neither did she have an accident on March 17th. She was killed, he said, by her only son, Donald Merrett.

The first day of the trial was occupied by police evidence. The first prosecution witness was Constable Thomas Middlemiss, first on the scene after the shooting. Right at the outset, it was obvious that Middlemiss had difficulty in remembering what he was expected to remember. Arriving with Constable Izatt and an ambulance, he met Merrett and Rita Sutherland at the front door of the building. Merrett told him his mother had shot herself. On going upstairs to the sitting room, Middlemiss found Mrs. Merrett lying on the floor. She was unconscious and was "making a choking sound as if there was blood in her throat." When asked about the positions of the furniture in the room, Middlemiss became vague and uncertain, saying, "About ten months have elapsed since I put in a report. I have been up and down a lot of places. I just cannot remember a lot of these things." Middlemiss said he picked up the pistol, rolled it up in a piece of paper, and put it into his pocket. Asked where exactly the pistol was lying, the constable was again indecisive, saying, "I don't know if I picked it up off the floor or the bureau."

Middlemiss said that Merrett told him he was on the other side of the room from his mother, that she was sitting writing, and that a shot went off. After seeing to his mother, said Merrett, he went into the kitchen and told the maid. After Merrett showed him a firearms certificate, Middlemiss reported the shooting as an attempted suicide.

The second police witness was Constable Izatt, Middlemiss's partner at the scene of the crime. Izatt testified that the pistol was lying on the floor near to Mrs. Merrett's right side. Izatt said Middlemiss bent down and picked it up. Izatt's evidence clashed with Middlemiss's version of events. According to Middlemiss, Merrett, when asked what could have made his mother shoot herself, replied, "Money matters."

"What do you mean by money matters?" asked Middlemiss. "Too much or too little?" "Just money matters," said Merrett.

Izatt's version was that Middlemiss asked if his mother was worried about money matters, and the youth replied, "Oh no, my mother is well off."

Rita Sutherland, said Middlemiss, told him that she was in the kitchen when she heard the shot. However, Inspector Fleming, who arrived at the apartment a little later, heard Rita say that she went into the lobby and saw Mrs. Merrett falling off her chair and saw the pistol dropping from her grasp. In evidence, Fleming said that he concluded that it was suicide because he read the two overdraft letters from the Clydesdale Bank, lying open on the writing bureau. At the end of the first day, the evidence for murder rather than suicide was, as yet, hardly convincing. The police evidence was flawed by inconsistencies and contradictions.

* * * * *

On the second day, the court was told about Mrs. Merrett's attitude, her statements and her questions as she lay in the infirmary. This evidence was hardly watertight, however. If the police had taken a sick-bed deposition from Mrs. Merrett, this could have been quoted directly in court. As it was, because of an apparent oversight, such a deposition was never obtained. Apparently, on March 19th, Constable William Watt went to the infirmary in response to a telephone call from Dr. Holcombe. From the infirmary, Watt rang the Edinburgh C.I.D. and asked if he should take a statement from Mrs. Merrett. Watt was told not to do so because a detective would be over to see Mrs. Merrett that afternoon. No detective appeared and no statement was taken. Any evidence about what Mrs. Merrett may or may not have said in the fortnight before her death was, therefore, only second-hand evidence which depended upon the memories of those concerned.

Mrs. Merrett gave the impression of not knowing that she had been shot. If she did realize it, she seemed not to believe that she had shot herself. She did remember that Donald had been standing by her as she sat at a table writing a letter. Perhaps she thought that Donald might simply have fired the weapon. Defending counsel Aitchison, in cross-examination of Dr. Holcombe, heard the doctor agree that Mrs. Merrett might not, after all, have told him Donald was actually standing beside her when she heard the shot. She may have said he was "standing in the room." Dr. Holcombe admitted that Mrs. Merrett told him she could not remember whom she was writing to at the time of the shot. In reply to Mr. Aitchison, the doctor agreed that "amnesia was a well-recognized feature with head injuries." On re-examination by Mr. Watson, Dr. Holcombe said Mrs. Merrett told him, "Donald was standing beside me." Having changed his mind twice, the doctor said, "I will stick to that."

In her cross-examination, Sister Grant said that she had known patients who had remembered nothing about the accident which had brought them into the hospital. She also said that she had known of a case where a would-be suicide had remembered nothing. Nurse Innes's evidence, in which she mentioned Mrs. Merrett's curiosity about what had happened to her, was to some extent nullified when, in cross-examination, the nurse admitted she had received coaching in her evidence from Sister Grant herself.

After Mrs. Hill had given evidence, Mrs. Merrett's sister, Alice Penn, went into the witness box. Again there was controversy over what Mrs. Merrett had said. Questioned about this by Mr. Watson, Mrs. Penn asked the judge, "Is this in order, my lord? Am I to answer this question?" Mrs. Penn testified that her sister had said she was sitting writing when "an explosion went off" in her head. She then asked Mrs. Penn if she would look after Donald. Still reluctant to speak, Mrs. Penn appealed again to the judge, "May I be excused, my lord?" She then said that Mrs. Merrett had told her, "It was as if Donald had shot me." Asked if she was quite certain of this, Mrs. Penn replied, "Yes, those words were burned into my mind."

The next witness, Walter Penn, recalled a conversation between Donald and Mrs. Penn in the nurses' room at the infirmary. According to Mr. Penn, Mrs. Penn said to Donald, "Donald, didn't you do it?" "No, auntie," he replied. "I did not do it, but if you like I will confess." At this, Mr. Penn said, "What a ridiculous thing, boy. You cannot do a thing like that."

Walter Penn was hard of hearing and wore a deaf aid. When Mr. Aitchison cross-examined him, the defence counsel adopted a clever method of casting doubt on what Donald actually said about a confession. Apparently, Mr. Penn was not wearing his aid when Donald was speaking. In the witness box, Penn said to Aitchison, "I will do it now to give you an idea what my normal hearing is like."

> Aitchison asked, "At the moment, is your hearing normal or abnormal?"
>
> "No, I cannot hear that," replied Penn. "I cannot hear that you are saying anything."
>
> Counsel stepped back to the dock rail and said, "I will confess if you like."
>
> "I can hear you talking," said Penn. "I can almost hear your articulation."
>
> Mr. Aitchison came nearer and repeated, "I will confess if you like."
>
> "It seems you are not trying to raise your voice at all," said Penn.
>
> Coming still nearer, to where he first was, Mr. Aitchison said again, "I will confess if you like."
>
> At last the words were understood. "You said, 'I will confess if you like.'"

"Was Donald's head as near your head as mine is to yours?" asked Aitchison. "That I cannot be quite sure of," said Penn. Knowing that Mrs. Penn had not mentioned Donald's offer to confess, Mr. Aitchison asked Penn, "Would your wife hear the words, 'I will confess if you like,'?" "Oh, I should think so. I feel quite sure she would." "And those words would burn themselves into her mind?" "That I don't know," said Penn. "It depends on what came after it or anything else." "And Mr. Jenks would have heard it as well, would he not?" "He must have, certainly."

Mr. Jenks was Penn's agent and was present at the time. Significantly, Jenks was not called as a witness to verify Donald's alleged remark. Aitchison's performance went a long way in casting doubt upon both the evidence of Walter Penn and that of Mrs. Penn.

* * * * *

The third day of the trial was occupied by scientific evidence for the prosecution. Mr. MacNaughton, a gunsmith, said Merrett's pistol a .25 automatic, was no good for rabbit shooting or target practice because of the shortness of its barrel. It was not a sporting weapon, but was more suitable for self-defence. Cross-examined, Mr. MacNaughton said that Merrett's cartridges contained a modified form of cordite known as "smokeless powder".

If Mrs. Merrett had shot herself, either deliberately or accidentally, one might expect that there would have been blackening of the skin around the entry wound, caused by the impact of hot cartridge powder on her skin. The absence of blackening would imply that she had been shot from a distance, in other words, that Merrett had fired the shot. None of the hospital staff could remember seeing any blackening around the wound after it had been washed with a moist swab.

The authorities contacted Professor Littlejohn of Edinburgh and Professor Glaister of Glasgow and asked them to carry out tests for blackening at different distances. Their tests were performed on December 8th 1926. Littlejohn and Glaister used cards to catch the black powder. The defence asked Sir Bernard Spilsbury and gunsmith Robert Churchill to do their own experiments. These took place in London on the Sunday before the trial began. They caught the blackening on fresh human skin. In both sets of experiments the range was varied from point-blank to six inches.

The results of the experiments did not agree with those from the defence. Littlejohn and Glaister could not remove blackening with a sponge wash when the pistol was discharged three inches away from the target. However, Spilsbury and Churchill found that the blackening at a range of one inch could be washed away by light pressure. Since the two sets of ballistic tests contradicted each other, they gave no real help to the jury in deciding the distance from Mrs. Merrett's ear at which the gun was fired and gave little guidance as to Merrett's culpability.

In cross-examination, Professor Littlejohn gave his opinion that, "suicide was not simply improbable, it was inconceivable." The credibility of Littlejohn's evidence was seriously weakened by the fact that in his report, dated 5th April 1926, he did not rule out suicide or accident, whereas in his second report, of 13th January 1927, the day before Merrett was charged with murder, Littlejohn ruled them out completely. "The wound," he said, "could not have been self-inflicted." The judge, knowing of the conflicting reports, asked Littlejohn to confirm that he had changed his opinion after a period of nine months. This confirmation, coming as it did at the very end of Littlejohn's spell in the box, could not have helped the prosecution case one iota.

After Littlejohn, Professor Glaister of Glasgow University gave his testimony. In cross-examination by Mr. Aitchison, Glaister discredited all the forensic evidence by making this remark, "You cannot tell a homicidal wound from a suicidal wound unless you are dealing with the actual weapon in your hand and see the wound produced."

Mr. Aitchison asked him, "Don't you agree the whole thing is in the region of conjecture?" Professor Glaister replied, "That is the truth of the whole case. It is problematic."

Mr. Watson completed the prosecution evidence at the end of the third day. The next two days were given over to evidence against Merrett on the forgery charge. On the sixth day of the trial, Monday, February 7th, Mr. Aitchison opened the case for the defence.

* * * * *

Did Rita Sutherland see Mrs. Merrett fall from her chair with the pistol in her hand? She had at first told Constable Middlemiss that she was in the kitchen, heard a shot, and saw nothing. About half an hour later Rita told Inspector Fleming she had run to the door of the sitting room and seen Mrs. Merrett falling. Later, she went back to her original story. For the defence, Mr. Aitchison called Dr. Rosa of Pitt Street, Edinburgh. He testified that on the evening after the shooting, Rita Sutherland telephoned him to say she was feeling unwell. Dr. Rosa said that when he talked to her at the apartment, Rita told him another version. Rita said she was in the sitting room. Mrs. Merrett was sitting at the table and Donald at a small table at the opposite end of the room. She said she saw Mrs. Merrett remove her false teeth. As she turned her back to leave the room, Mrs. Merrett shot herself. Detective Sergeant Henderson, who was with Fleming on the morning of the shooting, confirmed that he heard Rita say she saw Mrs. Merrett falling from her chair while Donald was across the room reading a book.

Sir Bernard Spilsbury and Robert Churchill described the results of their shooting experiments. Each of the two defence witnesses advanced theories as to how Mrs. Merrett could have either shot herself or been shot accidentally. Robert Churchill, gunsmith, of 39 Leicester Square, London, said that he knew of a case where a woman shot herself behind her right ear, in a direction roughly the same as in Mrs. Merrett's case. The wound, said Churchill, could have been produced without Mrs. Merrett moving her arm into an impossibly awkward position. It could, he said, have been caused by just an instinctive movement of her head. "Women," said Churchill, "instinctively flinch, close their eyes, and turn away from a discharge." The pistol, said Churchill, was of "a cheap Spanish make". The safety catch could have come off accidentally.

Sir Bernard Spilsbury, then a lecturer at St. Bartholomews's hospital, said the location of Mrs. Merrett's wound "was not inconsistent with suicide". He said also that he thought an accident unlikely. Spilsbury held the pistol himself and demonstrated how easy the position was. In cross-examination by Mr. Watson, Spilsbury said an accident could have occurred had Mrs. Merrett's elbow hit the edge or top of the bureau and applied pressure to the trigger. He showed his own dexterity by demonstrating for the jury how such an accident could have happened.

In evidence, George Robertson, Professor of Mental Diseases at Edinburgh Royal Infirmary, said he had not been directly involved in the investigation of the case. He had, he said, read the newspaper reports and been informed of the medical facts. Robertson stressed that patients who had sustained head injuries were very prone to suggestion and often suffered from memory loss. Mrs. Merrett's injuries, he said, would have included perforation of coverings of the brain, together with physical shock. Later, the brain would be inflamed, causing severe pain, and meningitis. Professor Robertson, who had been in charge of a hospital for shell-shocked soldiers in the Great War, said that head injuries often produced mental changes which he labelled "altered consciousness" or "dissociation". This condition might be "unrecognisable to an ordinary observer". Robertson quoted a case where a man had hanged himself and, while unconscious, been cut down by his wife. The man remembered nothing about the episode. When the injured man returned home after seeing a doctor, he told his parents it was the doctor who had caused the accident. Robertson said he could neither affirm nor deny that Mrs. Merrett suffered from dissociation. Nevertheless, he said, "Her statements must be viewed with caution."

If it were true that Mrs. Merrett suffered from memory loss or altered consciousness, she did say that she remembered Donald standing by her at her table and that later she heard an explosion under her ear. Any memory loss would seem to apply to the interval of time between these two events. During Robertson's evidence, the judge remarked, "Quite possibly, the interval of time between knowing her son was beside her and the explosion might have been considerable."

By the same token, if the two events were almost contemporaneous, one could conclude that Donald fired the pistol. This is the conclusion, despite her misgivings, that Mrs. Merrett seemed to have reached when she spoke to Mrs. Penn in the infirmary. As she said, Donald was "such a naughty boy". Mrs. Merrett may also have believed that Donald had simply fired the gun, but not at her. She seems to have been unaware that a bullet was lodged in her skull.

On the afternoon of the seventh day, following the defence evidence, Lord Advocate Watson addressed the jury on behalf of the Crown. Next morning, Mr. Aitchison began to speak in defence of Merrett.

Mr. Aitchison said, "This is a stale prosecution. The trial is taking place some ten months after the events, at a time when every circumstance that might have exonerated the accused has been obliterated. If there had been a proper investigation at the time, a murder charge would not have been brought. Analysed, the Crown's case amounts to Merrett being in the same room where his mother died."

In retrospect, the prosecution case did not seem convincing. Even if Rita Sutherland did not actually see anything happening in the sitting room, this hardly proved that Merrett fired the shot. Hearsay evidence about what Mrs. Merrett was alleged to have said when she was possibly suffering from brain damage might not convince the jury. There was, however, Merrett's callous behaviour towards his mother before and after her death. Would this prompt the jury to believe that he had shot his mother out of wilful spite? Mr. Aitchison explained Merrett's behaviour by saying it was "the apparently callous conduct of a youth who would be ashamed of showing anything that looked like emotion".

Mr. Aitchison ended his speech, "There are greater things in life than loyalty to one's own life, and there is no greater loyalty than to the memory of one's mother."

Referring to the absence of Merrett himself from the witness box, where he may well have said that his mother shot himself, Mr. Aitchison said, "There are people, and thank God there are people, who would rather go to their death with their lips sealed than that they should speak a single word that would reflect upon the name of a mother – a name which is incomparably the greatest name in all the vocabulary of our human life."

Finally, Mr. Aitchison said, "I leave the case there. Judge with truth and judge with insight. And I beseech you, if you have not got all the explanations you would have liked, do not jump to conclusions. There may be reasons which you do not know and of which you can know nothing. I need not remind you, members of the jury, of what your verdict means to the accused, who has undergone the ordeal of these trying days. Do not forget that he is without the guidance of a father, who should have been his guardian and his mentor as he was passing from boyhood into manhood. You have seen some of his relatives – and his mother is in her grave. But you have got to send him out to life; and I say to you, with the utmost respect, that if you send that lad out into life with a verdict of not proven, with a verdict that implies a stigma on him, upon the evidence that has been led in this case, then I say to you that you take a tremendous responsibility upon your shoulders.

Members of the jury, I claim from you with a clear conscience a verdict of not guilty upon both of these charges. Give him, by your verdict, a reputation up to which he will have to live for the rest of his life; and I will say this to you, as one who has been much and intimately in contact with him during these last few days – and it is my final word – send him out from this court-room this afternoon a free man with a clean bill and, as far as I can judge, he will never dishonour your verdict."

* * * * *

Lord Alness then gave his charge to the jury. The judge pointed out the weakening delay of the case for the Crown. Of the murder charge, the judge asked, "Is the Crown claiming at your hands a verdict against the accused upon the evidence which they deemed insufficient even to warrant his arrest upon this charge? Did the report of the forgeries induce the Crown to arrest him in December? Was that the new factor which induced the Crown, who had hitherto abstained from arresting the accused? Did the Crown conclude it had discovered a motive for the crime which until then had been lacking?"

The jury retired to consider their verdict at 4.35pm. They returned to court at 5.30pm. When asked for the verdict on the two charges, the jury foreman announced,

"The verdict under the first charge is not proven, by a majority, and on the second charge, uttering guilty, unanimously."

Lord Alness then sentenced Merrett on the forgery conviction to twelve months' imprisonment, limited because of his youth. After the trial it was revealed that the voting of the jury on the murder charge was 5 "guilty" and 10 "not proven". All the nine women jurors voted "not proven".

* * * * *

Twenty-seven years after being cleared of his mother's murder, Donald Merrett was again implicated in violent death. In the early hours of February 11th 1954, Merrett's wife, Isobel, whom he married in 1930, was found strangled in her bath at a nursing home for aged persons run by Merrett's mother-in-law at 22 Montpelier Road in Ealing. Isobel's mother, Mary Menzies, was found dead also. Her head had been battered and, like Isobel, she had been strangled.

Donald Merrett was now using the name "Ronald Chesney". During the Second World War, he had served as a lieutenant-commander in the Royal Naval Volunteer Reserve. During a life of crime, he had collected a string of convictions for cheque frauds, theft and currency trafficking. Five days after the discovery of the bodies of his wife and mother-in-law, Merrett, alias Chesney, was himself found dead in a wood near Cologne. He had been shot through the head. By his side was an American Colt .45 pistol. In his pocket was a British passport in the name of "John Donald Milner". A scrap of paper was also found on his body, on which he named a Fraulein Sonia Winnickes as his heir. He had written her a letter saying, "When you receive this I am no longer alive. After all I have gone through I have no chance."

At an inquest on the two women in March 1954, it was stated that Mrs. Chesney had been in fear of her life because she would not divorce her husband, who loved Sonia Winnickes. On his mother's death, Chesney, as Donald Merrett, had inherited her wealth. Ten thousand pounds was being held in trust for him and his wife in a marriage settlement. It seems that he blamed his mother-in-law for giving him away to the French police. A letter was found in which Chesney said he would not forget her betrayal.

Chesney had been trying to dispose of his wife Isobel for years. In 1951, a man called Pickersgill, whom Chesney knew in prison, had been offered £2,000 to kill her. Chesney gave him a plan of the Ealing house. Another former prisoner called Boyd said that Chesney told him how he tried to murder her by locking her in a bedroom and turning on the gas while she was asleep. Mrs. Chesney awoke in time and broke a window.

At the inquest, Chesney's solicitor read out a letter from him saying he was innocent of the two killings. Chesney wrote,

> "I have seen so much of prison that I have no wish to return there even for a day. The prospects of hanging appeal to me still less. I hope the police do find the doer of my deeds. I only wish to make sure that Miss Sonia Winnickes gets everything which devolved upon me, that is the settlement money of £10,000, the carpets, silver and chest of drawers at Montpelier Road."

At the close of the inquest, the jury returned a verdict of, "Murder committed by Ronald John Chesney." At the age of 46, Donald Merrett's role in the history of murder was, at last, at an end.

Chapter 3

The Savoy Hotel

At about 2.30am in the morning of Tuesday, July 10th 1923, in a suite on the fourth floor of London's Savoy Hotel, Prince Ali Kamel Fahmy Bey, a diplomat at the Egyptian legation in Paris and the son of a wealthy Egyptian landowner, was shot in the head by his French wife, Marie Marguerite Fahmy. At 2.55 the prince was admitted to Charing Cross hospital, where he died half an hour later from severe lacerations to the tissues of his brain.

Madame Fahmy was 32 when she shot her husband, who was ten years her junior. Born Marie Marguerite Alibert into a poor family, the future Madame Fahmy gave birth to a daughter, named Raymonde, when she was sixteen. The child was adopted by her grandmother. About twelve months later, Marguerite became engaged to André Mellor, the brother of a wealthy French racehorse owner. Dark-eyed, slim and attractive, the young Mademoiselle Alibert began to mix socially with wealthy people. In Bordeaux she lived with a married man. When this relationship ended, she returned to live in Paris, where, during the First World War, she lived as a kept woman with a variety of rich men. In 1919, at the age of 29, she married Charles Laurent, an interpreter at the Japanese consulate in Paris. The marriage ended in divorce a few months later.

As a result of a generous divorce settlement, Marguerite Laurent was now a wealthy woman in her own right, enjoying a comfortable life in fashionable Parisian society, a celebrated and popular member of the *beau monde*. As the year 1922 opened, Marguerite's star was very definitely in the ascendancy. Her life, however, was about to change, and not, as she had first anticipated, for the better. In January of that year, at the Majestic Hotel in Paris, she met the young, handsome, and incredibly wealthy Ali Fahmy.

If Maggie Alibert, who had trodden a path in life from rags to riches, could have been cast in the role of Cinderella, 21-year-old Prince Ali Kamel Fahmy was in no way a suitable candidate for her Prince Charming. For a long time at the start of his relationship with Marguerite, however, that is exactly the pantomime role he played.

Ali's father had died when he was a boy, leaving him a vast fortune and a huge annual income, chiefly from cotton plantations. If Marguerite had, at first, considered embarking simply on an entertaining fling with the young prince, then Ali himself did all he could to ensure that the affair would become more permanent. For this purpose he gave voice to persistent expressions of adoration and devotion, together with a generous profusion of expensive gifts. No expense or extravagance did he spare. When the couple were apart, Ali sent Marguerite a stream of passionate letters. When Ali was forced to return to Egypt, there were telegrams, in one of which he said, "I am dying. Your name alone is on my lips."

Dying or not, in November 1922, Marguerite agreed to visit Ali at his residence at Zamelek, on the coast, near Alexandria. It was now that Marguerite, who was herself long-accustomed to wealth and luxury, was to discover just how immensely rich her young lover was. The villa at Zamelek was, to all intents and purposes, a palace filled with a treasury of artefacts. The rooms were equipped with Louis XVI furniture, vast wall tapestries and Persian carpets. Marguerite was given a room designed for the King of Serbia. Her bathroom was made of white marble, with a solid silver bath and curtains of pure lace. At her disposal was a collection of sports cars, limousines, motor boats and a huge yacht, as well as a large staff of servants.

Prince Ali was not content to just live with Marguerite. He wanted her to become his wife. At the time, Ali believed that Marguerite was a widow named Maggie Mellor. If he knew any details of her career in Paris, it seemed to have no effect on his insistence that they should be married.

Eventually, Marguerite agreed to marry the prince. On December 26th 1922 there was a civil ceremony. After Marguerite had been converted to Islam, a religious wedding took place. Under Moslem law, after a great deal of hesitation, and great pressure from the Fahmy family, Marguerite waived the right to divorce and, in February 1923, became Madame Fahmy.

The newly-weds embarked upon a ten-day cruise on Ali's yacht, up the Nile to Luxor. They visited the temple at Karnak, the Valley of the Kings, and the tomb of Tutankhamun, discovered the previous November by Howard Carter, whom Ali entertained to dinner on his yacht. Local men would swim to the yacht begging for money. Ali beat them on the knuckles with a swagger stick as they came alongside. He read and censored Marguerite's outgoing letters and, after a heated disagreement about his cruel treatment of the crew, Ali stopped the vessel and went ashore in high dudgeon, leaving his new wife locked in her cabin. He later refused to allow her to leave the yacht at all until the end of the cruise.

The new Madame Fahmy was treated as a virtual prisoner in Ali's palace, under the ever-watchful eyes of his servants. Ali spent his nights in the fleshpots of Cairo. Instead of allowing the marriage a chance to blossom into friendship and affection, Ali seemed determined to behave as a master towards a female servant. Marguerite, who missed the company of her Parisian friends and contact with her parents and daughter, was quickly reduced to a condition of misery and desolation. Clearly, Ali had made a serious blunder by trying to control Marguerite by force. The mistake was compounded by the fact that she was a mature woman, who had for many years been accustomed to a great deal of independence and freedom of action. To Marguerite, the marriage, even at this very early stage, seemed doomed to failure. Unfortunately for her, she had already given up the right to divorce Ali, no matter how cruelly he might treat her, nor how many times he might be unfaithful.

* * * * *

In May 1923, after changing his mind several times, Ali took Marguerite to Paris. They stayed at the Majestic Hotel, where they had first been introduced. The prince's private secretary, Said Enani, went with them, together with a number of servants and Ali's pet dog. An Algerian bodyguard called 'La Costa', who terrified Marguerite by his malevolent expression and by his sheer bulk, was also present. She was strictly forbidden to travel in a motor car to call on her friends, having to ride on public trams accompanied continuously by one of Ali's black servants.

Ali decided they would make a tour of European cities. At the beginning of July, Ali, with Marguerite and his retinue of staff, left Paris for London. They booked into Suite 41 at the Savoy Hotel.

By the time the Fahmys arrived at the Savoy, their days together were regularly punctuated by heated arguments, usually over the most trifling matters. The exchange of insults and the trading of blows, even in public, had become commonplace. During their brief period as husband and wife, there had already been several quite serious incidents between them. Once, in Paris, after Marguerite returned home from a visit to a cinema, Ali struck her on the face so hard that her jaw was dislocated. He once threatened to get his Algerian guard to disfigure her face with acid from a car battery. On one occasion he said he would kill her with a pistol. To counteract Ali's malicious behaviour, Marguerite continually threatened to leave him. Each time she issued this threat, Ali became repentant and begged her for forgiveness. He would then continue his cruel treatment a day of two later.

At lunch on the day before the shooting, the conductor of the Savoy Orchestra asked Marguerite if she would care to choose a piece of music. "Thank you very much," she replied. "My husband is going to kill me in twenty-four hours' time, and I am not very anxious for music." Making light of the matter, the conductor commented, "I hope you will still be here tomorrow, Madame."

Arguments continued that evening at the theatre. Marguerite was talking about leaving on her own the next day, bound for Paris. Ali, who was trying to be pleasant to her for a change, begged her to stay with him in London. Marguerite insisted she would travel in the morning. At supper in the Savoy, the bickering continued apace. Eventually, at about 1.45am, Marguerite went up to the suite, followed a few moments later by Ali.

At about 2.30am, John Beattie, the night porter, was wheeling a trolley of luggage along the fourth floor corridor. The door of suite 41 opened and out came Ali in his pyjamas, followed closely by Marguerite in an evening dress. Both were in a state of frantic excitement. Ali approached Beattie and said to him, "Look what she has done!" He pointed to his cheek. Beattie could just about make out a small red mark. Marguerite started pointing towards her eyes, babbling excitedly in French. The porter, used to dealing with rather difficult guests, did his best to calm the couple and asked them to go back into their quarters, but to no avail. Tired and more than a little exasperated by the quarrelling pair, Beattie started to walk away along the corridor towards an end staircase.

Beattie then heard a whistle and, looking back, saw Ali crouching down, beckoning a small dog. It had evidently escaped from the suite. A few seconds later, the porter heard, in quick succession, three gunshots. Turning swiftly back towards the door of suite 41, Beattie was just in time to see Marguerite throwing a gun on to the floor. Ali lay slumped against a wall. Beattie went towards Marguerite, picked up the gun, and took hold, very gently, of her wrists. As Beattie began to lead her from the scene, Marguerite knelt down by Ali's body and spoke to him in French. Ali, unconscious, was unable to reply. Blood from a head wound began to seep into the corridor carpet. Marguerite's earlier agitation had disappeared. It had been replaced by an air of calm and detachment. The silence was broken by the whimpering of Ali's little dog.

* * * * *

Later in the morning of July 10th, Madame Fahmy, now widowed, appeared at Bow Street Magistrates Court, charged with murder. Escorted into court by a nurse, she looked pale and decidedly ill. The magistrate allowed her to sit in the dock. After a short hearing, she was remanded in custody and taken in a taxi to Holloway Prison.

At the present time, where there has been a suspicious death and when criminal proceedings are likely to be taken against an individual, an inquest is opened briefly, allowing formal evidence of identification and medical evidence as to the cause of death to be placed in front of the coroner. Once this has happened, the coroner usually adjourns the inquest until some distant future date. In this way, the body can be released for burial or cremation. In the 1920s, the coroner's inquest was played out in full. The proceedings could sometimes extend over two or three days. After hearing evidence from witnesses, the inquest jury would decide, on the guidance of the coroner, the cause of death. In a case of murder, the jury could name an individual culprit. Such an inquest was opened at Westminster Coroner's Court on July 12th 1923, just two days after the death of Prince Ali Fahmy. The coroner was Mr. Ingleby Oddie. Madame Fahmy did not attend the hearing, but she was represented by a solicitor, Mr. Freke Palmer.

In his evidence at the inquest, head porter John Beattie described what he had witnessed at the hotel on the night of the shooting. He said he had picked up three spent cartridge cases and a bullet in the corridor outside the Fahmy's suite. Evidence was given by Madame Fahmy's doctor, Dr. Gordon of Southampton Street, off the Strand. He said she had consulted him about a painful condition of haemorrhoids. The doctor suggested she should have an operation. Marguerite agreed to this and, on Monday, July 9th, it was arranged that she should enter a nursing home the following day. However, on the morning of the 10th, Dr. Gordon saw his patient earlier than he had expected. Informed of the shooting that early morning, he hurried to the Savoy.

Dr. Gordon told the inquest jury that he spoke to Madame Fahmy in suite 41 at about 2.30am. She confessed to him that she had shot her husband and asked the doctor what would happen. A police sergeant asked Dr. Gordon to question her because she spoke only French. "Did you do it?" asked Dr. Gordon. "Yes," she replied. "With that?" asked the doctor, pointing to the gun. "Yes."

Madame Fahmy told Dr. Gordon she had intended to go to Paris, have her operation there, and visit her family. She said Ali had been ill-treating her earlier that evening and had forced his attentions on her. Ali had, she said, threatened to kill her if she left him, even to go to Paris. At supper, she said he had threatened to hit her with a wine bottle. Madame Fahmy said that Ali, in the bedroom after supper, approached her and threatened her. To frighten him, she fired the pistol out of the open window and then, thinking the weapon was now unloaded, fired it again. When Ali fell, said Madame Fahmy, she thought he was shamming. It was not until she saw blood that she realised what she had done. The trigger, she said, had gone off so very easily.

Further evidence revealed how, at Bow Street police station, Marguerite appeared to be in a complete daze. She told Inspector Grosse, "I cannot understand what I have done. They say I have shot my husband. How many shots did I fire?"

When told Ali was dead, she broke down in tears. Under caution at the police station, she was alleged to have said, "I told the police I did it. I have told the truth. It does not matter. He has assaulted me in front of many people since we have been married. He has told me many times to kill him, and many people have heard him say so." When charged with murder, Madame Fahmy replied, "I understand. I lost my head."

After a summary of the evidence by Coroner Oddie, the inquest jury, without leaving the jury box, returned their verdict, "Wilful murder by Madame Fahmy."

Legal process moved swiftly. On Saturday, July 21st, after the preliminary hearing, at which the prosecution case was presented in front of magistrates, Marguerite Fahmy was committed for trial at the Central Criminal Court, Old Bailey.

* * * * *

The Old Bailey trial opened on Monday, September 10th 1923, only two months after the death of Prince Ali. Crown counsel were Percival Clarke and Eustace Fulton. Madame Fahmy, who was rich enough to afford the fees demanded by the very best criminal barristers of the time, had engaged the services of three – Sir Edward Marshall Hall K.C., Sir Henry Curtis-Bennett K.C., and Roland Oliver. The judge was Mr. Justice Rigby Swift. The proceedings were to be translated for Madame Fahmy by an interpreter. After the charge had been read out to her, Madame Fahmy, dressed in deep black mourning clothes, pleaded *"non coupable*".

After Percival Clarke had presented an outline of the Crown's case, he called his first witness. This was Prince Ali's personal private secretary, a man called Said Enani. Enani had a close relationship with his master. Unknown to the jury, critical comments and numerous satirical lampoons had appeared in the Cairo press, implying that Enani had complete control over the young prince, both in business and social matters. There was talk in Cairo that Ali had relationships with young boys and that he had formed a similar liaison with Enani, who was using the alliance to manipulate the prince like a puppet. None of this scandal could be made public at the trial.

Ali Fahmy was in no way related to the Egyptian royal family. He had been given the title "prince" for his charitable donations from his vast fortune. A cynic would have said that Fahmy had, in effect, purchased his title, a fact that was not lost on his numerous critics in his homeland.

During cross-examination by Sir Edward Marshall Hall, Enani agreed that he had tried to dissuade Fahmy from marrying Marguerite. When asked if he was "much attached" to Fahmy, Enani said that he was, but denied having any influence over him or that that influence made Marguerite jealous. His relationship with Ali, he said, was not just one of master and servant. They were "great friends". Enani said he did know about Fahmy's intimacies with many women, but he could not say they were treated brutally. Attempting to show that Marguerite may have been tricked into visiting Egypt, Hall forced Enani to admit that Fahmy used to pretend he was dangerously ill, and then write to Marguerite, saying that her presence was the only way of saving his life. On October 4th 1922, Enani sent a telegram to Marguerite, backing up Fahmy's pretence. It read,

"No news from you. Baba seriously ill since arrival.

Have not been able to write to you, being busy with him. Hope for prompt recovery. Telegraph from time to time."

Hall asked Enani, "Do you know she came out to Egypt in the belief that Fahmy had been dangerously ill?" "Yes," replied Enani, "but it was only a question of advancing the date." Questioned about Fahmy's guard and valet, La Costa, Enani said he had never told the black Algerian to watch Madame Fahmy. He said she became a Moslem to ensure that Fahmy would inherit his mother's legacy. Hall asked Enani if he knew that on February 21st, Fahmy swore on the Koran he would kill Marguerite. Enani said he did not know of such a pledge. The defence counsel showed Enani a letter written by Fahmy to Madeleine, Marguerite's sister. It included the passage:

> "Just now I am engaged in training her. Yesterday, to begin, I did not come into lunch or dinner, and I also left her at the theatre. This will teach her, I hope, to respect my wishes. With women one must act with energy and be severe."

Hall asked, "Did he say, 'I am taming her'?" "I do not know what you mean by 'taming'. He said that if she would obey him he would be nice to her."

"From being a gay, cheerful, entertaining and fascinating woman, was she not sad and broken, miserable and wretched?" asked Hall. "They were always quarrelling," said Enani. He also said he remembered Fahmy dislocating Marguerite's jaw. He knew nothing, he said, about Fahmy trying to strangle her.

Evidence from prosecution witnesses helped to build up a picture of Marguerite's manner after Fahmy was shot. Arthur Mariani, the night manager, whom the porter Beattie called to the scene, told the court how he asked Madame Fahmy why she had done such a terrible thing. She told Mariani, "Sir, I have been married for six months. It has been a torture for me. I have suffered terribly. I lost my head. I lost my head."

Then from the suite, she telephoned Enani and said, *"Venez vite. Venez vite. J'ai tiré sur Ali."* ("Come quickly. I have shot Ali.") Continuing in French, she told Enani, "I don't know how I did it." Enani ran downstairs to the fourth floor to find his master being carried away on a stretcher.

Could Madame Fahmy have fired three shots accidentally? The

pistol was a Browning .25 automatic. When a round was shot from the weapon, the spent cartridge case was automatically ejected and replaced by a fresh one. The gun did not have to be re-cocked to fire a second round. For the prosecution, gunsmith Robert Churchill agreed that each shot required a separate squeeze of the trigger. Three shots would, therefore, require three distinct pulls, making the accidental discharge of three shots extremely unlikely. In cross-examination, however, Churchill agreed with Marshall Hall that an inexperienced person might easily reload the weapon, thinking it was being emptied.

Marguerite's physician, Dr. Gordon, to whom she admitted having killed Ali, told the court how she was about to enter a nursing home for an operation on the morning of the shooting. Marguerite, said Gordon, had written a letter to him. It told him that instead of having the operation in England, she would be going to have it done in Paris. She gave the un-posted letter to him before she appeared at Bow Street. It read,

> "Doctor – affairs have come to a crisis. My husband refuses to take the responsibility for my operation. I am, therefore, returning to my family – that is to say, tomorrow I leave for Paris. Will you excuse me to the doctor who was kind enough to look after me, and believe me. Yours gratefully, M. Fahmy."

According to Dr. Gordon, the phrase "responsibility for my operation" did not only mean that Ali refused to pay for it. Dr. Gordon said Madame Fahmy meant that Ali refused to accept that he had been responsible for her condition, haemorrhoids, which the operations were designed to put right. In cross-examination, Dr. Gordon said that he believed Madame Fahmy's medical condition had been caused, or aggravated, by unnatural sexual acts. This bombshell was followed by Dr. Gordon's testimony that marks found on the back of Madame Fahmy's neck were consistent with Ali's hand having grasped her throat before the shooting.

After police evidence had been submitted by Detective-Inspector Grosse and Detective-Sergeant Allen, Mr. Percival Clarke declared the case for the prosecution closed. In the afternoon of the second day of trial, Sir Edward Marshall Hall stood up to make his opening remarks to the jury.

* * * * *

For Madame Fahmy to be acquitted of murder, the jury would have to believe that either the pistol went off accidentally, or that she shot Prince Ali in self-defence. The jury had the option of convicting Madame Fahmy of manslaughter if they believed that she was put under such severe provocation that she had little or no choice but to fire the pistol. Were she to be found guilty of murder, Marguerite Fahmy would automatically be sentenced to death.

In his opening remarks, Sir Edward Marshall Hall asked the jury for a not guilty verdict, not a conviction for manslaughter. He began by revealing to the jury the black side of Ali Fahmy's character. Speaking ill of the dead may be taboo, but it was Hall's duty to Madame Fahmy to speak against Ali. In this way, the killing might be justified in the eyes of the jury.

"Price Ali Fahmy," said Hall, "was a sadist who enjoyed the sufferings of women. He was abnormal and a brute." Under the marriage contract, Madame Fahmy, said Hall, was promised £2,000 by Ali. She received only £450 and an I.O.U. Madame Fahmy, said Hall, was "at the mercy of Ali and his entourage of black servants." In January 1923, she drew up a document, put it into a sealed envelope, and gave it to her lawyer. The envelope was to be opened after her death. She accused Prince Ali of having sworn a holy oath on the Koran that some time, some day, he would kill her. Ali took this extraordinary action, claimed Hall, because Madame Fahmy would not hand over to him her large collection of jewellery.

After the marriage, said Hall, Fahmy changed, "From the plausible, kind, attentive lover into a ferocious brute." Through Ali's cruelty, she became nervous and, at times, "almost in a dazed condition." He said the conditions under which she had to live "make one shudder." Ali, said Hall, inflicted numerous assaults upon Madame Fahmy, as well as insults. Once, when she asked him to pay a bill for 18,000 francs, he told her to "find a lover to pay for it." Far from wanting to divorce her, Ali dictated a document saying that whatever she did, he would never release her from the marriage. "He heaped every sort of indignity upon her," said Hall.

At the start of the proceedings on the third day, Hall told Mr. Justice Swift that he wished to argue a point of law. After the jury had left the court, Hall pointed out to the judge that Mr. Percival Clarke had said he proposed to cross-examine Madame Fahmy as to whether she had led an immoral life, and was, therefore, a woman of the world, well able to take care of herself. Hall objected to this line of cross-examination on the grounds that it might prejudice the jury against his client. Mr. Justice Swift ruled that Madame Fahmy should be cross-examined only about her relations with her husband. When the jury returned to their seats, the judge told them that they would be denied access to newspapers (which would record Hall's legal argument), until the trial was over.

It was now the turn of Madame Fahmy herself to give evidence. Her testimony was to occupy the next seven hours of the trial. Helped into the witness box by a wardress and replying to questions through a male interpreter, Madame Fahmy said she was 32. In 1919 she was married to a Monsieur Laurent, whom she divorced on the grounds of his desertion. Madame Fahmy said she first agreed to go to live with Ali in Egypt because she believed him when he said he was ill. She thought it necessary for his recovery. Madame Fahmy described how, at Ali's house on Christmas Day 1922, there was a quarrel. Believing Ali to be no longer sincere, she wanted to leave him and return to France. However, on the very next day, she signed a civil contract of marriage. The only reason she gave for this *volte-face* was, "He made a scene of desperation to make me stay."

Towards the end of January, said Madame Fahmy, there was yet another disagreement. Ali took the Koran in his hand and said, "I swear on the Koran that I will kill you, and that you shall die by my hand." She told her lawyer about this oath and sent a sealed document to be opened in the event of her death. Ali begged for her forgiveness, swearing now to love her in the future. However, on the very first day after they left Cairo, Ali tried to frighten her by firing a revolver over her head. He began to strike her and, during the three-days' journey to Luxor, he locked her in her cabin. They quarrelled violently during the entire journey. Marguerite said she was "in a state of terror, alone on board and surrounded by black men."

She again contacted her lawyer, asking for people to be sent to confirm that she had been injured by Ali's attacks. She told the lawyer that she had on her arms "the mark's of my husband's gentleness". This was her plea: "I ask you to send one or two persons who will have this condition established, so as to make use of it."

After promises of good behaviour from Ali, she sent the lawyer a wire, cancelling the arrangement: "Send nobody. Wait for new letter."

According to Marguerite, the state of sporadic warfare between herself and Ali continued in Paris. It was here that firearms appeared on the scene. She said that Ali threatened her with a horsewhip, seized her by the throat, and threw her backwards on to the floor. This attack was halted, she said, by her sister pointing a pistol at him. She herself began to keep a pistol close to hand. On one occasion, she said, she tried to frighten him with one, threatening to shoot him if he did not stop beating her.

Ali became obsessed with the idea that Marguerite might leave him. It was only by threatening to do so that she was able to control his wild behaviour. In retrospect, it might have been better had she gone through with her threat.

While staying at the Savoy, Madame Fahmy took the opportunity to visit her daughter Raymonde, now aged 16, and attending a school near London. Ali's behaviour, she said, did not change, in spite of his continual promises to improve. She told how, in the Riviera Club, he threatened to throw her in the Thames, saying, "I am tired of you." A night or two later, she told him she preferred to die rather than go on living as she had been doing. To this statement, said Marguerite, Ali said, "You have a revolver." Pointing to the window, he said, "It is quite easy, there are four floors."

* * * * *

In the afternoon of the third day of the trial, Madame Fahmy, from the witness box, gave her version of what happened on the night of Ali's death, and how she came to fire the gun. Ali found out that Marguerite had told Dr. Gordon about her condition and that she had made arrangements to have an operation in London. She said that Ali was angry when he knew she had consulted a doctor. He refused to pay for the operation. She told her maid to pack her luggage ready for her return to Paris. Ali was now furious. She said he ripped a photograph of himself out of its frame, tore it up, and threw the pieces into her face. If she left him, he said, his pride could not suffer the hurt. "You will see!" he said. "You will see!"

Marguerite said she believed he was so angry that he might kill her. She said she decided to frighten him with the pistol. To make the weapon safe, she said, she tried to remove the cartridges as she had seen Ali do it, but to no avail. She said she was shaking the pistol in front of an open window when it went off. Believing that the gun was now safe, she put it down the side of an easy chair. She then left with Ali and Enani for the theatre.

On returning to the hotel, Marguerite and the two men ate supper in the restaurant. More quarrelling broke out. Enani tried to pour oil on to troubled waters by getting Ali to calm down. At one point, Ali threatened to smash her head in with a wine bottle. In a violent temper, he shouted, "I will disfigure you, and after that you can go to the devil!"

There was a dreadful thunderstorm over central London that night. When Marguerite went up to her bedroom at about 1am, the storm, she said, "was raging terribly". She said, "I am afraid of thunder and lightning. I was very nervous and tired as well." Too scared to go to bed, she went into the sitting room and wrote two letters, one of which was to Dr. Gordon, explaining that she would be going to Paris later that morning to have her haemorrhoids operation there. About half an hour later, Ali came to the sitting room door and asked her what she was doing. She replied, "I have sent a cheque to the doctor. Are you going to give me any money to leave tomorrow?" "Come to my room," said Ali, "and see if I have any money for you." She went into his room. He showed her some pound notes and about two thousand francs. She asked Ali for the francs for the voyage to France. "I will give it to you if you earn it," he said. When Ali took told of her, she refused to co-operate. He started to tear off her dress. According to her testimony, Marguerite tried to get to the telephone to summon help. Ali grabbed hold of her hand and dragged her towards him. She hit him on the head. Ali responded by twisting her arms and punching her in the face. At this point, she said, she rushed out into the corridor. Ali followed her and ordered her back inside.

As things turned out, it might have been wise if Marguerite had sought help there and then, but she did not. Instead, she returned to her room. She described what happened next. Her account was translated into English by the interpreter.

"As soon as he got into my room, he advanced with a very threatening expression. He said, 'I will avenge myself.' I went out into the corridor. He seized me suddenly and brutally by the throat with his left hand. His thumb was on my windpipe, his fingers pressed into my neck. I got away. He crouched to spring at me, saying, 'I will kill you.' I raised my arm, and without looking, pulled the trigger. The next moment I saw him on the floor in front of me, without realizing what had happened. I do not know home many times the pistol went off. I did not know what had happened. I asked the people what all the trouble was. I saw my husband on the floor. I fell on my knees beside him. I caught hold of his hand and said, 'Sweetheart, it is nothing. Speak, please speak to me.' While I was on my knees, the porter arrived, but I was so touched that I understood nothing."

Madame Fahmy said the shooting was an accident. She said, "I thought there was no cartridge when you had pulled the barrel and that it could not be used." Asked by Marshall Hall why she pulled the trigger, she replied, "I was afraid he was going to jump on me."

As she told her story in the witness box, Madame Fahmy was frequently in tears. Once she seemed so overcome that the judge asked her if she needed time to compose herself. She declined his offer of an adjournment.

* * * * *

Towards the end of the third day, Crown counsel Percival Clarke began his cross-examination of Madame Fahmy. When he asked her if her father was a cab-driver, the judge intervened to enquire of Clarke if the question was relevant. Clarke did not pursue the matter. He tried to show that Madame Fahmy knew about the situation of rich, married women in Egypt and did not go to that country in total ignorance of Egyptian domestic arrangements. She said that she visited Egypt in 1915, travelling there with two men, one of whom was Egyptian. She said that she did know that Egyptian wives were attended by servants. Madame Fahmy said she met Prince Ali through a lady friend of hers. "When I went to Egypt to see Ali, I had decided nothing concerning marriage, I expected to be his *amie*." She said she was not ambitious to marry Ali, but she did love him. She denied ever threatening him, but she said she had once "boxed his ears when he had beaten me very much".

At the start of the fourth day, before Clarke began his cross-examination, Sir Edward Marshall Hall had the interpreter changed. The man was replaced by a Madame Simon, believed to be a French barrister. Marshall Hall explained to the judge that Madame Fahmy had found difficulty in understanding the male interpreter. The real reason for the change could have been that being a French woman, the new interpreter would, when standing and speaking alongside Madame Fahmy, make a more favourable impression upon the jury.

Concerning the signing-away of her rights to divorce Ali, Madame

Fahmy said that she had refused to sign the contract at first, but did so eventually, under pressure. A document, giving Ali the right to act in any way he wished without risk of divorce, was written by her, at Ali's dictation. Mr. Clarke asked her about it, "Did you write it to assist you in your divorce?" "I never produced it. It was so degrading to me." Here Madame Fahmy burst into tears and covered her face with her hands.

Madame Fahmy said she received from Laurent, her first husband, an annual allowance of 36,000 francs. She said her life in Paris had been "a gay life, but not immorally gay, going to dinners, theatres and the like". Of her married life with Prince Ali, she said, "I was always alternating between hope and fear. Some days he would be nice and I had a new confidence in him, but by the next day he would be bad again. It was always the same."

Sometimes, she said, she thought Enani was in league with Ali to ill treat her. If she ever spoke to Enani in confidence, he would carry tales to Ali. "He always did whatever he could to make things worse."

Asked by Clarke why she did not flee from Ali when he left her alone in Paris while he visited Stuttgart, she said, "I could not have escaped. Enani would have followed me." She said she kept her suffering to herself. "I did not tell my friends in Paris because I thought they would laugh at me."

Prosecuting counsel Clarke turned his attention to the shooting and to Madame Fahmy's gun. Clarke placed the weapon before her on the front edge of the witness box. He invited her to pick it up and examine it. Gingerly, she took hold of the weapon. The jury watched her intently. In response to Clarke's questioning, Madame Fahmy said, "I thought that when a bullet had been fired, the pistol was unloaded." Having earlier in the evening, before going to the theatre, fired the pistol through the open window, she said she believed the gun could not again fire a round without being adjusted.

"I never wanted to kill my husband," she said. "I only wanted to prevent him from killing me. I though the sight of the pistol might frighten him. I never wanted to do him any harm. I never did."

She said she pulled the trigger and saw Ali on the floor before she realized what had happened. "I never did anything intentionally. I just moved my arm when I saw he wanted to come at me. It was done instinctively. I just thought it might stop him."

At this point in her testimony, Madame Fahmy claimed that just before the shooting, Ali called up the night manager on the telephone. "I wanted to call the night manager," she said, "but my husband did so because I cannot speak English." To this, Clarke asked, "You don't suggest he called the night manager so that he might see him kill you?" Madame Fahmy replied, "He was not afraid of me. I was afraid of him." "Did you know your husband was absolutely unarmed when you pointed the weapon at him?" "I did not know. He often had a pistol in the pocket of his dressing gown. The thunderstorm was so awful. I was in such a terrible state of nerves. I do not know what I thought of it at the time."

Clarke continued, "Isn't that when you fired the shot out of the window – at the height of the storm – to see, as I suggest, if the pistol was in working order?" "No," she replied, "That shot was fired at half past eight." "Were you not fully aware that if your husband attacked you, you could immediately ring the telephone bell and get assistance?" "I could not speak English. What could I say?" "Could you not have got your maid to stay by you that night?" "She had gone to bed and was on the eighth floor. I had no telephone to her."

After Percival Clarke's cross-examination, Marshall Hall got to his feet again to re-examine Madame Fahmy. He read out, in French, the sealed letter she sent to her lawyer, Mrs. Assuard, from the honeymoon yacht at Luxor. The lady interpreter translated the letter into English as Hall read it out:

> "I, Marguerite Alibert, of full age, of sound mind and body, formally accuse, in case of death, violent or otherwise, Ali Bey Fahmy of having contributed to my disappearance. Yesterday, January 21, 1923 at 3 o'clock in the afternoon, he took his Bible or Koran – I don't know what it is called – kissed it, put his hand on it, swearing to avenge himself on me, tomorrow, in eight days, in a month, in three months, but I must disappear by his hand. This oath was taken without any reason, neither jealousy nor bad conduct, nor a scene on my part. I desire and demand justice for my daughter and for my family. Done at Zamelek, at about 11am, January 22, 1923 – Signed M. Marguerite Alibert.
>
> P.S. Today he wanted to take my jewellery from me. I refused, hence another scene."

* * * * *

After Hall had finished reading, Madame Fahmy left the witness box and returned to the dock. It was now time for Hall to speak to the jury on her behalf. Sir Edward Marshall Hall's two and a half hours' speech to the jury was in two parts. It began towards the end of proceedings on the fourth day and was resumed on the morning of the fifth. Hall did not suggest that Madame Fahmy had killed in self-defence alone. He also claimed it was a case of self-defence by accident. He said that Madame Fahmy pointed her pistol at Prince Ali in order to stop him attacking her. Then, because of her misunderstanding of how the gun worked, she fired it, believing the chamber of the pistol to be empty. Hall's theory gave the jury two ways to save Madame Fahmy from the gallows. However, his main platform was self-defence. He told the jury, "Either it was a deliberate, premeditated and cowardly murder, or it was a shot fired by a woman from a pistol she believed to be unloaded at a moment when she thought her life to be in danger."

In the 1920s there was a widespread belief that in the streets of English cities there were men lurking, ready when the opportunity arose, to inveigle innocent young girls into their clutches, hold them prisoner, and smuggle them out to a life of prostitution and slavery in the Orient. Many were the cautionary tales with which mothers warned their daughters about the dreadful danger of being friendly towards strange men, who could, for all they knew, be "white slavers", ready in the twinkling of any eye to capture them and take them away to a fate worse than death in the bazaars and harems of the East. It was against this background that Marshall Hall painted a picture to the jury of Madame Fahmy, a beautiful European woman, coming under the cruel influence of an Arab Prince, imprisoned inside a marriage to a wicked and sadistic "Oriental". "Madame Fahmy's great mistake," said Hall, "possibly the greatest a woman could make, was, as a woman of the West, marrying an Oriental. It is common knowledge," he said, "that the Oriental's treatment of women does not fit in with the idea the Western woman has of the proper way she should be treated by her husband." Warming to his theme, Hall continued, "The curse of this case is the atmosphere which we cannot understand – the Eastern feeling of possession of the woman, the Turk in his harem, the man who is entitled to have four wives, if he likes, for chattels. That is something we cannot quite deal with."

Marshall Hall's comments about Egyptian men were later to cause a distinct chill in the temperature of Anglo-Egyptian relations. After singing the praises of ancient Egyptian civilization, Hall said, "I suppose there are many magnificent Egyptians today, but if you strip off the external civilization of the Oriental, you have the real Oriental underneath."

The fact that neither Crown counsel Clarke nor Mr. Justice Swift interrupted Hall's racial comments speaks volumes for the way nations beyond the shores of Great Britain were often viewed at the time. Hall's remarks, if uttered in a court-room today, would quite possibly result in a barrister being disciplined. As it was, they formed a main plank of Hall's defence.

"Prince Ali," said Hall, "struck Madame Fahmy to show his mastership of this Western woman. He wished to tame her, to destroy her will-power and her self-control."

Enani, said Hall, was hostile to Madame Fahmy and played a role of "Eastern duplicity". Hall told the jury, "You have seen Said Enani, and have heard something about him. Is he the kind of man you would have as the sole buffer between yourself and a man like Fahmy?" Fahmy, said Hall, developed "abnormal tendencies" in his relations with his wife. "It is," said Hall, "the abuses and not the uses of a great natural function that are the curse of mankind."

At the conclusion of his remarks to the jury, Hall showed them what he suggested were the final seconds before the fatal shots were fired. Stooping down to the floor of the Old Bailey, Sir Edward acted out the last attack of Prince Ali upon his wife. As he did so, Hall said this: "In sheer desperation, as he crouched for the last time, crouched like an animal, like an Oriental, retired for the last time to get a bound forward, she turned the pistol and put it to his face and, to her horror, the thing went off." Hall let the pistol drop from his hand to the court-room floor. Peering intently into the faces of the watching jurors, Hall asked, "Was that deliberate and wilful murder?"

Marshall Hall's final words were, "To use the words of my learned friend's great father, (Percival Clarke was the son of Sir Edward Clarke, a celebrated criminal defence lawyer in Victorian times), many years ago in another case at the Old Bailey, 'I don't ask you for a verdict. I demand a verdict at your hands.'"

* * * * *

In reply, Percival Clarke told the jury that he had to bring them back "from the theatrical atmosphere which has pervaded the court for the past three days". Clarke said that Hall had tried to make the jury believe that Fahmy deserved death at the hands of his wife, and "that the world was well rid of a brute". Clarke said, "The civil contract of marriage gave to his proposed wife more liberty and freedom than was known in any other family in Egypt. I have no brief for the dead man," said Clarke, "it is for the Crown that I appear."

Percival Clarke made three telling points to the jury. Firstly, he reminded them that Madame Fahmy was quite used to handling guns. Clarke said, "Although she said she knew nothing about pistols, she had had one for years." Implying that Madame Fahmy had made plans before the fatal shooting, Clarke said, "Did not the shooting out of the window seem to indicate that Madame Fahmy anticipated a hell of a row?" Clarke's third point was in sharp contrast to the theatrical demonstration from Marshall Hall of the creeping, crouching prince. He reminded the jury that the porter, Beattie, the only third party near the scene of the killing, said he heard a whistle and, turning round, saw Prince Ali beckoning his frightened little dog. Clarke asked the jury, "Was there any doubt that the accused seized the pistol and shot her husband while he was playing with a dog?"

If the jury were to believe that Prince Ali was crouching down in the hotel corridor, not to jump on top of his wife, but to attract the attention of a pet animal, then Hall's self-defence theory would be in tatters.

Finally, Clarke told the jury, "I do not demand a verdict from you, I only ask you to return a true verdict according to the evidence."

* * * * *

In his summing-up, Mr. Justice Swift warned the jury that they should not allow themselves to be prejudiced by the character of the dead man. He said, "It is no reason or excuse for homicide that the person killed is believed to be a weak, depraved, or despicable person. You are not trying the dead man, but the woman in the dock."

Putting some of Hall's remarks into perspective, the judge said, "The accused's story of self-defence was not concocted by legal advisers. It is the same story as told to Dr. Gordon immediately after the tragedy."

Realizing that the trial might not be completed that evening, Mr. Justice Swift asked the jury if they wished to have a short adjournment or whether they would prefer to adjourn for the day. After the foreman had passed a paper round the jury members for them to vote on the adjournment, he announced a majority for going on with the trial. The judge said that as the jury were not unanimous, some of them might be too tired to finish the case that night. He adjourned for the day. Madame Fahmy seemed to be almost overcome. Perhaps she may have believed the jury were actually voting on her fate. She had to be helped from the dock.

Resuming his summing-up the next morning, Saturday, September 15th, Mr. Justice Swift told the jury that, when considering their verdict, they were not entitled to say, "Here is an Oriental man married to a French woman, and therefore things were likely to be so-and-so." Advising the jury in law, the judge said,

"A manslaughter verdict implies extreme provocation. Apart from the evidence that Fahmy spat in the accused's eyes, there appears to be nothing at the moment of shooting. If he seized her by the throat, I consider a verdict of manslaughter would be right. The contention of the defence is that she is guilty of nothing at all. If she thought the pistol was unloaded, it was excusable homicide, but was she protecting her own life? A person who honestly and reasonably believes that his life is in danger is entitled to kill his assailant, if that is the only way he honestly and reasonably believes he can defend himself. But he must be in real danger, and it must be the only way out of it."

The jury were out for an hour and eight minutes, during which time Madame Fahmy sat in a basement cell. On the jury's return, she was brought back into the dock. She sat, seemingly quite composed, her chin resting on one hand, her elbow on the dock rail.

The verdict was "Not Guilty". Cheering broke out in the court and was continued outside in the street. Marguerite left via a side entrance. She was driven away by car to a West End hotel. There she told pressmen, "I want to thank everyone whose sympathy was with me throughout my terrible ordeal. I am very moved. I think British justice is too wonderful for words." Madame Fahmy said she would send a telegram and a letter of thanks to Sir Edward Marshall Hall. Next morning, on his 66th birthday, the *Daily Express* dubbed him "the last of the orators".

Chapter 4

The Hearn Case

In the summer of 1930, at Trenhorne Farm in the Cornish village of Lewannick, near Launceston, there lived a married couple, William Thomas and his wife Alice. William and Alice, now in their forties, were married in 1910. They took over Trenhorne Farm at the end of the First World War in 1918. A short distance from the farm, there stood a large building known as Trenhorne House. By 1930 this house had been divided into two separate dwellings. One part was occupied by a widow named Elizabeth Spear. The other part of Trenhorne House was the home of two sisters, Lydia Everard and Sarah Ann Hearn. The sisters had been living there for five years.

Lydia Everard, who was always known to her friends as "Minnie", was 52 in 1930, nine years older than her sister Annie. Minnie, who had suffered ill-health for most of her adult life, took a turn for the worse in the spring of 1930. On July 21st of that year, she passed away, leaving Annie alone in Trenhorne House. Before she died, Minnie lost the use of her legs. They were extremely painful. She suffered also from neuritis and pins and needles in her arms and hands. Minnie's doctor attributed her death to colitis and gastric catarrh.

From the time of their arrival at Trenhorne House, sisters Minnie and Annie had struck up a friendship with William and Alice Thomas of Trenhorne Farm. Mrs. Thomas often called on the sisters and, when Minnie died, Alice continued to visit Annie. Sometimes Mr. and Mrs. Thomas visited together. At other times, William Thomas went over to the house on his own. In 1930, during Minnie's fatal illness, Mr. Thomas used to go over to the house nearly every day, taking newspapers, items from Launceston, and gifts of junkets and cream which Mrs. Thomas made as a special treat for the unfortunate Minnie. Occasionally, Mr. Thomas took the sisters for drives in his car. If Minnie was unable to go, he took Annie instead. In December 1928, Mr. Thomas lent Annie £38.

In September 1930, Mr. Thomas's mother came to stay with her son and daughter-in-law at Trenhorne Farm. While she was there,

there came the dreadful news about the R-101 airship. On October 5th, en route for India, the R-101 had crashed in flames as it was landing at Beauvais in France. The tragic event was preserved for posterity by newsreel cameras. Air travel was increasing in popularity in the thirties. In May 1930, just a few months before the airship crash, aviation pioneer Amy Johnson completed a solo flight from England to Australia. It took her nineteen days.

On Saturday October 18th 1930, Mr. Thomas's mother was due to return home after her stay at Trenhorne Farm. William Thomas was going to drive her there. Before he left, Mr. Thomas went over to Trenhorne House and asked Mrs. Hearn if she would like to come along in the car too. He suggested that after leaving Mrs. Thomas senior, Mrs. Hearn could join Alice and himself in a drive to the seaside at Bude, where the three friends could spend the rest of the day. Annie Hearn said she would love to go. The party of four drive out of Lewannick at two in the afternoon.

It was a mild, sunny Autumn day. Mr. and Mrs. Thomas and Mrs. Hearn passed a pleasant afternoon strolling around Bude and, at about 5.00pm, they went into Littlejohn's Cafe to have their tea. A pot of tea, bread and butter and cakes were ordered. Annie Hearn had brought with her some chocolate cake and some fish sandwiches. She put the packet of sandwiches on the cafe table and asked William and Alice to have some. Each of them ate one sandwich.

After tea, William Thomas went away from the cafe for a little while. When he returned to the ladies, it was approaching 6.30pm. Alice Thomas complained of a sweet taste in her mouth. "Are there any fruit shops?" she asked. They found one, and William bought his wife some bananas. At a quarter to seven, the trio left Bude on the drive back to Lewannick.

On the way home, Mrs. Thomas began to feel quite sick. William stopped the car while Alice was sick at the roadside. In fact, during their ten-minute stop, Alice vomited three times. When they reached Launceston, it was 8.00pm. William parked the car and went away, saying he had to meet someone on farming business. Alice Thomas and Annie Hearn stayed in the car. When Mr. Thomas returned, at about 9.20pm, he found that Alice had been sick again. About five minutes later, they reached the farm at Lewannick.

Mrs. Thomas was by now very ill. William got her some brandy and telephoned for the doctor. With Mrs. Hearn's help, he managed to get Alice to bed. Mrs. Hearn agreed to stay at the farm that night. When Dr. Eric Saunders arrived, he found Alice suffering from cramps in her legs and a pain in her abdomen. Her pulse was rapid. The doctor said it looked as if she had food poisoning. He prescribed kaolin mixture and advised Mrs. Thomas to live on a diet of whitebait and water. Mr. Thomas and Mrs. Hearn looked after her. Next day, Mrs. Hearn told Mr. Thomas that she herself had not felt at all well after the tea at Bude. Mr. Thomas asked Mrs. Hearn what was in the sandwiches she brought with her to the cafe. She told him it was tinned salmon. Dr. Saunders came again. Alice was vomiting. She had cramps in her legs and diarrhoea. The doctor said he would call daily to monitor her progress.

On Tuesday the 21st there was still no improvement, but the cramp was a little less severe. Alice was in a state of severe anxiety and mental agitation. It was something much more than worry over her illness. She began to develop tingling sensations in her feet, as well as being unable to sleep for more than a few minutes at a time. By the 27th, sores had appeared on her upper body. On the 29th, Alice was vomiting again.

After October 29th, Mrs. Thomas's condition improved. On Friday the 31st, William carried her downstairs. Dr. Saunders prescribed a fuller diet. He said the first symptoms had cleared up but she was very weak. On November 2nd, Alice felt well enough to eat some mutton for her Sunday lunch. However, she was soon vomiting again, saying she felt worse. At 10pm that evening, William carried her up to bed and gave her three aspirin tablets to help her sleep.

At about 4am on November 3rd, Mr. Thomas was awakened by Alice calling out for him. He got up and carried her to his own bed. Next morning, her nose began to bleed copiously. Dr. Saunders was called in again. He got to the farm at about 9.30am. When he examined Mrs. Thomas, Dr. Saunders began to believe that this might not be a case of food poisoning at all. To get a second opinion, he called in Dr. William Lister, a consultant from Plymouth Hospital. Dr. Lister said Mrs. Thomas was suffering from peripheral neuritis, possibly caused by arsenic poisoning.

Alice Thomas was admitted to Plymouth Hospital at 1.30am on the morning of November 4th, seventeen days after the tea party at Bude. Her case was now quite hopeless. She died at 9.35am that morning.

* * * * *

A post-mortem examination revealed that Mrs. Thomas's liver and heart had been affected by arsenic. Dr. Thomas Tickle, Public Analyst, found over four-fifths of a grain of white arsenic in the internal organs. It looked as if Alice Thomas had not been affected simply by bad fish sandwiches. She had probably been poisoned deliberately, and seemingly not only on a single occasion. Suspicion fell upon Mrs. Thomas's companions at Bude – her husband William and her friend Annie Hearn.

The funeral was held on Saturday, November 8th 1930. On the following Monday, Mrs. Hearn, who had lived at Trenhorne Farm since Alice's death, told Mr. Thomas that she was going over to Trenhorne House to attend to things there. That evening, Mr. Thomas went to the house but found it locked and empty. Next morning, he received a letter from Mrs. Hearn. It read,

> "Dear Mr. Thomas, Goodbye. I am going out if I can. I cannot forget that awful man and the things he said. I am innocent, but she is dead and it was my lunch she ate. I cannot stay. When I am dead they will be sure I am guilty and you, at least, will be clear. May your dear wife's presence guard and comfort you still. Yours A.H."

The day after Mrs. Hearn's departure from Lewannick, her coat was found on a cliff top at Looe. A thorough search of the area at the base of the cliffs was made but no body was found. On Monday, November 24th, an inquest into Mrs. Thomas's death was opened at Plymouth. After a two-day hearing, it was decided the cause of death was arsenic poisoning. The death was homicidal, but the jury said there was not enough evidence to show by whom, or by what means, the poison was administered.

While the police continued to search for Mrs. Hearn, they decided that she might have been involved in two other poisonings. On December 9th, the bodies of Mrs. Hearn's sister, Minnie, and that of her maiden aunt, Mary Ann Everard, were exhumed from the churchyard at Lewannick. Minnie's remains contained arsenic.

On November 11th, the day after Mrs. Hearn's disappearance, a woman resembling her took lodgings at a house in Ellacombe Church Road, Torquay. The householder, a Mrs. Marker, told the police that the woman gave her name as "Mrs. Faithful". She told Mrs. Marker she was waiting for her husband to be discharged from Torbay Hospital. The woman stayed for a week and left on the 18th. Some two months later, the police were contacted by a Mr. Cecil Powell of Brooksby Street, off Hesketh Road in Torquay. Mr. Powell said he thought a woman living in his house, and working for him and his wife as a cook and general servant, might be the woman the police were looking for. Mr. Powell knew the woman as "Mrs. Dennis". He also knew that she had given him false references.

Before the Torquay police swooped on the house in Brooksby Street, they called in Sergeant Trebilcock of Lewannick so that he could identify her. The sergeant arrived in Torquay on Monday, January 5th 1931. In the afternoon of the 5th, the woman went shopping. At 6.30pm that evening she was seen on a bus by a plain clothes detective. He boarded the bus. Meanwhile, Detective-Sergeant Milford and Sergeant Trebilcock were waiting in Hesketh Road. The woman left the bus and walked towards Mr. Powell's house. Milford and Trebilcock went up to her.

"I believe I know you," said Trebilcock. There was no reply. "I believe you know Lewannick," said the sergeant. "I don't think so," said the woman, in a monotone.

Milford said, "You have been definitely identified as Mrs. Hearn. You must go to the police station with the sergeant. He has something to say to you." The woman was ushered into an awaiting unmarked police car and taken to the Torquay police station. In the charge room, Superintendent Martin told her why she had been brought in. She then admitted she was Sarah Ann Hearn. Superintendent Pill from Launceston went over to Torquay, arriving at the police station at 11pm. At 3.30am the next morning, Mrs. Hearn was taken to Launceston and charged with the murder of Alice Thomas. Later that morning, at the Launceston Magistrates Court, she was remanded in custody.

* * * * *

By the start of the committal hearing on February 24th, Mrs. Hearn faced two murder charges – of Alice Thomas and of her own sister, Minnie Everard, who had died in the previous July. The proceedings spread over ten days because of the large number of prosecution witnesses and ended on March 19th. Mrs. Hearn was ordered to be tried at the Assize Court.

On Monday, June 15th 1931, Mrs. Hearn's trial opened at Bodmin Assizes before Mr. Justice Roche and a jury. Mr. H. du Parcq K.C. led for the Crown. His junior counsel was Patrick Devlin who, in later years, was to serve as Lord Chief Justice. The defence case was in the hands of Norman Birkett K.C. and Dingle Foot, brother of future Labour Party leader, Michael Foot.

Before starting to outline the background to the case, Mr. du Parcq announced that he would be proceeding first on the murder count relating to Mrs. Thomas. The gist of the Crown's case on this charge was that Mrs. Hearn administered arsenic to Mrs. Thomas in the salmon sandwiches she took with her on the day trip to Bude on October 18th, and that she gave her a second dose of the poison some time before October 29th. Mr. du Parcq claimed that Mrs. Hearn bought weed-killer from a local chemist. The chemical, he said, contained seventy per cent of white arsenic. To prove that she bought it, he read out a letter received from the chemist concerned. Until October 29th, said Mr. du Parcq, Mrs. Hearn had the opportunity to give Mrs. Thomas a dose or doses of arsenic. He also claimed that no-one else had a similar opportunity to do so.

Mr. du Parcq said that on November 5th, the day after Mrs. Thomas's death, and before chemical analysis had revealed the presence of arsenic in the body, there was a conversation between Mrs. Hearn and William Thomas. According to Mrs. Hearn, Mr. Thomas told Mrs. Hearn that there had been a post-mortem and there would be an inquest. Mr. Thomas was alleged to have said, "They are going to send some organs for analysis. They will blame one of us, but the blame will come heavier on you than on me. People are saying so. A detective may be here at any time. Whatever there is, they will find it out."

Three days after this conversation, immediately after Mrs. Thomas's funeral, Mrs. Hearn came into contact with a number of the dead woman's relatives at Trenhorne Farm. Mrs. Thomas's brother, a farmer called Percy Parsons, was there. Mr. Parsons, in the midst of the throng, associated his sister's death with the sandwiches prepared by Mrs. Hearn. He had at first thought they had been made at the farm, but Mrs. Thomas's mother corrected him, saying, "Mrs. Hearn made those sandwiches and brought them with her." Mr. Parsons's response was to say, "This looks serious. It will have to be seen into."

According to Mr. du Parcq, Mrs. Hearn, realizing she was in danger of being arrested, fled from the village. Concerning Mrs. Hearn's motive for flight, he asked the jury, "Did Mrs. Hearn intend to commit suicide, or did she want to escape and to delude people into thinking she had killed herself? By leaving her coat on the cliff top at Looe, was she possibly trying to make it seem that she had thrown herself over and that her body had been swept away to sea?"

Mr. du Parcq read out from a long statement taken down by the police after her arrest. She admitted cutting the sandwiches and, as she had on many previous car trips with the Thomas's, took them with her to Bude. Mrs. Hearn said that all three of them ate a sandwich, "Mrs. Thomas took the first, I the second, and Mr. Thomas the third."

In her signed statement, Mrs. Hearn gave her reasons for running away. She said, "I felt people were suspecting me of having poisoned Mrs. Thomas. It appeared that either Mr. Thomas or I would have to suffer. I felt I could not face the ordeal. It appeared as if somebody was going to be charged with the murder. I could not think of anyone but us two. I thought I would go my own way and take my life. I went to Looe with the intention, and left my coat there, but I found I could not do what I thought of doing."

At this point in his opening remarks, Mr. du Parcq told the judge he intended to introduce evidence concerning the death of Minnie Everard. In order to illustrate Mrs. Hearn's method of killing Mrs. Thomas, Crown counsel wanted to prove to the jury that Minnie had died from arsenic too. There was also the matter of quoting extracts from Minnie's diary. Mr. Birkett objected. He claimed that the evidence was inadmissible. Before the judge heard the legal arguments on this, he sent the jury out for an extended lunch break. Mr. Birkett submitted that Miss Everard's death was not relevant to the case against Mrs. Hearn on the first charge. He said the jury ought not be allowed to hear any evidence about it. The judge decided that the evidence was admissible, but he disallowed any quotation from the diary.

On the first afternoon of the trial, Mr. du Parcq described some of the events surrounding Minnie Everard's death. He claimed that she died from the effects of arsenic, given to her in small quantities over a period of about seven months. Minnie's final illness began on January 17th 1930. Dr. Galbraith, a partner of Dr. Gibson of Launceston, found that Miss Everard was vomiting, had severe abdominal pain, and a feverish high temperature. Mrs. Poskitt, a married sister from Doncaster, visited Minnie and found her ill. Apart from this visit, Minnie was alone in Trenhorne House with Mrs. Hearn. On April 19th, said Mr. du Parcq, Minnie complained that her medicine was too strong. She said it was causing her pain. Dr. Galbraith suggested she take part doses only. On April 26th she still complained. On May 2nd, Dr. Gibson saw her and prescribed an effervescent mixture. On the 8th, Miss Everard said she felt as if she were being poisoned. She said the medicine was "going into her hands and feet". She said it was causing her legs to be paralysed – a symptom, said Mr. du Parcq, of arsenic poisoning.

Mrs. Hearn explained away Minnie's suspicious symptoms by saying that she thought the medicine was too strong because it was actually an emergency medicine to be given when there was extra pain. The doctors denied that this was so. No medicine at all was prescribed, they said, after Dr. Gibsons's visit on May 2nd, some ten weeks before Minnie's death. Forensic evidence, said Mr. du Parcq, showed that Miss Everard's hair was contaminated with arsenic for some distance along each strand away from the scalp. The extension of poison along the hair showed, he said, that arsenic had been consumed over a period of about seven months before death.

* * * * *

The next five days of the trial were to be occupied by evidence from witnesses for the prosecution. The first of them was Mrs. Thomas's husband, William Thomas. He was the Crown's chief witness. The Crown relied upon his evidence to provide the jury with an account of the circumstances surrounding his wife's death. He told the jury that he used to take Mrs. Hearn and her sister Minnie out together in his car, and sometimes separately. Concerning the visit to Littlejohn's Cafe, Mr. Thomas said that the fish sandwiches, brought by Mrs. Hearn, were placed between her and his wife. Mrs. Hearn invited them to have some. He thought there were six sandwiches altogether. They took one each, so that there were three left uneaten. After tea, said Mr. Thomas, he left his wife and Mrs. Hearn and walked down the street.

It was then that he began to feel "a little bit sick". He went into the Grove Hotel and had "two drops of whisky". The sickness, he said, passed off. On rejoining the ladies at about 6.30pm, his wife complained of a sweet taste in her mouth. Mr. Thomas went into a shop and bought some bananas for her. Mrs. Hearn, he said, made no complaint then about feeling ill.

Mr. Thomas said that from the onset of his wife's illness until October 29th, he and Mrs. Hearn nursed Alice. Mrs. Hearn did the cooking, while Alice ate invalid's food. A day or two after the Bude trip, Mrs. Hearn told him it was tinned salmon that she put in the sandwiches. She told him that she herself had "felt funny" after eating one. According to Mr. Thomas, after her first bout of illness Alice seemed to get better, and then relapsed into a second bout. On October 29th, he drove over to Eglosberry and collected his wife's mother, Mrs. Parsons. The idea was that Mrs. Parsons should stay at the farm and nurse Alice, generally look after her, and cheer her up. After October 29th, said Mr. Thomas, Mrs. Hearn and Mrs. Parsons shared the cooking between them. Mrs. Parsons did all the nursing of her daughter and slept with her.

Mr. Thomas said he remembered telling Mrs. Hearn, on November 5th, that he had been to Plymouth. He was very upset. According to Mr. Thomas, he told Mrs. Hearn there had been a post-mortem and that they would likely be taking something away to be analysed. "Whatever is the matter they will find out," he told her. He did not, he said, remember Mrs. Hearn's reply.

In 1928 Mr. Thomas lent Mrs. Hearn £38. On the evening of the 5th, he asked for an acknowledgement of the money he had lent her. He said she gave him the money. He told her, in a kindly way, that he would not be needing her services after the funeral and inquest had been held. On November 10th he went to look for Mrs. Hearn at Trenhorne House. The doors were locked. He did not, he said, see her again until she appeared before the magistrates at Launceston.

Mr. Birkett, in cross-examination, asked Mr. Thomas for more details of the events in the cafe. Mr. Thomas said that the salmon sandwiches were put down in two piles of three. There was, he said, no adjustment of the plate, nor any juggling around with the sandwiches. About his conversation with Mrs. Hearn on November 5th, her version did not match up with his. Pressed on this discrepancy by Mr. Birkett, Mr. Thomas denied he had made any mention of blame falling on anyone. He denied he had said, "They will blame one of us," or that he said, "The blame will fall heavier on you than on me, people are saying so." He may, he said, have told Mrs. Hearn that people were talking. However, he said that Mrs. Hearn did say to him, "If people are thinking like that, I had better go to my own house."

Mr. Birkett was now hinting that William Thomas himself might be under suspicion, and perhaps with good reason. Mrs. Hearn had written Mr. Thomas a letter in which she said, "Goodbye. I am going out if I can." Birkett asked Thomas what he thought she meant by that. He replied that he thought she was going to take her own life. At the end of Mr. Thomas's cross-examination, the judge put to him the question, "Did you, from first to last, ever yourself give your wife any arsenic?" "No, sir, never in my life." "Are you sure?" "I have never had any arsenic in my possession, except sheep dip and worm tablets, which are things any farmer might have."

Mrs. Elizabeth Thomas, William's mother, testified that she had been at the farm after the funeral. She heard Percy Parsons say, "It is the woman." She said Parsons believed that Mrs. Hearn had a lot to do with Alice's death. On the day she disappeared, Mrs. Hearn told Mrs. Thomas she could not forget what "that horrid man" had said. Mrs. Hearn asked Mrs. Thomas if she could pop over to Trenhorne House to have a look around. "Certainly," said Mrs. Thomas. After Mrs. Hearn left the farm that day, Mrs. Thomas next saw her at the magistrates' court. In the kitchen one day, Mrs. Hearn, who seemed very quiet, said to Mrs. Thomas, "I do not think life is worth living."

Nobody seemed to know what happened to the sandwiches that were left over after the cafe tea. In cross-examination, Ivy Willshire, the waitress who served the three companions at Bude, said she did remember the sandwiches being on the table. She said they were wrapped in paper. After the people had gone, she saw no sign of the sandwiches nor of the wrapping.

Dr. Eric Saunders, called out to Trenhorne Farm on October 18th, described what he remembered of Mrs. Thomas's illness. On the 29th, he suggested to her that she might like to go into hospital for treatment. Mrs. Thomas said she preferred to stay at home. At this stage, said the doctor, Mrs. Thomas was too weak to stand and complained of weakness and tingling in her limbs. Dr. Saunders did not, as yet, think that she was suffering from anything other than food poisoning. Later, said Dr. Saunders, she was much worse, more or less delirious, and could hardly move her legs at all. There were no reflexes.

It was then, said the doctor, that he suspected arsenic poisoning and sent for Dr. Lister. To the judge, Dr. Saunders said he had "a fleeting suspicion" about arsenic on October 28th or 29th. He had never seen an arsenic case before. It was the neuritis on November

3rd that suggested it. Dr. Lister, who immediately diagnosed arsenic poisoning, had Mrs. Thomas taken to hospital. He discounted Mr. Birkett's suggestion that it was food poisoning at first and that arsenic was given later. The doctor said he thought Mrs. Thomas had received two doses of poison, the last one four or five days before death. Dr. Eric Wordley, County Pathologist, who carried out the post-mortem, admitted that food poisoning and arsenic symptoms were, up to a point, the same. He said he did not think death was due to the arsenic taken on October 18th. There was too much arsenic in the liver for a fatal dose to have been taken then, seventeen days before death. Dr. Wordley said that arsenic was definitely given before Sunday 2nd November, two days before death. Dr. Wordley's answers provided some support for Mr. Birkett's contention that no arsenic at all was put into the salmon sandwiches.

Mrs. Thomas's brother, Percy Parsons, was a controversial witness. Had he not been called by the prosecution, he might well have qualified as one of Mr. Birkett's defence witnesses. This was because Mrs. Hearn claimed that Parsons' hostile attitude frightened her away from her home and caused her to contemplate suicide. At the funeral of Mrs. Thomas, said Parsons, he asked Mrs. Hearn about the food eaten at Bude. There were several people present when he started questioning Mrs. Hearn. Someone, said Parsons, asked her where the sandwiches came from. Mrs. Hearn replied, "We brought them with us." Parsons said this led him to believe that they came from the farmhouse. Old Mrs. Thomas said, "Mrs. Hearn made them and brought them with her." Parsons then said, "This looks serious. It will have to be seen into."

So far, there was little in Parsons' evidence to account for Mrs. Hearn's fears. Under cross-examination, however, Parsons admitted he may have said the words in a raised voice and with a threatening attitude. He denied, however, having ever said, "It is that woman." Old Mrs. Thomas was mistaken about that, said Parsons. He introduced a new slant on the whole affair when he testified that relations between William and Alice Thomas were not all they might have seemed. Parsons said, "I know my sister and her husband did not get along together from the first." He said he had not spoken to William Thomas for about ten years.

Mr. Thomas had, for a second time, been shown in a bad light. To counter this development, Mr. du Parcq called him back into the witness box. Thomas said Alice had left him just over a hundred pounds. There was no will and her life was not insured. He had, therefore, little to gain financially from his wife's demise. Mr. Thomas admitted he had arsenic chemicals in his possession, in the form of sheep dip and worm tablets. Superintendent Pill, in cross-examination, said the only arsenic found in Mrs. Hearn's possession was an old tin of weed-killer bought in 1926. Asked to describe Mrs. Hearn's demeanour when she was being questioned in the police station, Superintendent Pill said she appeared "cool and un-flustered". She answered readily and, according to Pill, "seemed anxious to help".

In evidence, Sergeant Trebilcock introduced an alleged verbal comment which he said Mrs. Hearn made to him in the police station while Superintendent Pill was taking down her statement. All too often, accused persons have been plagued in court by alleged remarks made to the police but unrecorded at the time. Such was part of Trebilcock's evidence. He said that Mrs. Hearn said to him, in a low voice, outside the hearing of Superintendent Pill, "Mr. Thomas used to come to our house every day with the paper. Of course, that was only a blind." When Mr. Birkett tackled the sergeant about this, he asked him if she might have said, "He was very kind." Trebilcock said he was not mistaken. On this point he could not be shaken. Did this mean, perhaps, that Mr. Thomas visited Mrs. Hearn daily on some innocuous pretext, but that in reality, according to Mrs. Hearn at any rate, he came because he was fond of her. Were that so, was that all there was to it?

* * * * *

On the fourth day of the trial, Crown counsel du Parcq began to present evidence about the death of Mrs. Hearn's sister, Minnie Everard. Mrs. Elizabeth Spear, who lived in the other part of Trenhorne House, testified how, some time in April or May of 1930, Mrs. Hearn asked her to help with Minnie, who had become quite poorly. Mrs. Spear found Minnie in bed. They read a chapter from the Bible and prayed together. Some time in May, said Mrs. Spear, Mrs. Hearn came to her again and told her Minnie was worse. She went to see her. Minnie complained to her about "dreadful pains in her legs". She could not move them. Minnie blamed the medicine she was taking. She said it was too strong for her and it was "going into" her hands and legs and "deadening them".

Mrs. Hearn explained to Mrs. Spear that the medicine was to be taken in an emergency, when Minnie's pain was more severe than usual. As far as she knew, only Mrs. Hearn looked after Minnie. A Mr. Roberts lodged with the sisters for a short time and Mrs. Hearn's sister, Mrs. Poskitt, stayed in February. She saw Mr. Thomas visit the house only twice. Mrs. Spear declared that she did notice that the illnesses of Minnie and Alice Thomas were very similar. Both women lost the use of their legs. At Mrs. Thomas's funeral, Mrs. Hearn came back from the farm and told her she could not stay there any longer because people thought the tinned food was poisonous. Mrs. Poskitt, in evidence, said that her sister was ill "on and off for twenty or thirty years". Dr. Charles Gibson, who attended Minnie, said that no emergency medicine was ever prescribed. None of his medicines, he said, would cause pain in the arms and legs, nor sickness.

Dr. Galbraith carried out an examination of Minnie's body, exhumed from the churchyard on December 9th. The autopsy was done at the graveside. As it turned out, the doctor's evidence was not as damaging to Mrs. Hearn as might have been expected. This was due to Mr. Birkett's skilful cross-examination. Dr. Galbraith said Miss Everard's body was remarkably well preserved. The skin was intact, apart from the tip of the nose. (Prolonged preservation of a body is a feature of arsenic poisoning.) Mr. Birkett aimed to show that earth from the grave may have come into contact with the body and thereby artificially caused an apparent high arsenic content. Dr. Galbraith said that the soil above the coffin contained 125 parts per million of arsenic. The soil beneath contained 62 p.p.m. Cornish tin soil was always contaminated with a substantial amount of arsenic. Mr. Birkett asked Dr. Galbraith, "Would a piece of soil, so small that you could not hold it between your fingers, dropped on to this body, make all calculations wrong?" "Yes," replied the doctor. "A mere pinch would vitiate all analyses. That is quite clear, is it not?" "Yes."

Dr. Galbraith said the shroud was partly stained, but was not analysed. Mr. Birkett asked him, "As the skin of the body was intact, does it not look as if the staining of the shroud came from a source other than the body?" "Yes," said the doctor. "Putting aside arsenic for a moment, what you found might have been connected with death from many other causes?" "Yes."

If the jury now doubted that arsenic had killed Minnie Everard, the next day's evidence from Home Office analyst, Dr. Roche Lynth, could only have convinced them that arsenic was responsible for Alice Thomas's death.

Dr. Lynch was in the witness box all day. He testified that, in his opinion, Mrs. Thomas received no less than ten grains of arsenic on October 18th, the day of the trip to Bude. There was, he said, another later dose or doses. A total of three-quarters of a grain was found in the body organs. Moreover, arsenic had enough time to find its way into the fabric of Mrs. Thomas's hair and into her nails. Dr. Lynch's evidence concluded the case for the prosecution.

On the morning of the sixth day, Saturday June 20th, Mr. Birkett opened the defence case. He began by submitting to the judge that there was insufficient evidence to go to the jury on the charge of Mrs. Thomas's murder. Not surprisingly, Mr. Justice Roche said there was "ample evidence". Nevertheless, the fact that Mr. Birkett had made the submission could well have impressed itself on the jury.

Mr. Birkett called Mrs. Hearn into the witness box. She could now give her version of events leading up to Mrs. Thomas's death, and tell the jury just why she fled from the village with the intention of killing herself. The judge allowed her to sit down to give her evidence.

Mrs. Hearn said she regarded herself as a widow. Her husband left her in 1919. She had not seen nor heard of him since. Born in Market Rasen, a farmer's daughter, she was unsure of her age. She said she was "over forty". Mr. Birkett asked her, "Mrs. Hearn, have you ever, at any time or in any form, given arsenic to Mrs. Thomas?" "No, sir," was the clear and definite reply. "Have you, at any time or in any form, given arsenic to your dead sister Minnie?" "No, sir," repeated Mrs. Hearn.

Mrs. Hearn told the court how, when she was about twenty, she went to Sutton-on-Sea to help Mrs. Poskitt in a dressmaking business. About a year before that, she went to live in Harrogate, with an aunt who kept a cookery school there. It was becoming clear that Mr. Birkett was leading his client gently forward, beginning with simple questions which were not in dispute. His intention was perhaps to give Mrs. Hearn confidence and to accustom the jury to accept her responses as truthful. In 1917, Mrs. Hearn moved from Harrogate to live with her parents at Grindleford. From there, she moved again to Harrogate, to help nurse two of her sisters, Minnie and Mabel. Minnie, she said, was suffering, as she had all her life, from an inability to digest food, and a consequent, almost permanent, sickness. Mrs.

Hearn said that she was married in 1919. Her husband left her in the same year. After Mabel died, Minnie and Mrs. Hearn lived together in Harrogate.

Mrs. Hearn described some of Minnie's illnesses. She said that in 1921 they moved to Cornwall because of Minnie's poor health. That winter, Minnie was very ill. She had inflammation of her stomach and bowels, eye trouble, and neuritis in her hands and feet. It was too painful for her to walk. When they moved into Trenhorne house in 1925, Minnie was so weak that she could not even sit up in bed. The doctor took her there in his car. Describing Minnie's final illness, Mrs. Hearn said that "on May 8th or 9th" Minnie said to her, "I think the medicine is too strong. I feel like I have been poisoned." The doctor, she said, told her to take half doses. Mrs. Hearn was adamant that she never gave Minnie any other medicine except what the doctor sent. "Did you put the sandwiches in any special position on the table?" asked Mr. Birkett. "I do not exactly remember," said Mrs. Hearn. "I think about the middle." "What did you say about the food you brought?" "I said, 'I have brought a few sandwiches, would you care for one?'. I took the sandwiches from my bag and put them on the table. Mrs. Thomas and myself were seated side by side and Mr. Thomas was opposite, on my right-hand. Mrs. Thomas took one, and Mr. Thomas one, but I could not be positive now whether Mrs. Thomas or myself took the next." "Did anyone have any more of the sandwiches?" "I had another, but I could not be sure whether anyone else had one. Mrs. Thomas had some chocolate cake. There was," she said, "one sandwich left over, and some cake."

Mrs. Hearn described how Mr. Thomas said that the blame for his wife's death would fall heavier on her. On the day of the funeral, said Mrs. Hearn, she was preparing food to be taken into people at the lunch table. Nearly all present were strangers to her. Percy Parsons was sitting in the middle of the far side of the table. She said she did not know who he was then. Mrs. Hearn described how several ladies asked her about Mrs. Thomas's illness. Mrs. Hearn then told the court what happened next, "I told them what I knew. Someone mentioned sandwiches. Parsons said, 'Oh, sandwiches! Who took them?' I said, 'I did.' He said, 'Where did you get them? Were they taken from here?' – two or three questions before I had answered a word. At first he spoke in an inquiring tone. When I said about the sandwiches, he stood up, and for the rest of the conversation, he shouted. 'Where did you get the salmon from?' he asked. 'From Shuker and Reed,' I said. 'Were they made there?' he asked, pointing towards the house. I said, 'I took them with me. They were made there.'"

Mr. Birkett asked Mrs. Hearn, "When you wrote that letter to Mr. Thomas, what were your intentions?" "I had decided to end my life." "Do you mean you intended to commit suicide?" "Yes." "Were your able to do so?" "No."

Mr. Birkett asked, "Did it occur to you that by going on November 10th, if people were saying things about you, they might say more things about you?" "It did afterwards," she replied. "What was your reason for hiding in Torquay?" "The fact that I could not forget the things that were said about me. If people were saying things like that, they would still be saying those things."

About Sergeant Trebilcock's claim that Mrs. Hearn said to him, in an undertone, about Mr. Thomas's regular visits to her home, "It's only a blind." Mrs. Hearn denied she had ever said that to the sergeant, nor anything of the kind.

Mr. du Parcq began his cross-examination by asking Mrs. Hearn about her marital status. She said she married in 1919 at a register office near Bedford Square in London. Her husband was a medical student called Leonard Wilmot Hearn. She later read in a Harrogate newspaper that her husband had died on June 12th 1919, six days after the marriage. On the assumption that he was dead and she was a widow, the two newly-weds, according to Mrs. Hearn, parted company. Mrs. Hearn said she could name no-one who ever knew her husband.

"Did you ever had a husband," asked du Parcq. "Only for a very short time, but I did," she said. "Answer yes or no." "Yes, I did, certainly," said Mrs. Hearn.

Mrs. Hearn said she gave the uneaten sandwiches to her dog. It was not ill afterwards. She said it was not until she read a paper at Torquay that she realised Mrs. Thomas had died from arsenic. Until then she believed it was food poisoning. She did not think Parsons was accusing her of only supplying poisoned food to Mrs. Thomas, but of murdering her. When, after the funeral, a lady asked if Mrs. Thomas had looked well on the day she went to Bude, Parsons said, "The strongest person in the world would die if they were poisoned."

"Did it occur to you," asked Mr. du Parcq, "that people might be saying here is a husband and here is another woman, and between them they wanted to get rid of the wife?" "No," said Mrs. Hearn. "If you had put a little of the weed-killer into the sandwich you had a great deal to fear?" "Yes, a very great deal" "Let me put it quite plainly," said Mr. du Parcq, "is it not a fact that you did put some weed-killer in that sandwich?" "No, it is not a fact." "Is it not a fact that you made up your mind to run away?" "What do you mean by run away?" asked Mrs. Hearn. "Not to commit suicide, but to run away?" "No, I did not," said Mrs. Hearn. "Did you ever think Mr. Thomas coming to see you was a blind?" "No." "If you had no suspicion that arsenic would be found, the completer the investigation the better for you?" "The more true the findings the better for me," said Mrs. Hearn. "Inside of an hour you made up your mind all at once?" "I did not make up my mind until I got near the edge of the cliff."

"Was it your idea to throw yourself over the cliff or into the sea?" "Over the cliff," she said.

Asked by Mr. du Parcq what she was running away from, Mrs. Hearn replied, "I did not know exactly." "Did it occur to you," asked Mr. du Parcq, that if at any time Mrs. Thomas died, Mr. Thomas might have made a match with you?" "No, never," said Mrs. Hearn.

The prosecution had, at this very late stage, suggested a motive to explain why Mrs. Hearn should have wanted to get rid of Mrs. Thomas. Mr. Birkett did not let this suggestion go unchallenged. In re-examination, he asked Mrs. Hearn about the possibility of her marrying Mr. Thomas. She agreed that until that very moment, no-one in the world had ever suggested that she wanted to marry him. Mr. Birkett said, "I want you to understand that it is now suggested that you killed Mrs. Thomas in order to do that. Is there a word of truth in that?" "No, not an atom." "Did you ever conceive a passion, guilty or otherwise, for Mr. Thomas?" "No." "It is suggested that on October 18th you gave Mrs. Thomas a poisoned sandwich in order to marry Mr. Thomas. Is there a shadow of truth in that?" "Not a shadow of truth," she replied. "It is suggested that because you were poor and had a hard life, it would have been a good thing if Mr. Thomas had made a match of it. Did anything of that kind ever happen in your mind?" "No." "Counsel for the Crown suggests you killed your sister by putting something into her medicine. Are you sure there were two medicines?" "Yes," she replied. "With regard to the sandwiches, you did not even know that Mrs. Thomas would take a sandwich if you offered it to her?" "No, I did not."

Birkett's last question was, "From first to last in this matter, have you administered or given, in any shape or form, arsenic either to Mrs. Thomas or to your sister?" "No, I have not, never." "That is the case for the defence," announced Birkett, and sat down.

* * * * *

The following Monday, June 22nd, was devoted to final speeches from the two opposing counsels. Mr. du Parcq, for the Crown, spoke first. When he came to describe the way arsenic was allegedly administered by Mrs. Hearn to Mrs. Thomas, his face turned dreadfully pale. After trying to continue his speech, Mr. du Parcq collapsed into his seat, unable to go on. He staggered out of the court, supported by Mr. Birkett and Mr. Devlin. On reaching an ante-room, he fainted. The judge adjourned proceedings for an hour and a half to enable Crown counsel to recover.

When Mr. du Parcq resumed his speech, he said the defence had called no medical expert to refute the fact that Mrs. Thomas's death was caused by arsenic. "Why," he asked, "should Mrs. Hearn have been so frightened as to think of suicide or flight?" He asked the jury, "Would anyone have run away until everything pointed to her? What had she to fear?" Mr. du Parcq submitted that Mrs. Hearn, "Had knowledge of her guilt and had no intention of suicide. She was fleeing to escape justice, and detection."

Of the letter Mrs. Hearn sent to Mr. Thomas before she fled, Mr. du Parcq said, "Mrs. Hearn wrote that letter to give the impression of a martyr. When she was gone, they would think her guilty and Mr. Thomas would be cleared. If she showed the letter to anyone, they would think her involved."

It was as if the Crown counsel were accusing Mr. Thomas of involvement in the crime. Then, in the next breath, Mr. du Parcq said, "Mr. Thomas sent the letter to the police anyway, since he had an innocent conscience. Because Mr. Thomas visited Mrs. Hearn regularly," said Mr. du Parcq, "she might have thought she had a chance of being the second Mrs. Thomas."

The fact that the Crown seemed to have stumbled upon this motive, almost as an afterthought, was not lost on Mr. Birkett. When he began his final speech for the defence, he made quite sure that the jury received this impression also. He said, "At twenty minutes past four," pointing to the clock, "the Crown on Saturday suggested that there might be a motive – a motive so fanciful and fantastic – that

Mrs. Hearn had conceived some kind of idea that if Mrs. Thomas were not there, Mr. Thomas would marry her. With the one exception, which was made by Sergeant Trebilcock, there is not a breath nor a hint of any such motive. That ascription of motive was made after every Crown witness had left the box. Mr. Thomas was never once asked whether, by word or by gesture, or in any way, Mrs. Hearn had shown she was fond of him."

Mr. Birkett then sought to show that the day trip to Bude provided Mrs. Hearn with little opportunity for an act of poisoning. He told the jury, "It is remarkable that the invitation Mrs. Hearn received to go to Bude on October 18th was utterly unexpected by her. Yet on that day, according to the Crown, that foul design was carried out. It is strange and quite inexplicable that so utterly unexpected an invitation should be the occasion of it, and that there should be in the house a tin of salmon, and poison which, according to the Crown, had been there for over four years."

Mr. Birkett then shifted the jury's attention away from Mrs. Hearn and on to William Thomas. He said, "Where is the evidence of possession? No evidence has been called to carry the matter further than 1926, but from October 18th to November 10th there were Cooper's Worm Tablets in the farmhouse. Those tablets contained arsenic and contained that which the weed-killer did not contain – copper. In the organs of Mrs. Thomas there was found copper."

Mr. Birkett claimed that Mrs. Thomas suffered from food poisoning on October 18th, followed by arsenic poisoning on November 2nd. Knowing that Dr. Lynch had said that ten grains of arsenic were received on the 18th, Mr. Birkett said, "Dr. Roche Lynch has never attended one person suffering from arsenic poisoning, yet he spoke of symptoms with exactly the same confidence as he spoke of other matters. Let the cobbler stick to his last."

In evidence, Mr. Thomas denied he had ever told Mrs. Hearn, "The blame will fall heavier on you than on me." Mr. Birkett claimed that Mr. Thomas did say it and he lied about it. He told the jury, "When Mr. Thomas said what he did say, he did not speak the truth, and, moreover, he did not speak the truth because there was a purpose in what he said to this court." Referring to the loan of £38, Mr. Birkett said, "Counsel for the crown had represented Mr. Thomas as a loving husband, with an occasional quarrel making affection deeper, but the loving husband – that distraught and grief-stricken husband – went for the first time to Mrs. Hearn and said, 'Give me an acknowledgement of the money I lent you,'. I suggest he was putting her as far from himself as he could."

Mr. Birkett continued, "The fact that arsenic was found in Mrs. Thomas's body does not prove that she died from arsenic poisoning. Even if you are satisfied, is it proved that Mrs. Hearn occasioned it? Suspicion and speculation will not do. Blue weed-killer which Mrs. Hearn had, she had since 1926. It would have turned the sandwich blue. There is no evidence that Mrs. Hearn administered arsenic after October 18th. Others had equal opportunity. The worm tablets, containing 14 per cent arsenic, can be cut across and swallowed like aspirin."

Turning again to Mr. Thomas's role, Mr. Birkett said, "When Mr. Thomas mentioned blame, what a statement to make for a distraught, innocent, unsuspecting husband?"

Defence counsel ended his speech by telling the jury, "If all these things do not put the greatest doubt in your minds, then it is beyond the powers of men and angels to do it. It is not for me to say that I have to prove that someone else did it. God forbid that burden should fall on me. But the Crown must prove beyond all reasonable doubt that Mrs. Hearn did it. Have they done so? Mrs. Hearn went into the witness box at her own request and was unshaken under a searching cross-examination. The Crown's case is not proved." Mr. Birkett's speech lasted four hours.

* * * * *

On the eighth and final day of the trial, Tuesday, June 23rd 1931, Mr. Justice Roche spent four hours going over the evidence for the jury and summing-up. He said, "The issue is now down to two people – Mrs. Hearn and Mr. Thomas. It lies between them. I do not suppose any other person can occur to you. It is no use beating about the bush or refusing to face facts. To my mind it does lie between these two people. Here, as elsewhere, it is for the prosecution to satisfy you that it was not Mr. Thomas. It is not for the defence to satisfy you that it was. Mr. Norman Birkett has never undertaken the burden of satisfying you that it was Mr. Thomas. If at the end of this case you cannot say which it was, you ought to acquit Mrs. Hearn, just as if you were trying Mr. Thomas you would have to acquit him."

The judge dismissed the idea that Mrs. Hearn and Mr. Thomas plotted together to dispose of Alice, but left it to the jury to decide if

Mrs. Hearn had disposed of her alone. He said, "There was no suggestion that there was any misconduct between Mrs. Hearn and Mr. Thomas. Did Mrs. Hearn, in straitened circumstances, knowing that Mr. Thomas had been very friendly towards her, conceive the idea that if Mrs. Thomas was not there, she, with her attractions and capabilities, would have a strong prospect of becoming Mrs. Thomas? The prosecution had said that Mrs. Hearn was not normal, not that she was insane, but that in relation to life and truth she lived in a different world from that of ordinary people. The promise of leftover money when she died, going to Mr. Thomas, showed he occupied first place in her feeling. However, the letter from Mrs. Hearn to Mr. Thomas after the wife's death was certainly written under the idea that the wife was dear; otherwise it would be the merest mockery. It appears inconceivable that the letter was written by one conspirator to another."

When the judge had ended his summing-up, the jury left to consider their verdict. They returned 55 minutes later. The verdict, on the charge of murdering Mrs. Thomas, was, "Not guilty".

The jury was re-sworn and the second charge, that of the murder of Minnie Everard, was read out. Mr. du Parcq halted proceedings by saying that the Crown offered no evidence. The judge then directed the jury to return a not guilty verdict on the second charge. This they immediately did.

The judge then announced, "Sarah Ann Hearn, you are discharged."

Mrs. Hearn walked out of court, supported by a nurse on one side and a wardress on the other. No-one else was charged with the murders of Alice Thomas and Miss Everard.

Chapter 5

Stella Maris

At about 11.20pm on Thursday, August 12th 1926, James Barton was walking his dog along St. Anne's Road in the Tankerton district of Whitstable in Kent. As Mr. Barton approached a house called *Stella Maris*, he saw that the curtains in the front downstairs room had been left drawn. The light within shone out onto the footpath. When he reached the illuminated windows, Mr. Barton saw a man and a woman standing near the centre of the room. A second man stood with his back to the window. The man next to the woman had his right arm outstretched. She stood beside him, a little behind his extended arm. Mr. Barton walked past the window. A second or two later, the sound of a gun shot rang through the night air.

James Barton, darting quickly back, looked again through the window of *Stella Maris*. This time he saw the man and woman rushing towards the man by the window. The couple pushed him against the window. The man fell. There was the crash of a broken glass pane. The man who had made the rush raised his arm and began to strike downwards at the fallen man. After several blows, he got up on his feet again, apparently pressing something against his midriff. The woman shrieked out, "Don't, don't!" The man then handed her what looked like a revolver.

The man Mr. Barton had seen clutching his stomach was John Derham. A few moments later, Derham staggered out of the house and collapsed on the pavement. He had been shot. In the early hours of Saturday August 14th, John Derham died in a Whitstable nursing home. That morning, Derham's adversary in the struggle in the front room, 40-year-old Francis Austin Smith, described as a married man "of independent means", who had the previous day been charged with trying to kill Derham, appeared before the Canterbury magistrates on a murder charge. He was remanded in custody. On September 3rd 1926, Smith reappeared at the Police Court. He was ordered to stand trial by jury at the next session of the Maidstone Assizes.

The fatal struggle which James Barton witnessed through the lighted window of *Stella Maris* on August 12th had involved a woman. This was Smith's wife Kathleen. It was the relationship between Kathleen Smith and John Derham that had led to Derham's death at the age of 37. What chain of events could have given rise to that fatal shooting in a quiet, residential corner of sleepy Whitstable, disturbing so violently the peaceful stillness of that summer night?

At the end of 1925, Smith and his wife were living in a flat in Herne Bay. Derham and Smith, who were both Old Etonians, became friendly. Derham was soon a frequent visitor to the Smiths' flat, and the friendship later continued at a house in Herne Bay called *Llangollen*. Derham, who was living apart from his wife, became more than friendly with Kathleen Smith. During the summer of 1926, Derham visited the Smiths constantly, and in particular, Mrs. Smith. Towards the end of June, it had become clear to Francis Smith that Derham and Kathleen were lovers. Smith had been forced to play the role of a cuckold. He left his wife and went to live in lodgings in London, at Dollis Hill. Kathleen prepared a deed of separation and had it served upon Francis. Early in July 1926, Derham, who was now living with Kathleen Smith at Herne Bay, moved with her to his mother's property in Gladstone Park Gardens in Cricklewood.

Consumed by jealousy and humiliation, Smith broke into Derham's house and took away two photographs of Kathleen from the sitting room. By this time, Kathleen had rented another Herne Bay flat, called *Claverhouse*. While she was away with Derham, Smith got into *Claverhouse* and took a letter from her room. The letter was to Kathleen from Derham. Incensed by his discovery, Smith inflicted a good deal of damage to his wife's flat and belongings.

From July 15th to July 26th, Kathleen Smith stayed with her parents in London. She then took a lease on the house called *Stella Maris* in Whitstable. A few days later, Mrs. Smith's teenage sister, 15-year-old Lilian Wright, arrived at *Stella Maris* with the Smith children. In the meantime, Smith, who had as yet not visited his estranged wife, wrote a letter to Derham. Dated July 16th, the letter did not make pleasant reading,

> "You damned swine. I only wish you had the courage to meet me. You have seduced my wife and for that you think you will get off easily in the divorce court. You took my wife. I have taken something from you. Go and find out what. You dirty white-livered fool. You lied to me and now you are going to suffer. If you are any sort of a man you will meet me face to face. You must realize that you ruined not only a very sweet girl, but

> the woman that I, not you, love. If you really loved her you would not have done it."

On August 9th, Smith borrowed, from a friend, a service revolver and ammunition. He said he was going to Ireland and wanted the weapon "for protection against Sinn Feiners" who, he said, had already burned down his home. Smith then went to *Stella Maris*, now occupied by Kathleen, young Lilian and the children. He got there at about 8pm on the 9th. Next morning, Mrs. Smith and Lilian searched the house for the revolver. They found it in a coal box in the drawing room. They hid it again in a glove box in the hall-way. On the morning of August 12th, Lilian found that the revolver had been removed from the glove box. On the 12th also, Smith sent a telegram to Derham at his lodgings in Dollis Hill. Made to appear as if it had come from Kathleen, the telegram said,

> "Will you come down for a few hours tonight. Urgent. Wire K.I.Smith, G.P.O. Whitstable, not house. Come house if I am not at station - Kathleen."

Derham arrived at *Stella Maris* on the evening of the 12th. Some time after Derham's arrival, young Lilian, passing the open door of the drawing room, saw, inside the room, Kathleen, Smith and Derham. As she hovered near the door, someone closed it. Beyond the closed door, Lilian could hear voices raised in conflict and argument. Later that evening, Kathleen asked Lilian to help her find the revolver again. She found it in the kitchen. Kathleen held the weapon under a running water tap in an attempt to disable it. It was loaded at the time. Smith then appeared on the scene, seized hold of the gun, took out the cartridges, and put it into his pocket.

At about 8.30pm Kathleen and Francis Smith left the house with John Derham. They went together to the Marine Hotel, where they ate dinner. Leaving the hotel at about 10pm, the three reached *Stella Maris* shortly before 11pm.

Soon after 11pm, Lilian Wright heard the sound of raised voices from the sitting room. She heard Smith saying, "I won't have this other lover of yours sleeping in the house." A few minutes later, she heard Smith leave the sitting room and go to the kitchen. Something was said about a game of bridge. At about 11.20pm, Lilian was in her bedroom. She heard a loud bang. Running downstairs to the front room, she found Smith lying on the floor with Derham sitting across him, beating him on the head and shoulders with some kind of object. It looked like a gun. Mrs. Smith was trying to drag Derham off her husband. Finally, she succeeded and, as could be seen by James Barton through the window, Derham handed the gun to Kathleen. Derham left the room, clutching his stomach, walked through the front door, and collapsed on the pavement in front of the house.

Mr. Barton and two other men arrived on the scene. While Derham lay bleeding on the pavement, Smith, who was still inside the house, his face covered with blood, spoke to the men. He was extremely agitated and smelled of drink. He said to them, "You three gentlemen will make a good jury, I know you will give an honest verdict. I loved my wife dearly, She invited him here. One of us had to go." Before he was taken away by police, Smith handed a sealed envelope to the sergeant and said, "I have written a letter to my wife. You may as well have it now." He opened the letter, saying, "This letter will explain matters. My wife started to talk about divorce proceedings. I would not listen to her. I intended to shoot myself, but in the struggle for the revolver, it went off and shot Derham."

When told he would be arrested, Smith said, "How is he? Where is the seducer?" Blood continued to flow down Smith's face from two deep cuts in his forehead.

If Smith was telling the truth when he said that the gun went off accidentally during a struggle with Derham, then, at most, Smith could be considered guilty of only manslaughter. There was, however, evidence pointing to a deliberate act on Smith's part. It looked as if Derham's fatal wound had been caused by a shot from behind him, and in a downward direction, as if Derham had his back turned to the gun when the shot was fired.

* * * * *

Francis Smith's trial for murder opened at Maidstone on November 25th 1926 before Mr. Justice Avory and a jury of ten men and two women. His defence counsel was Sir Edward Marshall Hall K.C. Leading prosecution counsel was Roland Oliver K.C.. Smith, who pleaded not guilty, wore in his buttonhole a sprig of white heather.

The shooting of John Derham, if it was murder or manslaughter, was clearly a crime of passion caused, it would seem, by jealousy, disappointment and hatred. However, as Roland Oliver was quick to point out in his opening remarks to the jury, a deliberate shooting, in the absence of direct and immediate provocation, is murder. It was therefore punishable by death on the gallows. "In this country," said Mr. Oliver, "there is no unwritten law, as it has sometimes been called. It might be said that the motive that prompted the prisoner to fire the revolver was one of jealousy, but that is no answer in this court. Our law accepts no such answer, and it does not take into consideration whether he had good or bad reasons to be jealous of Derham on account of Derham's association with his wife. No civilized community could carry on at all if people having grievances against each other were in a position to take the law into their own hands."

The Crown's case was that Smith's gun did not, as Smith claimed, go off during the struggle with Derham. Mr. Oliver contended that Smith deliberately shot Derham first. Then, he said, Derham sprang on Smith, got the revolver from him and struck Smith on the head to disable him. Although Lilian Wright and James Barton saw something of what happened after the shot was fired, only Smith and Kathleen were present when the gun was discharged. The prosecution, therefore, were unable to call witnesses to the act of killing itself. Smith, of course, was going to claim that it was accidental. Kathleen Smith's version of events would not be heard in court. She could not be used as a witness because a wife cannot be compelled to testify against her husband. Marshall Hall was not going to call her either. The absence of eye-witnesses had the effect of making the shooting a subject of speculation and conjecture rather than a cut and dried matter of fact. It remained to be seen whether the prosecution would be able to convince the jury of Smith's guilt.

There was the matter of the letter which Smith said he had written to his wife and kept ready in a sealed envelope. He gave it to the police almost immediately after the shooting while he was first being taken into custody. In the letter, Smith threatened to kill himself. Mr. Oliver, who did not believe that Smith had any intention of giving the letter to Kathleen, read it out during his opening statement. The letter said,

> "My dear girl, this problem can only be resolved in one way, the removal of your lover Derham or myself. With the characteristic cowardice which that individual has shown throughout your mean and sordid intrigue, he moved himself from his room, fearing, I presume, a second visit from me. Whether he imagines he would have a comfortable second home in any house you live in and a mistress gratis on my money, or whether he thought that, I being out of the way, you would be an easy victim, I know

> not, but this I do know, that his pursuit of you – a young married woman with three children, babies, and a little money – knowing in full that marriage – he being already married – was impossible, was a despicable and damnable thing. Nor are you much less to blame with your constant lies and enlistment of your reputable friends to cover up your affairs. I was hard up, and you had his car. A life for a Morris Cowley is in your opinion a fair exchange. The whole thing is too mean and disgusting for me. I can't stand still while I live and go on supporting this great agony of mind and heart. May God forgive you and for what I am about to do and may he forgive you, the cause of it all. As to your lover, you will always have this between you, and if you can go on after it there are no sentences in the language which could be construed to express what you both are. You have £2,000 of mine and after this, £5,000 and other monies will be yours and the children's. I have no more to say. My heart is broken and there is nothing in life for me. If you hold something sacred in this world or the next, look after the children. They and you, God help me, are my only regret. I still love you too much. Your husband, Frank."

Taken at face value, the letter shows that Smith intended to kill himself. However, the letter, which Kathleen never saw, might well have been a smoke-screen set up by Smith to obscure his murderous intent against Derham. It was also possible that after putting his thoughts on paper, Smith simply changed his mind about suicide. After all, with Derham out of the way, Smith might have believed that everything he seemed to have lost would be restored to him. It was reasoning and argument on these lines that the jury would be asked to consider when assessing Smith's culpability, but first, they would have to hear all the evidence presented to them. It is notable that at an inquest into Derham's death held at Whitstable, a month before the trial, a coroner's jury had returned an open verdict. Proof of murderous intent was, therefore, not going to be easy for the prosecution.

Did Smith's behaviour in the weeks before the shooting give any clue to his state of mind and intentions on August 12th? Clearly, the struggle and shooting at *Stella Maris* was the culmination of months of bad feeling between Smith and Derham, as well as between Smith and Kathleen. The Smith family's nanny, a Miss Wyatt, said in evidence that while Smith was living away from his wife, John Derham virtually lived with Kathleen. Miss Wyatt did say that Derham never stayed overnight. One morning, during the time when Kathleen was living at *Claverhouse*, Smith arrived. He went up to the bedroom and came down with a letter. Miss Wyatt said that at that stage, Smith appeared calm. He took the children out and returned in the afternoon, slightly the worse for drink. Smith told Miss Wyatt that she was to take the children away to their grandfather in London. He said he was going to smash up the house, kill Kathleen, and then kill Derham too. For safety's sake, Miss Wyatt took the children upstairs into her own room. For about a quarter of an hour, said Miss Wyatt, she could hear the crashing sounds of Smith breaking and smashing things downstairs. Miss Wyatt also testified that on one occasion she had seen Smith and Derham fighting.

The difficulty that Smith faced was compounded by the fact that although he wanted his wife back, should the Smiths simply separate, Kathleen would receive a sum of £140 a year out of Smith's own money, an amount which would have enabled her to live with Derham without impunity. Smith, however, refused to sign the document. Instead, he went to the office of Kathleen's solicitors, where he told managing clerk, Henry Barwood, that he would not be going through with a legal separation. He wanted a divorce. According to Mr. Barwood, Smith left the office "very excited". He said he would find Derham and "smash him up".

As far as Kathleen was concerned, it was in her interest not to divorce, so that she would continue to receive an allowance of the interest on some of Smith's investments. The money would allow her to surmount the awkward problem of Derham's own wife refusing to divorce him. Derham's father, in evidence, said that Mrs. Derham, who was a devout Roman Catholic, would not even entertain the idea of divorcing John. This meant that should Derham set up a home with Kathleen on a permanent basis, he would still be obliged to support his own wife, a situation that would strain his finances to the absolute limit.

Three days before the shooting – on August 9th – Smith armed himself with a revolver. David Harrower, formerly of the Royal Naval Division, testified that Smith called on him at his lodgings in Maida Vale and asked him for a loan of his service revolver and some ammunition to go with it. Smith told him he had to make a trip to Ireland and wanted to carry the gun to protect himself against a gang of Irish Nationalists who, he said, had burned down his house and were seeking to kill him. Whether Harrower really believed this tale or not, he lent him the weapon and six cartridges.

In cross-examination by Sir Edward Marshall Hall, Harrower said that when Smith took the revolver from him he put it into his hip pocket. The muzzle was pointing upwards. Harrower agreed with Hall that if a man drew the gun in that position, and another man tried to seize it from him, the first part of the gun he would seize would be the barrel.

Kathleen Smith's sister, Lilian, described finding and hiding the revolver on August 10th, and its subsequent disappearance. On the night of August 12th, said Lilian, her sister gave her the loaded revolver, which she hid. Smith twice asked Lilian where it was. She told him she did not know. Lilian then gave the revolver to her sister. Kathleen put it under a running water tap in the kitchen. While Kathleen was doing this, Smith came into the kitchen and said to his wife, "Give it to me. I want to sell this." Kathleen handed it over. Derham was also in the kitchen at the time and must have been aware that Smith had control of a loaded gun. In cross-examination, Lilian said that after the shooting and the struggle were over, Derham walked out of the house with the revolver in his hand. She followed him into the street and saw him fall on to the pavement. She knelt down, took the weapon from Derham's hand, and put it, out of harm's way, into some bushes.

According to James Barton's evidence, he was not looking through the front window at the moment the revolver was fired. He had already reached a point a yard or two beyond the window when he heard the explosion of the weapon. Doubling back, he saw, he said, Derham and Kathleen rushing at Smith. In cross-examination, Hall suggested to Barton that Derham and Kathleen jumped towards Smith before the shot went off. "No," said Barton. "I was not looking when the shot was fired. When I looked round, the two others were actually in contact with the prisoner." In an attempt to clarify what Barton did see, Mr. Justice Avory intervened and asked Barton, "Were Derham and Mrs. Smith moving towards the prisoner after the shot was fired?" "They were still moving towards the prisoner," said Barton. "All had their hands up. Derham was moving backwards towards the window."

Barton, who had the best view of what happened in the sitting room, had really not given consistent evidence. Firstly, he said he saw Derham and Kathleen "moving" or "rushing" at Smith. Next he said they were in contact with him when he first saw them after hearing the shot. Finally, in response to the judge's question, Barton said they were still "moving towards" Smith. Neither Barton's evidence, nor that of Lilian Wright, did anything to settle the matter of whether the gun went off during a struggle, or whether Smith shot first and was then overpowered. However, there must have been quite a time lapse between Lilian hearing the shot and her rushing down stairs to see a struggle taking place. Barton would have been able to get his second look through the window before Lilian reached the front room. If Barton had convincingly stated that Derham and Kathleen rushed at Smith after the shot had been fired – and only one shot was fired – then this would strongly imply that Smith shot Derham first. As it was, his evidence left a great cloud of uncertainty and doubt as to the exact sequence of events in the sitting room.

The forensic evidence tended to favour the theory that the bullet was fired into Derham's body from some distance. If the weapon had been discharged very close to his body, one would expect there to have been charring and blackening of Derham's flesh, produced from the hot cartridge powder. No such blackening was found. The trajectory of the bullet also did not exactly fit in with a close struggle, although it did not rule one out completely. The bullet travelled from behind Derham, and in a downwards direction. Such a trajectory could match a scenario in which Derham was shot when his body was turned slightly away from the gun, as if trying instinctively to protect himself from the bullet.

Derham's fatal wound, and the bullet's trajectory, were described in court by Dr. Ernest Whitby, who carried out the post-mortem examination. Hall suggested to the doctor that the wound might have been caused during a struggle. Dr. Whitby did agree with Hall that the wound could have been caused while one man was trying to wrench the weapon from another as it was being drawn out of a hip pocket. The doctor said that when he examined Smith, who had cuts on his head, the man was not drunk but, said Dr. Whitby, "he certainly had been drinking."

Roland Oliver closed the case for the prosecution on the first day. The following morning, Hall called upon Smith to leave the dock and go into the witness box.

* * * * *

Smith described how, when he and his wife were living in the house called *Llangollen* at Herne Bay, he had rows with Derham on two occasions. During the second of these rows, Derham was knocked unconscious. Smith said he went upstairs for some water and bathed Derham's face. After that, said Smith, he did not see much of him. One day, Smith drive to *Llangollen* in a taxi. When he arrived, Kathleen was out. As he waited for her to return to the house, he saw a car drew up on the road behind the house. Smith then saw his wife sneaking in through the back door. Seemingly, Kathleen had been brought home by Derham. When Smith tackled her about this, she told him she had indeed spent some time with him, but that it was all quite innocent.

A few days after this incident, said Smith, he left *Llangollen* and returned to London. Shortly after that, he received a draft deed of separation from Kathleen's solicitors. According to Smith, he never gave authority to anyone to prepare a deed. He said he had no idea that his wife was preparing such a document.

In July, Kathleen had a summons of some sort. She had to appear before the Registrar in London. She went to London but did not notify Smith. Smith said he went to see her at the Mayor's Court. At this time, said Smith, Derham was living in lodgings at Dollis Hill. Kathleen was staying next door to Derham. Angry about the situation, Smith went to Derham's room while he was out and took away photographs of this wife. Smith said he then went to Herne Bay.

By now, said Smith, he was drinking heavily, trying to alleviate the distress he was suffering over the loss of his wife. He was, he said, "frantic". "Drink was no solace," he said. While Smith was in London, he arranged to meet Kathleen, at her suggestion, at the Grosvenor Hotel. She failed to turn up.

"Why did you procure a revolver," asked Hall. "I was going to commit suicide," Smith replied.

Determined to discuss the whole situation with Kathleen, on Monday, August 9th, Smith sent her a telegram, asking if he could come over to talk to her. He got a favourable reply. He went to see her that day. Questioned By Hall, Smith then described his brief reunion with Kathleen at *Stella Maris*.

On the evening of the 9th, said Smith, he mentioned to Kathleen that he was contemplating committing suicide. He said he showed her the revolver he had obtained for the purpose. He said he placed it in the coal box, unloaded. He begged her, he said, to give up Derham. Kathleen said she would think it over that night and would talk it over again in the morning. That night, said Smith, he slept in Kathleen's bedroom while she slept in the spare room.

The next day, said Smith, they discussed the whole issue. Kathleen agreed to give up Derham and return to him. That night, the couple slept together. Smith described how, on the morning of Wednesday the 11th, Kathleen went on a visit to Herne Bay. Before she left, he wrote her a letter in which, he said, he put his feelings down in words. The letter said,

> "My own adorable little wife – you have made me happier than ever I hoped to be. I have been mad lately and in hell. Now you have given me glimpses of the heaven which, with your help, my wife, I leave no stone unturned to reach. The mad, the criminal, folly I have been steeped in is a thing of the past from yesterday for ever. You must forgive me as you forgave me last night and, although you will learn of two reckless and foolish things I have done, they all belong to that nightmare of the past. You asked me to forgive you last night. I could only say 'I love you' and that covers everything. I bury yours, will let me bury mine? Atonement I must make some day, and punishment I deserve. These will be easier now because of you. I feel like a man who has been in a terrible fever, delirious and wandering, and am just waking from a deep, refreshing and life-giving sleep. Do not throw a lifebelt to me and then draw it away at my last grasp. You have a great heart and courageous. I need it always and I want it. Your words last night will never leave my memory. I could never love anyone like you. God bless you with all the love in my heart, your own husband, Frank."

When Hall had finished reading out the letter, he asked Smith, "Is that letter an honest expression of your feelings towards your wife on Wednesday, August 11th 1926?" Tears streaming down his face, Smith replied, "It is."

A plaintive cry rang out in the court. One of the two women jurors became hysterical and then collapsed. Women in the public gallery began to sob. The judge ordered an adjournment. The distraught juror left the court and returned five minutes later.

Smith said he handed his letter to Kathleen in the morning. She said she would read it on the bus down to Herne Bay. Soon after she left, the postman knocked on the door and handed Smith a letter, addressed to Kathleen. It was a love letter from Derham. Smith said he read it and immediately ripped it up.

When Kathleen returned from town, her previously warm manner towards Smith had undergone a distinct change. She was now decidedly chilly. The night before, when they were reconciled, she had suggested Frank should return to her; now she said she wanted him to go. That night, the couple slept apart.

In evidence, Smith admitted sending a telegram to Derham in his wife's name, inviting him to come over to *Stella Maris* on the evening of the 12th. Smith denied asking Derham to come so that he could kill him. It was, he said, simply a way of getting Derham to the house so that all three of them could have a proper discussion about just what should be done to resolve the situation. Smith said he suggested that both he and Derham should leave Kathleen alone for three months or so. Neither man should see her during that time. Far from agreeing to Smith's proposal, Derham and Kathleen joined forces and, said Smith, suggested that he himself should go away. Derham, said Smith, advised him to go to Paris, where he could be divorced from Kathleen quite cheaply.

The discussion, said Smith, took place after they had returned from the Marine Hotel. Inside Smith's pocket was the loaded revolver. When the lovers mentioned Paris, said Smith, he took the weapon out of his pocket and told them he would shoot himself. They snatched it away from him. He said that he then went upstairs and asked Kathleen why she was preparing a bed in the spare room. It looked as if Derham was planning to stay the night. Whether Derham intended to sleep in Kathleen's bed Smith did not mention, but when he asked Kathleen what was going on, she apparently laughed at him. She went downstairs to the sitting room where, in the middle of what seemed to Smith to be a serious domestic crisis, she and Derham proceeded to sort playing cards for a convivial game of bridge. To Smith, the situation must have seemed at least bizarre, if not quite outrageous.

Smith had apparently not quite reached breaking point yet. He said he went to look for a chair to sit on at the card table. Events then moved quickly, as described by Smith, "I went to get a chair to draw up. I did not want to play cards. I told them I was going to do away with myself. They did not seem to believe it. It all happened in a flash. I went to get a chair, and as I did so, I put my hand to unbutton the back pocket of my trousers, to take out the revolver." (Smith showed how he did this.) He said he was standing with his back to the window. Contradicting Mr. Barton's evidence, Smith continued, "I was getting the chair and pulling out the revolver. The next thing that happened, all I know is there was a terrific struggle. I was hit on the head, the revolver went off and the next thing I am absolutely conscious of was speaking to Inspector Rivers. I had a faint recollection of Barton. I knew there was someone but I could not distinguish him. I remember walking about the room and he seemed to be following me. It was all very hazy."

Hall asked Smith, "Have you any recollection of yourself ever pulling the trigger?" "I swear I never touched the trigger," said Smith.

After Sir Edward Marshall Hall had sat down, Roland Oliver began his cross-examination of Smith. He asked him, "Do you think a man who behaved like Derham behaved deserves to be killed?" Smith replied, "I cannot form a judgement on that." He then added, "I do not think any man deserves to be killed."

Smith said that he had never at any time threatened to kill Derham, nor to injure him, except for the night he fought with him at *Llangollen*. When he wrote to Derham threatening to "break him up", he said he meant he would go down to *Claverhouse* and break Derham's house up.

Mr. Oliver read out a letter written by Smith and sent to Derham's mother. (She was then at a hospital in Dollis Hill.) This letter seemed to contain an unmistakable threat of physical violence. Smith had written,

> "Dear Mrs. Derham, No doubt you are aware that your son Jack has seduced my wife. She is somewhere with him now and he confesses to the attraction he holds. I have sufficient proof for my solicitors, but the satisfaction I will obtain with my own hands."

"What did you mean by that?" asked Mr. Oliver. Avoiding the issue, Smith said, "After writing that letter I went straight down to *Claverhouse* at Herne Bay." "Your satisfaction was in breaking up *Claverhouse*?" "Yes," said Smith. "In another letter," said Mr. Oliver, "you wrote 'you lied to me. Now, by God, you are going to suffer.' Does that not refer to physical violence?" "I should not think so," said Smith. "Derham was a big man compared with me." "You said you knocked him out once, and intended to give him a hiding?" "To try," said Smith. "In another letter you said, 'You seduced my wife and for that you will not get off easily in the divorce court.' What else did that mean but a threat?" "I did not know what I was doing," said Smith, "I was in such a state of mind that I did not know what I was doing. The use of force did not occur to me."

The prosecuting counsel then gave Smith a letter in his own writing, dated August 2nd. It was to his wife. Invited by Mr. Oliver to read it out, Smith did so, very slowly and carefully. The letter ended:

> "Let me know by return, even if it is only the word 'No' on a postcard, as otherwise I shall go mad and come down and deal with you both in a fashion that cannot be mended. Jackie (Smith's son) won't want to have fingers pointed at him as the son of a murderer of an unfaithful wife and her lover, and of a suicide. Come back to me, my girl, my little white heather. Your heartbroken husband."

Whether or not Smith's remarks were real threats of idle menaces, he had clearly threatened to kill Derham, and Kathleen as well. "What did you mean by that?" asked Oliver. Smith replied, "I never had murder in my heart."

Determined to show that Smith had thought about killing Derham, Mr. Oliver quoted from another of Smith's letters to his wife. It said,

> "I have got to see you, and all the police in Europe will not keep me away. If I do not hear from you on Monday I will do something really desperate. All you write is that the children are well. That is not what I want. I want to see them. Even you will admit that I love them. What is your idea? Are you living with this man? I really think you are driving me crazy."

The postscript was, "God help Derham if he is coming to Tankerton. I have not started on him yet."

This last letter was written on August 9th, the day Smith got the gun and went to Tankerton. Mr. Oliver asked him, "When you say, 'God help Derham,' does that refer to doing something desperate?" "No." "What was on your mind when you wrote that?" "Certainly not murder or anything like it," replied Smith.

Mr. Oliver asked Smith to describe again the events immediately before the gun went off. Smith, for a second time, demonstrated how he removed the gun from his hip pocket. Turning to the jury, Smith then said, very emphatically, "I swear no finger of mine ever touched the trigger, and that I will swear before God to my dying day."

Here, the judge intervened. He asked Smith, "Why did you pull out that gun?" "To show I had the means of shooting myself." "Then I want to know this," said the judge. "In that state of affairs, how could you think that getting Derham to the house on the evening of the 12th would assist a reconciliation?"

Smith replied, "She had become reconciled the day before, but she was blowing hot and cold. I was doing everything in my power. I thought I could even persuade Derham to see the folly of it all." "How could you suppose that the presence of Derham would assist in effecting a reconciliation with your wife?"

"My strongest argument was that of the children. My wife is a Catholic. Derham could not marry her." "She knew that already without him being present, did she not?" "Derham was a gentleman," said Smith. "I might have appealed to his better nature."

Mr. Justice Avory then asked Smith, "After you called him 'a damned swine', could you really appeal to his better nature?" "I described him in those terms in a fit of temper," said Smith. After giving evidence for three hours, Frank Smith left the witness box and returned to the dock. After Sir Edward Marshall Hall and Mr. Roland Oliver had each made their closing speeches to the jury, proceedings were adjourned until the next morning.

* * * * *

On the Saturday, Mr. Justice Avory began his summing-up. After going over the evidence, the judge reminded the jury of the issues they should consider. He pointed out that Kathleen Smith, as the third party present in the sitting room when Derham was shot, would have had the best view of the sequence of events which led to the revolver being fired. She could not be forced to testify against Smith because she was his wife. She was not, however, called upon to speak in his defence either. Mr. Justice Avory put Kathleen's position to the jury in this way, "There were only three persons present. Smith has said what happened. Mrs. Smith has not been called. Is it conceivable that the prisoner's wife, if she could support the statement he had made, would not have been called as a witness for the defence? You must say what inference ought probably to be drawn from the fact that Mrs. Smith has not been called. She can not be called for the prosecution. Can there be any possible explanation for her not being called by the defence, other than the fact that she is unable to support her husband's story?"

The judge pointed out that Smith's story was that the gun went off in a struggle for possession of the weapon. If Smith drew the gun with the intention of committing suicide, then the jury should return a verdict of manslaughter. This was because suicide itself was an illegal act. The judge said, "If the prisoner did not intend injury, either to himself or anyone else, why was there a desperate struggle for the revolver?"

Concerning Smith's actions in the days leading up to the shooting, the judge told the jury to ask themselves just what were Smith's intentions when he sent the bogus telegram to Derham, inviting him to come to Stella Maris on the evening of August 12th. "What purpose," said the judge, "was in Smith's mind when he got the revolver and loaded it?"

Forensic evidence showed that the gun had been fired at least twelve inches away from Derham. Looking through the window, James Barton saw Derham with his right arm outstretched, with Mrs. Smith behind it. The judge asked, "Was Derham trying to protect Mrs. Smith from something and she, sheltering behind his arm, turned away from Smith, exposing his left side, where the bullet did enter?"

Smith told Superintendent Quested on the night of the shooting that he intended suicide, "I intended to shoot myself, but in the struggle for the revolver, it went off and shot Derham." In evidence, Smith said he did not use the word 'but'. He said he was not actually trying to shoot himself at the time. This part of his police statement should, said Smith, have been read as two separate sentences. Smith also claimed that he did not intend to use the gun at all when he took it out of his pocket. Why then should Smith, after Kathleen had run water over the gun, go to the trouble of washing the cartridges so carefully, and reload, unless perhaps he intended to fire them? Smith denied having told Lilian he would kill her, and Kathleen as well, but Lilian had, from the witness box, sworn that he did threaten to kill them both.

Before they left the court to consider their verdict, the jury were given a warning. The judge said, "I have told you the law of this country, as it must be applied. If you apply any other law, or any notion of your own, you are violating the oaths you have taken."

The jury returned at 12.05pm. After 15 minutes, they sent a message to the Clerk of the Court, asking for the revolver. The judge had invited them to examine it and to experiment with it during their deliberations.

The jury returned at 2.15pm. The verdicts were, "Not guilty of murder," and, "Not guilty of manslaughter."

In his final words to Smith, Mr. Justice Avory said, "The jury have taken upon your trial the most lenient view possible of the circumstances of this case. In view of the verdict of the jury, I must assume that you had this weapon and this ammunition in your possession with the intent of endangering no other person than yourself. I must assume that. I have my own opinion on it."

Frank Smith was sentenced to twelve months imprisonment with hard labour for possession of a firearm with the intention of endangering life.

Chapter 6

The Green Bicycle Case

It was a pleasant summer evening on July 5th 1919 in the village of Little Stretton, a few miles from the city of Leicester. Just after 9pm, Joseph Cowell of Elm Farm, as generations of his forebears had done before him, was driving his herd of cattle along a quiet country lane, up to the top meadow for the night. As the cattle ambled steadily along the earthy track which formed the road to Gartree, each beast took up its accustomed position within the herd. The more bold and intelligent cows, instead of leading the way forward, kept, as always, to their more sheltered and protected places in the centre of the group. Cattle lower in the bovine pecking order brought up the rear, while the least favoured ones were forced to lead the way, their heads bent low, as if in submission to their allocated role.

After he had let his cattle into their appointed field for the night, and as the slanting sunlight began to fade down to twilight, farmer Cowell closed and tied the five-barred field gate. He then set off back towards the supper and the bed that awaited him back at Elm Farm. It was the first summer after the Great War. The conflict in Europe had exacted a dreadful toll of the nation's menfolk. Very few were the settlements, no matter how tiny, that had not lost at least one of their young men in the service of their country. The villages around Leicester were no exception to the tragic rule. Little Stretton, Gaulby, Stoughton and other villages had their share of the Grim Reaper's work on the fields of Flanders, and in Leicester itself there were thousands of mothers and sweethearts lamenting their losses. As he made his way home that beautiful July night, Joseph Cowell might well have spared some time to think of absent friends.

Cowell had walked only a few hundred yards when he saw, ahead of him, a young woman lying in the roadway. When Cowell reached her, he found that she was near the grass verge, lying partly on her back and partly on her left side. She was wearing a hat. The hem of her summer frock had ridden above her knees. The girl's face was covered with blood. A sticky pool had formed around the spot where her head lay. It looked as if the unfortunate girl had fallen from her bicycle and struck her head on the ground as she did so. There was no sign of life in her. Clearly, there had been a dreadful accident. Perhaps the poor girl had fainted with exhaustion and tumbled off her machine to her death. Cowell hurried off into the village of Long Stretton and reported his discovery to Police Constable Alfred Hall.

The dead girl was 21-year-old Annie Bella Wright. Bella lived with her parents at Stoughton. She worked at a tyre factory in Leicester. Each day, like many local villagers, she would cycle to and from her work in the city. She was going out, at the time, with a Navy stoker. He was expecting to be demobilized in about a month's time.

At 10.50pm that Saturday night, Joseph Cowell, on P.C. Hall's instructions, managed to telephone Dr. Edward Williams at his home in nearby Gaulby. The doctor immediately drove in his car to the accident scene on the Gartree road, where Hall was waiting for him. Dr. Williams briefly examined the girl and confirmed that she was dead. Her body was then taken by ambulance to the mortuary. Dr. Williams judged that Bella had died within the previous 1½ hours, possibly only minutes before Joseph Cowell found her body.

Dr. Williams felt that Bella Wright's death was an accident. However, P.C. Alfred Hall had some misgivings about the matter. It bothered him at intervals as he spent a rather restless night. Early on the Sunday morning at 6am, Hall, a tall man with a military bearing and a bristling handlebar moustache, found a spot of blood on one of the pedals of Bella Wright's bicycle. Hall then rode out to the place on the Gartree road where Bella had fallen. He began a thorough and systematic search of the ground near the spot where she had been lying. At about 7.30am, Hall found, trodden into the roadway by the hooves of a passing horse, a lead bullet. It lay embedded near the centre of the carriageway, six yards from the pool of dried blood.

P.C. Hall, who was now convinced that he had a suspicious death on his hands, decided to get in touch with Dr. Williams again. Before Hall contacted the doctor, he paid a visit to the mortuary. He made a more thorough examination of Bella's head. The left side of her face was caked with dried blood. Hall washed it gently with moistened swabs of cotton wool. Beneath the blood, the side of the face was bruised black. On the left cheek, about an inch below and an inch behind the left eye, there was, without doubt, a bullet hole.

Dr. Williams looked at Bella's wound at about 8.30 that Sunday evening. He then began to look for an exit wound. Sure enough, a larger, more jagged bullet hole was found on top of the head. Until then it had been covered by the girl's hair. Bella Wright had not died through collapsing from her bicycle with exhaustion. She had, either accidentally or deliberately, been shot through the brain. The Leicestershire Constabulary now treated Bella Wright's death as murder.

* * * * *

Police inquiries revealed that on the night before her death Bella went into work on the night shift. When she got home on the morning of July 5th, she went to bed. She got up again at about 4pm. At about 6pm that evening, Bella rode on her bicycle to the post office at Evington, where she bought some stamps. She cycled back and got home at about 6.30pm. Soon afterwards, she left the house again. At about 7.30pm, Bella arrived at the house of her uncle, George Measures, at Gaulby. By now, she was not alone. She reached her uncle's cottage accompanied by a man. He was riding a green bicycle. Bella was inside the house for about an hour. The man waited for her outside. She told her uncle that the man was a complete stranger to her. She said he had asked her the way to a certain village. It had looked as if they were on friendly terms, and this was again apparent when they rode off together. Less than an hour later, Bella was dead.

Earlier on the evening of July 5th, at about 5.30pm, two little girls, 11-year-old Valerie Cavan and her friend, Muriel Nunney, aged 13, were cycling along the Leicester to Stretton road. The girls came upon a man riding in the opposite direction, towards Leicester. He smiled and spoke to them as he rode past. The man then turned around, followed and overtook them. The girls became frightened by the man and rode back towards Leicester. They left the man standing by his bicycle near a farm gate. According to the girls, the strange man's bicycle was enamelled in green. The road on which they said they met the man connected with the road where Bella Wright's body was found.

A month elapsed. The police had not made an arrest. On Monday August 4th they announced that they were anxious to trace a man who spoke to a cycle repairer at Leicester, with whom he left a green bicycle. Thus was on July 2nd, three days before Bella Wright's shooting. The man said to the shop keeper, a Mr. Cox, "I am a demobilized officer. I've just had a month's leave. I went back to my firm. They said I could have another two or three weeks on pay, so I took advantage of the offer and came to Leicester to visit some friends. I was working for a firm in London before the war."

The man with the green bicycle was between 35 and 40, about 5ft 8in tall, with dark hair turning grey, a broad, full face, and a broad build. He was said to speak in "a squeaking voice" and "in a low tone". When Mr. Cox saw him, the man was badly in need of a shave, his face covered with stubble.

It was not until eight months later, during the month of March 1920, that the police achieved a breakthrough. Enoch Whitehouse, a boatman, was plying his vessel along the local canal. His tow rope, attached to the harness of his draught horse, became caught up on an obstruction on the canal bed, a common occurrence near large towns. Whitehouse took out his barge pole and fished out of the canal a bicycle frame, coloured green. On March 12th, after dragging the canal, police recovered the rear wheel of the same bicycle. Attached to the wheel was a three-speed gear. A week later, on March 19th, the canal yielded up a third set of interesting items – a gun holster containing cartridges, both live and blank, such as were used in an army service revolver.

One of the identity numbers had been filed away from the metal frame of the green bicycle. There was, however, another number on the inner part of the front fork. The number was traced to a cycle shop in Derby, run by the Orton brothers. The green B.S.A. machine, Number 103,648, was sold on May 13th 1910 to a Mr. Light. The police had found their man. On Wednesday, May 24th 1920, after a two-day hearing at Leicester County Magistrates court, Ronald Vivian Light, aged 35, was committed for trial at the next Leicester Assizes on a charge of wilful murder.

* * * * *

Ronald Light was a native of Leicester. He was a qualified civil engineer from a family who were quite comfortably off. For some eight years he worked as a draughtsman for the Midland Railway at Derby. In October 1914, Light returned from Derby to live with his parents in Leicester. Having volunteered for the army, he was soon commissioned into the Royal Engineers. He served with that regiment in France during part of the First World War, later enlisting in the Honourable Artillery Company. Demobilized in February 1919, Light became a mathematics master at Dean Close School in Cheltenham. He was arrested at the school on March 4th 1920. When charged with the murder of Bella Wright, Light said, "It is absurd." Absurd or not, Light was brought to trial for his life at Leicester Assizes on Wednesday, June 9th 1920.

An interval of almost twelve months between the commission of a criminal offence and the trial of a defendant is quite normal nowadays. In 1919, such a time lag was extraordinarily long. Consequently, if the memories of prosecution witnesses had not truly faded when they were required to describe distant events, then certainly a defence counsel could justifiably claim that their powers of recall had, indeed, diminished. Prosecution evidence was therefore rendered more susceptible to doubt. Light's counsel at his trial, the redoubtable and extremely successful Sir Edward Marshall Hall, was most eager to stress that hindsight can often produce in a witness a distorted image of the truth.

Leading counsel for the Crown was the incumbent Attorney-General, Sir George Hewart. He was later to serve for many years as the Lord Chief Justice of England. In that capacity, Hewart presided with steely obduracy over the Court of Criminal Appeal. The judge at Light's trial was Mr. Justice Horridge. Acting as junior defence counsel was a fledgling barrister destined for a distinguished legal career – Norman Birkett. After Light had pleaded not guilty, Sir George Hewart stood up to outline the case for the Crown.

On the night of the shooting, July 5th 1919, Light was seen with Bella Wright less than an hour before her death. They were seen riding away from George Measures's house at Gaulby. Light was riding a green bicycle. Earlier in the evening, a man on a similar green bicycle had encountered and alarmed two schoolgirls on a nearby road. The man, whom the Crown claimed was Light, had apparently engaged the girls in some kind of conversation after turning his bike round and following them. Hewart said that Light was in the habit of making solitary evening cycle rides that summer, returning to his parents' house for dinner at 8pm. On the night of Bella Wright's murder, Light returned at 10pm, dusty and dishevelled. He said his bike had broken down and he had been forced to walk home. Light, it seemed, never rode his green bicycle again after that night.

Hewart alleged that Light filed off the serial number of the bicycle and then threw it, in pieces, into a nearby canal, together with a holster and some ammunition. Hewart said the holster had been used by Light to carry a service revolver. It was this weapon, which was never recovered, that Light was alleged to have used to kill Miss Wright. Light's motive, suggested Hewart, was that he had "made certain overtures" towards his victim. When these were resisted by the woman, Light had killed her, said Hewart, possibly because of "his anger or a desire to conceal what had been attempted".

The first witness for the prosecution was Bella Wright's mother. She was followed in the witness box by Joseph Cowell and Police Constable Hall. It was clear that had Hall not returned to the scene of the crime early the next morning, knowledge of a shooting would have been delayed, at least until a surgeon performed an autopsy. Dr. Williams's initial thoughts did not include the possibility of foul play. The doctor had cause to be embarrassed by his failure to discover a bullet wound on the night of the shooting, but the actions of the police that night, as Sir Edward Marshall Hall was quick to point out during his cross-examination of P.C. Hall, left a great deal to be desired. No attempt was made to cordon off the stretch of roadway where the body was found. The body itself was simply carried away to the mortuary and the fallen bicycle removed from the scene. This allowed traffic, pedestrians and animals to move freely along the road all night. The start of the police inquiries, in spite of P.C. Hall's diligence, had been far from auspicious. This would have impressed itself upon the jury and worked in favour of Light.

The next witnesses were the two schoolgirls who were harassed and frightened on the Leicester-Stretton road by a man on a green bicycle. The elder girl, Muriel Nunney, dressed in a belted raincoat and school boater, gave her evidence first.

Muriel described how she and her friend Valerie Cavan were passed by a man riding in the opposite direction, towards Leicester. The time was about 5.30pm on the day of the shooting. She described this man. She said he was wearing a light suit and carried a raincoat draped over his shoulder. Muriel had picked out Light from a line of twelve men at an identity parade. She pointed out Light in the dock as the man involved. The green bicycle, she said, had "funny handle-bars".

During cross-examination by Marshall Hall, Muriel Nunney's evidence was seriously weakened. This happened because, although the encounter she described occurred before Bella Wright was shot, she was not questioned about it until the following March, some eight months after the event. Muriel also admitted that she and Valerie

Cavan had read about the green bicycle case in the newspapers. They had also seen a photograph of the bicycle itself. Muriel testified that she and Valerie had then concluded that it was Ronald Light that they saw when they had talked the matter over with some of their school friends. It was then that they decided it was on July 5th that they met him. Significantly, when questioned further by Marshall Hall, Muriel said the date of July 5th had been suggested to them by the police. She said she could not herself remember the exact date at first.

The younger girl, Valerie Cavan, said she could not remember which summer it was that she and Muriel Nunney met the man. After he had caught them up, said Valerie, he rode along with them towards Stretton. At the foot of a hill, the two girls dismounted, whereupon the man, whom she now believed was Light, spoke to them. She said that Light asked Muriel to lead the way. When Muriel refused, he asked Valerie to lead the way. She also refused. Details of what was said were not asked for in evidence. Both girls said that they were alarmed by him and, while Light was attending to some defect in his machine, the girls turned their bikes round and headed back towards Leicester. Valerie, like Muriel, identified Light in court. She, too, had picked him out in a police line-up.

Marshall Hall said that the girls' part of the story "would be denied entirely" by the defence. He would point out that the girls did not give statements to the police "until March 9th 1920, statements about something said to have occurred in July 1919". It was a telling point to put to the jury. The unreliability of the girls' evidence must have been made clear to them.

Dr. Edward Williams came into the witness box next. As a general practitioner, Dr. Williams was asked by the prosecution to play the part of an expert medical witness, a role which he was ill-equipped to perform. He estimated the time of death as no earlier than 9.20pm. His failure to notice the bullet wound in Bella's head, until his attention was drawn to it by P.C. Hall, was put right when he carried out a post-mortem examination on Monday July 7th. He said the wound could have been caused by the bullet found by P.C. Hall at the scene of the crime.

When cross-examined by Marshall Hall, Dr. Williams admitted to having little experience of gunshot wounds. Then, instead of refusing to commit himself further, the doctor got into a tangle with Hall over the likely range over which the bullet had travelled before it entered

Miss Wright's head. Dr. Williams said he believed that the fatal bullet was fired at a distance of "not more than six or seven feet". Marshall Hall expressed surprise at this, suggesting that a bullet fired so close to the victim's head would have produced such a tiny amount of damage and, in particular, such a small exit hole. Dr. Williams said he did not think the exit hole should have been much larger. His lack of knowledge of firearms was evident when he admitted he was unaware that an army service revolver would throw a bullet more than half a mile. The doctor did agree with Marshall Hall that the clean-cut hole indicated a high velocity bullet. Marshall Hall was implying that the gun could have been fired a long distance away from Miss Wright and have, quite by chance, passed through her head. Marshall Hall suggested to the doctor that it was absurd that the bullet should have passed through the woman's head and yet had been found only six yards or so away from her body. Dr. Williams agreed that it did seem absurd. He then said, "The bullet must have hit something first," before landing in the roadway.

To illustrate to the jury the smallness of the entry hole, Marshall Hall asked Dr. Williams to give him an autopsy sample. The doctor produced from his bag a piece of face skin, in which was a small puncture wound. Hall then held the piece of skin up in front of the jury and showed them that the hole was so narrow that his propelling pencil could not pass through it.

The next set of prosecution witnesses was called to show that Light and Bella cycled together to Bella's uncle's house on the evening in question.

Mrs. Kathleen Power, a postmistress, testified that on the evening of July 5th, soon after 6pm, Bella Wright called at her post office in Evington. She bought some stamps and gave Mrs. Power some letters for the post. She then rode off towards her home in Stoughton.

Thomas Nourish, of Glebe Farm, Little Stretton, told the court he was driving cattle along the Little Stretton-Gaulby road on the 5th of July. A man and a girl on bicycles rode past him in the direction of Gaulby. It was between 7 and 7.30pm. After driving his herd into a field, Nourish came back to the road and saw 'a gentleman' waiting there. He wore a grey suit and was in need of a shave. He looked about 35 years old. Nourish was unable positively to identify Light as the man he saw with the girl, but he said it looked like him. When Hewart showed him a photograph of Bella Wright, Nourish said, "It's very like the girl I seen."

John Henry Atkins testified that he was on the Stoughton-Gaulby road between 7 and 7.30pm. He said he saw a man and a woman riding bicycles. Although Atkins did not hear what the man said, he heard him speak "in a highish tone".

* * * * *

Witness testimony moved next to the arrival of Bella and the man at her uncle's cottage in Gaulby. A resident of Gaulby, Mrs. Elizabeth Palmer, described how she saw a man and a girl on cycles riding past her near Gaulby village. She saw the girl dismount and walk to Mr. Measures's gate. Mrs. Palmer identified Light in the dock as being the man she saw.

Bella Wright's uncle, George Measures, who worked as a roadmender, testified that Bella came to visit him on the evening of the 5th. She arrived at his cottage at about 7.30pm. His daughter and his son-in-law, James Evans, were in the cottage with him when she arrived. Measures said he noticed a man with a green bicycle outside the cottage, apparently waiting for Bella to come out. When she did leave, the man said to her, "Bella, you were a long time. I thought you were gone the other way home." They rode off together. This was, said Measures, at about 8.45pm.

Cross-examined by Marshall Hall, Measures said that Bella told him the man was 'a perfect stranger' to her. She said he had overtaken her and asked the name of the village. In re-examination by Hewart, Measures testified that while the man was waiting outside, Bella said, "I'll sit down here a little while and he will perhaps be gone."

James Evans, George Measures's son-in-law, gave evidence next. He said that when Bella was ready to leave the cottage, it was found that the front tyre of her bicycle needed fixing. Bella, James Evans and his wife went out to the front gate to mend it. Evans testified that the man said to Miss Wright, "Bella, I thought you had gone the other way." Evans then spoke to the man. He asked him how long he had owned the bike. The man said he had had it a long time. The machine, said Evans, was a "pea-green" colour. There was a three-speed gear and a back-pedalling brake. Looking at the bike in court, Evans said the one he saw was similar, except that the carrier was now different and the three-speed gear lever was missing from the handlebar. Evans followed previous witnesses in identifying the man as "the prisoner". He pointed to Light in the dock.

The judge, Mr. Justice Horridge, then asked Evans a question of his own. He said, “Did the man say ‘Hello’ or ‘Bella’?” “It was ‘Bella’,” replied Evans.

When asked by Hewart to describe the man’s voice, Evans said, “He had a high-pitched, squeaky voice, more like a woman’s than a man’s.”

Before the close of the first day of the trial, Sir George Hewart called two witnesses to prove that Light did, indeed, own a green bicycle. The first of these witnesses was Ethel May Tunnicliffe. She said she had known Ronald Light for nine or ten years. She said she had many times gone for cycle rides with him. Miss Tunnicliffe described how, the previous July, in his mother’s house, she and Light discussed the murder. Light’s mother said what a terrible thing it was. Ethel said that they asked Light if he did not agree. He said, “Yes, it’s a terrible thing.” Intervening, the judge said to Ethel, “Did you call it murder?” “Yes, Sir,” she replied. Hall then jumped to his feet and asked her, “Would you expect anybody to do the same thing?” “Yes, certainly,” she replied. To this the judge said, quite acidly, “That depends, of course, on the their knowledge of the thing.”

Cross-examined by Norman Birkett, Ethel Tunnicliffe said that she did remember that Light had a green B.S.A. bicycle. She also admitted that in 1916, during the war, she received from Light a parcel containing a revolver. She was told to take it to his home in Leicester. This she did. She remembered that Light himself opened the parcel containing the gun.

The last witness on the first day was Frederick Morris. He told how, in 1911, Light had been a lodger at his house in St. Giles Road, Derby. Light was then working in Derby at the offices of the Midland Railway. In 1914, Light moved with Mr. and Mrs. Morris to their new address in Hartington Street. Throughout the time he lodged with Morris, Light had a green bicycle. It was similar to the exhibit in court. Morris said Light took it with him when he left for Leicester at the beginning of the war in 1914.

* * * * *

On the morning of the second day, evidence was heard from Mary Webb. She had been employed as a servant by Light’s mother for the past eight years. Miss Webb was able to provide some details of Light’s behaviour before and after the shooting, and on July 5th itself. When Light returned from his lodgings in Derby to live at his parents’ home at Highfield Street in Leicester, he brought a green bicycle with him.

It was fitted with a three-speed gear, controlled by a black disc on the handlebar. While Light was away on military service, the bike stayed at Highfield Street, in a box room. When he returned from the war, he started to use the machine again. During the summer of 1919, he rode it regularly. Miss Webb said that Light used to leave the house at about 9.30am, return for lunch, go out again, and return for tea at 4pm. Normally, said Miss Webb, he used to go out on his bicycle in the morning and in the afternoon. She said she did not know where he went, but he once told her he was "helping a man with a business".

Mary Webb was able to fix upon certain dates in July 1919. This was because she remembered that on July 8th, a Tuesday, Mrs. Light went away on holiday to Rhyl. This was three days after the shooting. She said she recalled Light taking his bike to be repaired shortly before his mother went away. He brought it back on a Saturday, and on that day, which Miss Webb believed was July 5th, the day of the shooting, Light went out on it. He arrived home at 10pm, looking dusty and tired. Mary Webb asked him, "Why are you so late?" Light replied, "My bike broke down again and I had to walk back." He ate his supper and went to bed.

After July 5th, the green bicycle stayed in the back kitchen for a few days. Miss Webb said Light then took it upstairs to the box room at the back of the house. One evening, before Christmas, Light took the bike out of the house. He never brought it back again. Later, Light told Mary he had sold it.

On the evening that she heard about the murder of Bella Light, Mary asked Light is he had seen the newspapers. She said to him, "There has been a dreadful murder." To this, Light, seemingly uninterested, simply said, "Oh." Mary Webb mentioned that Light generally wore grey. He had several raincoats, some of which were grey. She also said that, before Christmas, some of his clothes were sold.

The next prosecution witness was a Leicester gunsmith called Henry Clarke. He was questioned first by Mr. Maddocks, junior counsel for the Crown. Arranged on a tray were several bullets. Some were from the cartridges found in the canal. One was the spent bullet which P.C. Hall found in the roadway. Mr. Maddocks asked Mr. Clarke to examine the bullets. Clarke said that the round which P.C. Hall found was .455 calibre, adapted for use in a revolver. He said the bullet was identical to one from a cartridge found in the canal.

Marshall Hall then subjected Clarke to a lengthy and rigorous cross-examination. Hall suggested that there were marks on the spent bullet, caused by it having been fired from a gun with a rifled barrel. Clarke examined the bullet with a magnifying glass and agreed that it had passed through such a barrel. He said he could not give the length of the barrel used, but he did say that the bullet might just as well have been fired from a rifle as a revolver. Service revolvers, said Clarke, had a considerable range. He said he had tested some service revolvers with the cartridges from the canal and had found that they would propel a bullet up to a distance of 50 to 60 yards. They could discharge a high velocity bullet which could penetrate an inch of deal wood.

Marshall Hall asked Clarke if he might have expected a service revolver to produce a wound with a much larger exit hole in the woman's head. Did not an exit hole of 1 inches by inch seem unusually small? Henry Clarke said he did not think so. He thought the size of the exit hole showed that the bullet "had been deflected from end-to-end motion after it entered the head". There was, said Clarke, a set of three distinct marks on the bullet. One was caused by a horse's hoof, another by it striking the road, and the third by passing through the head.

Throughout his cross-examination of Henry Clarke, Marshall Hall was seeking to show that the bullet which killed Bella Weight was fired from some distance, well away from the road, and, therefore, possibly by accident. Hall was also suggesting that the fatal bullet was discharged from a rifle and not from a Webley-Scott service revolver. Hall asked Clarke, "Have you ever seen a humanbeing who has been shot at a distance of within five yards with a service revolver?" "No, sir," replied Clarke. "I suggest to you that the effect of such a bullet on the skull of a humanbeing is almost to blow the side of the head off?" "It depends on the velocity, sir." "Of course it does," said Hall.

Since nobody reported hearing the sound of a gunshot near the road, Hall asked Clarke if the discharge of a cordite cartridge would have been audible over a very long distance, in quiet surroundings. "Yes, sir, it would," said Clarke.

After Marshall Hall had finished with Mr. Clarke, he was re-examined by Mr. Maddocks. Clarke said the barrel of a service revolver was rifled. The spent bullet showed, he said, "Marks consistent with it having been fired from a revolver." Clarke also said a badly worn revolver barrel could reduce a bullet's velocity and, therefore, also reduce its penetrating force.

The arresting officer, Detective-Superintendent Taylor, furnished the jury with a few verbal titbits from Light. On first being told he was on a murder charge, he denied owning a bicycle at all. The Superintendent said he went to Dean Close School on March 4th 1920 and asked Light what had become of his green bicycle. Light replied, "I never had a green bicycle." At Cheltenham police station, Light said to Taylor, "What is this stunt?" Later he said, "I sold a bicycle to Mr. Bourne of Wilmot Street, Derby." Light said he had also sold another one. He was identified by Harry Cox, a Leicester cycle repairer. According to Superintendent Taylor, as he and Light walked back to the charge room after Cox had picked Light out from a line, Light said, "My word, that fellow had me spotted all right." In evidence, Cox said Light brought a green bicycle to him on July 2nd, three days before the shooting. He asked Cox to repair the three-speed gear. He collected it on Saturday July 5th, the day Bella Wright was killed.

The Attorney-General declared the prosecution case closed at lunch on the second day.

* * * * *

Opening the case for the defence, Sir Edward Marshall Hall told the jury that the Crown had produced no evidence to place Light on the Gartree Road at the time Bella was killed. Neither, said Hall, was there any evidence of a link between Bella and Light before the evening of her death. Hall asked Ronald Light to go into the witness box.

In direct evidence, Light said he went to France in November 1915 and again in November 1917. On the latter occasion, he was a gunner in the Honourable Artillery Company. He said that he first had a revolver, a Webley-Scott service weapon, in July 1915. When he was finally invalided out of the army owing to shell shock and deafness in August 1918, the revolver and the whole of his kit were taken from him. He had not, he said, seen the revolver since then. The holster belonged to the revolver he left behind in England on his second visit to France. Light agreed that the bicycle part, fished from the canal and exhibited in court, was a part of his bicycle. He denied having a revolver on July 5th, but he did admit he had a cartridge.

Next, questioned by Hall, Light gave his version of his experiences on the evening of the shooting. He said that he left home at about

5.30pm and cycled away from Highfield Street in the direction of Little Stretton. He denied ever meeting two schoolgirls. Intending to get back home for about 8.30pm, said Light, he turned into the upper road. He saw a young woman stooping over her bike. He had never seen her before. As he approached, she looked up, and asked him if she could borrow a spanner. He had no spanner with him. They walked up the road for some distance, and then rode along together. At Gaulby, the woman said she was going to see some friends, adding, "I shall only be ten minutes or a quarter of an hour." By this, said Light, he understood that he should wait for her. He waited for a quarter of an hour and then, setting off back to Leicester, found that his back tyre was flat. He repaired it. It was them said Light, about 8.15pm.

Light said he thought he would ride back "to see where the girl had got to". He saw her coming out of her friend's house. He said to her, "Hello, you've been a long time." He did not, he said, call her 'Bella'. He did not know her name until he read it in the papers. He had a few words with James Evans and rode off with the woman. They pushed their bikes uphill. Yet again, said Light, his tyre went flat. At this, the girl told him she worked at a tyre factory and got tyres at cost price. They rode onwards to a road junction.

Light said that at the junction he turned to the right, towards Leicester. The girl dismounted and, pointing to the left, said to him, "I must say goodbye to you here." Light then said, "But isn't this the shortest way to Leicester?" "Yes," replied the girl, "but I don't live there." As Light rode down the hill, he saw the girl just starting to move off. He said he never saw her again.

Light told how, on his way home, he had to pump up his leaking tyre several times. Eventually, he had to walk. He learned of the death from a Leicester newspaper on the following Tuesday. When he saw a description of a bike and a man, he concluded that the dead girl was the girl he was with.

Concerning his actions after the shooting, Light said that about ten days later, he moved the bicycle into the box room. He did not tell the police because he "could not have assisted them in detecting the crime". In October, he removed the loose parts from the bicycle, loosened some nuts, and threw the machine into the canal. He also admitted throwing in a holster and some cartridges. Asked by Hall why he threw the bike away, Light replied, "Every paper suggested the man who rode the bike was the man who murdered the girl."

"Did you shoot this unfortunate girl?" asked Hall. "Certainly not," replied Light.

Now it was time for Light to be cross-examined. Conspicuous by his absence from court was Attorney-General Hewart. He had left Leicester and abandoned his junior counsel to handle the rest of the case, including the important cross-examination of the accused and the closing speech for the Crown. It was later reported that Sir George Hewart had been called down to London to assist Lloyd George in the drafting of peace proposals. It has also been suggested that Hewart left the court because he was already convinced that the case against Light would eventually be lost and did not want to face the defeat in person.

In cross-examination by Mr. Maddocks, Light said that every word the two little girls had said in the witness box about him was untrue. He said, "I never saw or spoke to those girls on any occasion."

On July 5th, said Light, he had no trouble with his bike until 6.45pm, when he had ridden seven or eight miles. Again he said he met Bella Wright by the roadside. He helped her with her bike for two or three minutes. When he parted from her it was, he said, about 8.45pm. Light said he walked most of the way home because of a puncture. He had, he said, intended to get home by 8pm.

Mr. Maddocks asked Light why, when he saw police notices appealing for information, he did not come forward. Light replied, "I was absolutely dazed about the whole thing. I could not think clearly about the matter. I could not make up my mind what to do." Mr. Maddocks produced a newspaper for Tuesday July 8th. Light said he found out about the death from it.

"Why didn't you give information to the police, say you were the man on the green bicycle, and explain your movements that night?" "Because apparently everyone jumped to the conclusion that the man on the green bicycle had murdered the girl."

Here the judge intervened and asked Light, "Don't you see that if you had gone to the police with the true story, you would have put them off a false scent and enabled them to look for the right one?" "I see it now, my lord," replied Light. "I did not make up my mind deliberately not to come forward. I was so astounded and frightened that I kept on hesitating and in the end I did nothing at all."

The exchanges continued:

Maddocks: "The police could then have examined the bicycle to see if there was a puncture?"

Light: "They can do it now. I have never touched the bicycle since in the way of repairs."

Maddocks: "Did you think your story at that time would not be believed?"

Light: "I did not think so."

Judge: "Did you talk to your mother and tell her you were perfectly innocent?"

Light: "No. One of the chief reasons why I did not come forward was because I did not want to worry her. I did not tell Mary Webb because I had not made my mind up to come forward."

Judge: "You did not think it difficult to get people to believe you?"

Light: "I did not think so"

Judge: "Don't you see it was still more extraordinary then if you did not come forward to tell people?"

Light: "There was the unpleasant publicity about it, which I shrank from, and I failed to realize what a position I was putting myself in."

Judge: "You could have given information to the police, saying, 'You are all wrong about the green bicycle.'. Don't you see that would have been of immense value to the police?"

Light: "I see it now."

Mr. Maddocks handed Light a letter, written to him by his mother on July 11th. She was then at Rhyl. The letter contained the sentence, "What is the news at home? We are interested in a cycle mystery." "Why did you not go to Rhyl or write to your mother?" asked Maddocks.

Light: "Because of all people, mother was the last one I wanted to know about it. It was to save her worry that I did not come forward."

Maddocks: "But she, of all persons, would accept your word?"

Light: "Certainly."

Light said he put the green bicycle into the box room after ten days because he read about the case. Mr. Justice Horridge asked him, "Did you put it there to avoid being identified by it?"

Light: "Yes."

Maddocks: "Why did you file off the serial number?"

Light: "If the bicycle had been found, I did not want it to be traced to me."

Light said he at first denied ever having a green bicycle because it was the first thing that came into his head. When the name of Orton, the cycle agent, was mentioned, it occurred to him that it might be identified.

Maddocks: "You replied, 'Yes, but I sold it years ago.' What made you say that?"

Light: "I had drifted into this policy of concealing the fact that I had been out riding that night. I had to go along with it."

Maddocks: "Why did you not make a statement to the police court?"

Light: "I was prepared to, but I was advised not to."

This last question of Maddocks was unfair and prejudicial. The judge, intervening to admonish the junior counsel, said, "Once a man is in custody he is quite at liberty to reserve his defence, and say nothing. If a prisoner merely sits tight, and says he will wait until he is tried, I think very often he is a wise man."

Re-examined by Marshall Hall, Light said his mother had been through a great deal of trouble in the last few years. His father had been killed by falling from a window. Light said he himself "had been the cause of very great expense to her one way or another". Her health, said Light, was poor. She had been "under doctor's orders for many years with a bad heart".

At the end of Light's testimony, after Hall's re-examination, the judge said to Light, "I am asking for all that passed between you and the girl about your parting. Have you told us all that passed between you?" Light said nothing. "Have you told us all the conversation that passed between you about your parting?" Light at last replied, "Oh yes, that was all, my lord, yes."

* * * * *

Light said he heard no shot as he rode back home. He completed his evidence shortly after 12 noon on the third day. Light's two stints in the witness box had lasted, in total, over four and a half hours. Mr. Maddocks then summed up the case against him. Referring to a suggestion by Marshall Hall that Bella Wright's death was an accident, caused by someone out shooting in a nearby field, Maddocks advised the jury that her head wound was inconsistent with that scenario. "Within a quarter hour of Light leaving the girl, she was found dead." The bullet found by the spot was the same, he said, as in Light's holster. Mr. Maddocks then put this to the jury, "If the prisoner is not the man, somebody else did it, and that somebody else had not been heard of." The prisoner's actions were, said Maddocks, "Those of a guilty man, anxious to cover up his guilt." Paying Light a back-handed compliment, he said, "The thoroughness with which he disposed of the bicycle shows that he is no ordinary man, but a clever and deliberate man."

Guilty or not, Light had stood up to his cross-examination, both by prosecuting counsel and judge, with remarkable composure and aplomb. There was little doubt that Light had displayed considerable courage in the witness box, a quality that fitted well with Hall's portrayal of Light as a soldier who had served his country in war and had been discharged with his health in tatters.

There was a distinct weight of circumstantial evidence against Light but, as Marshall Hall pointed out in his final remarks to the jury, there had been nothing to prove that Light and Bella knew of each other's existence before the night of her death. One might wonder if they had met before, and perhaps if they were having some kind of clandestine relationship, but no evidence for any such thing was ever produced. Idle speculation could not play a part in the jury's considerations. They had to decide the case on the evidence put before them. Since there was no apparent connection between Bella Wright and Ronald Light, there was, as Hall told the jury, "throughout the case an entire absence of motive". One can speculate that Light may have made some kind of sexual approach to the girl, but there was just no evidence at all to back up this theory. No forensic evidence had been given of any sign of physical interference whatsoever. As far as was known, the only injuries Bella Wright sustained were those to her head, caused by the impact of a bullet, and perhaps, to a lesser extent, by her falling from her bicycle.

In a murder trial there is no legal requirement for the prosecution to establish a motive for the killing. However, its case is, understandably, greatly weakened if the jury cannot find any good reason, from the rest of the evidence, for the defendant having committed murder. Much had been made of Light having owned a service revolver. He may, of course, have secretly disposed of it, but there was no direct evidence that Light had the weapon in 1919. As Hall said, "Among all the witnesses called to identify the prisoner, no-one could speak of having seen anything about him which could be described as in any way similar to such a bulky article as a service revolver."

Mr. Justice Horridge referred to Light's long silence about his movements on the night of July 5th, and to his disposal of the bicycle. In his summing-up to the jury, the judge said, "Do you think it is credible or possible that an innocent man should have behaved in the way that he did? He gave the reason that he was dazed and did not know what to do. The other motive is the guilty motive. If his conduct is compatible with innocence, then you must give him the benefit of the doubt. The question you have to decide is whether that deception could have been practised by an innocent man, or whether it points the finger at the guilty man."

Having heard the judge's summary, the jury retired at 4.35pm. Three hours later, they were called back and asked by the judge if there was any chance of agreement. The jury foreman said they hoped to return a verdict in about ten minutes. The jury retired again. Five minutes later, they reappeared and returned a verdict of not guilty. The outcome was greeted by cheering, both inside the court-room and outside in the street. Ronald Light was set free. When the verdict was announced, Light, through either relief, surprise or sheer exhaustion, fell back from his standing position in the dock and into his chair.

* * * * *

To avoid the possibility of prejudice against Light at his trial, much of his background was kept from the jury. Light, who held the position of a mathematics teacher at a Cheltenham school, had been appointed there on the strength of forged testimonials. Amongst other things, he had falsely claimed to have been an ex-pupil of Rugby School. In fact, at the age of seventeen, Light had been expelled from Oakham School for lifting a little girl's clothes over her head. In 1914, while employed as an apprentice engineer for the Midland Railway, he was sacked after being suspected of setting fire to a cupboard and making rude drawings on lavatory walls. He was 29 years old at the time.

From about 1910, Light formed a liaison with Ethel Tunnicliffe. She worked in the same office at the Derby Railway Works. Light's army record was bad. As a second lieutenant in the Royal Engineers he was dismissed the service and sent to England in 1916. There were rumours of an assault on a postmistress in a French village. Later that year, Light enlisted as a private in the Honourable Artillery Company.

In 1917, Light was involved in another escapade. Having already served as an officer in France, and in grave danger of being sent there again, this time as a private and a gunner, Light took action to forestall his posting to the front line. He got hold of some War Office stationery and forged a series of telegrams. These false messages were designed to ensure that Light's own gun battery's call to arms was repeatedly postponed. He was court-martialled at Westminster and, having served four months in the glasshouse, was shipped over to France to perform his military duty.

By 1919, the Leicester police already knew a good deal about Ronald Light and his green bicycle. The Essex Constabulary was investigating Light over an alleged illegal abortion in Southend. On October 28th 1919, Light was taken to a Leicester police station on suspicion of improper conduct with an eight-year-old girl. Although Light apparently admitted an offence, the child's parents did not wish to press charges. While he was awaiting his trial for murder, a 38-year-old pregnant woman alleged that Light was the cause of her condition. The Leicester police had a lengthy file on Light, chiefly for wandering about on his bicycle, pestering women and children. Ronald Light had ample time to remember his murder trial. He died at Sittingbourne, Kent in 1975 at the age of 89.

Chapter 7

The Camden Town Murder

At 4.30pm on the afternoon of Wednesday, September 11th 1907, a young man named Bertram Shaw set out from his lodgings at 29 St. Paul's Road in Camden Town and walked to London St. Pancras railway station. (The road is today known as Agar Grove.) Within the hour, Shaw was at work, cooking food in the dining-car of a Midland Railway train heading north out of the metropolis.

For some eight months, Bert Shaw had been living with a 23-year-old woman, Emily Elizabeth Dimmock. The couple had taken a two-room apartment at St. Paul's Road some eight weeks earlier, in July 1907. Bert and Emily were not married, but Shaw had led his mother, and numerous other people, to believe that they were.

Emily Dimmock was a tall, slim woman with fair hair. She dressed attractively and usually displayed a pleasant and accommodating manner. Born in Walworth, the youngest of fifteen children, Emily Dimmock grew up in Wellingborough. After working in a straw hat factory there, she moved to her native London when she was eighteen. She obtained a position as a housemaid in East Finchley. An accomplished pianist, Emily quickly tired of a servant's life and moved into the Gray's Inn Road district where, based at a variety of addresses, she worked the Euston Road as a prostitute. Her adopted name was "Phyllis".

Bert Shaw was blissfully unaware of Emily's double life. During the day, she was a housewife at St. Paul's Road. At night she visited pubs and entertained men, specializing in soldiers and sailors on shore leave. Bert's hours of work on the railway meant that he was out of London most evenings and nights.

Having left St. Pancras on the afternoon of September 11th, Shaw arrived back there the following morning at 10.40am. Forty minutes later, Shaw let himself through the house door at 29 St. Paul's Road. When he tried the front door of the apartment he shared with Emily, Shaw found that it was locked against him. No amount of knocking could bring Emily to open the door. Annoyed, and slightly uneasy about the situation, Shaw walked up to the first floor and reported his difficulty to the landlady, Mrs. Sarah Stocks. Using her own key, Mrs. Stocks let Shaw into the front room of the apartment and went inside with him. The accommodation was really one large room, divided into two by connecting folding doors. These doors were now also locked. Alarmingly, the front room was in great disorder. A chest of drawers had been rifled, its contents strewn about the room. Shaw's cut-throat razor lay open on top of the chest. As Emily had the key for the inner doors, Shaw forced them open with a series of kicks.

Emily Dimmock was lying in bed, naked beneath the bedclothes, face down, and dead. Her body was cold and rigid. In the bedroom were the remains of a supper for two people. Two plates, two knives and two forks lay discarded on a table. A basin on the wash stand held bloodstained water. Emily's throat had been cut. In the window, the shutters of the venetian blind had been pulled slightly aside, admitting a narrow strip of daylight. A sliver of light fell on to Emily's post card album, lying open on a chair. It looked as if someone had been searching through it. Post cards lay scattered across the bedroom floor. Missing from the ransacked chest of drawers were several items of Emily's jewellery, including a silver cigarette case and a watch on a chain. Curiously, two gold rings lay exposed on top of the chest, lying side by side. Bert Shaw ran for the police.

* * * * *

After Emily's brother Henry, a plasterer's labourer from Luton, had formally identified Emily's body, an inquest into her death opened at St. Pancras Coroner's Court on Monday, September 16th 1907 before Dr. Danford-Thomas, the Central London Coroner.

In evidence at the inquest, police surgeon Dr. John Thompson, who examined the body at 1pm, said he estimated the time of death as between 5am and 7am that morning of September 12th. The doctor also said that Emily's fatal wound could not have been self-inflicted, such was the force which must have been exerted to create it. He believed she may have been asleep when she was killed. A cut on her right elbow was probably caused accidentally after her death. After a fortnight's adjournment, Dr. Thompson, on September 30th, gave further evidence. The autopsy showed that Emily had eaten about three hours before she died. Because the landlady, Mrs. Stocks, knew she used to eat her supper at about midnight, the time of death was adjusted to between 3am and 4am. Emily usually went out between

8pm and 8.30pm and usually came home after Mrs. Stocks had gone to bed.

It was a clear case of murder. However, in those days it was customary for an inquest jury, if they could, to attribute a killing to a particular individual. When the inquest was resumed on October 21st, the police had already, on October 4th, charged a man with the murder. The accused was Robert William Thomas George Cavers Wood, "Bob" to his friends.

Robert Wood was living in his father's house in Frederick Street, off Gray's Inn Road. He had worked for fourteen years as an artistic designer with the London Sand Glass Company in Gray's Inn Road itself. Wood also drew cartoons for several newspapers on a freelance basis. He was a tall, dark-haired man with sensitive features and a long aquiline nose. He walked with a slightly stooping gait. Wood was born in Glasgow, and his mother died soon after he was born. His father moved to London and remarried. A clever schoolboy, one of his teachers got Wood a job as a steward at the Australian Medical Students Club in Chancery Lane. It was here that Wood's artistic talent became apparent. He became skilled in copying illustrations for students from expensive medical text-books. At 58A Gray's Inn Road, Wood designed figures and patterns for fancy glassware. Everyone who knew him found Wood to be a kind, amiable and courteous man, popular with both clients and colleagues. He was 28 years old when he was arrested.

Nowadays, the inquest would have been adjourned until after the accused had been tried. In 1907, the testimony of numerous witnesses was heard, after which a guilty person could be named. So, after hearing a further two days of evidence, the inquest jury brought in a verdict of "wilful murder against Robert Wood". After the verdict, coroner Thomas said of Wood, "Before the magistrate, the grand jury, and a final jury, he will have every opportunity of proving that he is not the person who did the murder."

The coroner was right about the three sets of proceedings which lay ahead for Wood. However, he was wrong when he said that Wood might prove his innocence. It was not up to Wood or his counsel to prove he was innocent. It was for the Crown to prove he was guilty, beyond a reasonable doubt, to the satisfaction of a jury. At that time, the jury's verdict had to be unanimous. Neither did it have to be proved that any other particular person committed the crime.

After a hearing before the Clerkenwell Magistrates, it was decided that the case against Wood was strong enough to warrant his being tried on a murder charge. Consequently, he was committed for trial by jury. In 1907, the antiquated "grand jury" system was still in operation. The process involved a panel of worthies, usually land-owners and businessmen, being addressed by the judge on the salient points of the Crown's case against an individual. If the panel, or "grand jury", believed that the accused should face a jury trial, they would issue a "true bill". In Robert Wood's case, the grand jury met on December 10th and, as used to happen in virtually all cases, a true bill was issued. Cumbersome and outmoded as the pre-trial process was in those days, it was usually swift. There was a period of only just over two months between Wood's arrest and his trial.

* * * * *

On February 27th 1907, the Central Criminal Court, frequently known as the Old Bailey, was opened for business on the site of the old Newgate Prison. It was here that Robert Wood came to trial on Thursday, December 12th 1907 for the murder of Emily Dimmock. A guilty verdict would mean an automatic death sentence for Wood. The judge was Mr. Justice Grantham. Leading counsel for the Crown was Sir Charles Matthews, senior Treasury Counsel and a future Director of Public Prosecutions. The defence was led by Edward Marshall Hall, as yet un-knighted. As Sir Charles began to outline the case for the Crown, the puzzling story of the murder of Emily Dimmock started to unfold.

Bert Shaw and Sarah Stocks found Emily dead on the morning of September 12th. The previous morning, Alice Lancaster, a widow who also had rooms at 29 St. Paul's Road, took two letters from the postman when he knocked on the house door at about 7.45pm. They were both addressed to "Mrs. B. Shaw", the name by which Mrs. Lancaster knew Emily Dimmock. Mrs. Lancaster knocked twice at Emily's apartment door. Saying, "Two letters," she pushed them under the door.

Robert Percival Roberts, a ship's cook living at 31 College Place, was paid off from his ship in August 1907. On Sunday September 8th, he met Emily in Euston Road. He went with her into a pub called the *Rising Sun*. Roberts testified that he left the pub with Emily, whom he then knew as "Phyllis", between 10pm and 11pm. They went to the apartment at 29 St. Paul's Road. Roberts said he stayed there overnight and left at 7.30am the next morning. The next night, Monday the 9th, Roberts returned to the *Rising Sun*. He got there at about 6pm. He said that Emily came into the pub at about 8pm. They exchanged a few words and then, soon afterwards, Robert Wood arrived on the scene. Emily immediately made a bee-line for Wood and, after drinking with him at the bar for about half an hour, left with him. Roberts stayed at the pub.

Emily and Wood came back into the *Rising Sun* at about 11pm. They stayed until 12.20am and then went out together again. Roberts said that a few minutes later, Emily returned alone and went with him to number 29. Roberts described how, in the apartment, Emily took a postcard out of her bodice and showed it to him. He noticed that it was signed "Alice". The message on it said, "If it pleases you, meet me 8.15pm at the *Rising Sun*. Yours to a cinder." The title of the pub was represented by a sketch of the sun peeping over the horizon and winking its left eye. Roberts and Emily talked about the card for a few moments and then Emily put it into the top left-hand drawer of the chest in the sitting room.

Roberts said that he met Emily again on the Tuesday evening. They went to a theatre, to the *Rising Sun*, and then back to number 29. On the Wednesday morning, Roberts was lying in bed when he heard a knock on the door. Two letters were delivered, presumably by Alice Lancaster. Emily opened the letters and read them. One was an advertising circular from a ladies' tailor; the other was a letter written on three sides of a folded sheet of paper. Roberts read this second letter also. Emily went over to the top drawer, took out the post card from "Alice" and showed him the card and the letter together. Roberts noticed they were both in the same handwriting.

Roberts testified that there was writing on three sides of the paper. On the third side he remembered seeing the following words, 'Dear Phyllis – will you meet me at the bar of the *Eagle* at Camden Town 8.30 tonight, Wednesday, Bert.'

Roberts said there was a postscript and other words on the paper, but that was all Emily showed him. She then, said Roberts, put the letter and the advertisement into one envelope, set fire to them with a match, and threw them into the fire grate. She put the post card back into the top drawer. Roberts said that both the letter and the post card had been written with an indelible lead pencil.

At 8.30am on the morning of Wednesday the 11th, Roberts left number 29, having spent three consecutive nights there. That morning, said Roberts, was the last time he saw Emily Dimmock, the woman he knew as Phyllis.

According to Roberts's testimony, at 5.30pm the following day, he was in the *Rising Sun*. The head barman told him Phyllis had been murdered. Two detectives came into the pub and he went with them to Somers Town police station. There, Roberts dictated and signed a statement. On October 5th, he identified Wood as the man he saw with Emily on the Monday.

Cross-examined by Marshall Hall, Roberts said that when he was told of the murder, he stayed at the *Rising Sun* to wait for the police to come to him. He told people there that he intended to stay so he could tell the police what he knew. He knew Wood because, during the time he was in the *Rising Sun*, they "looked very hard at each other". On the night of the murder, said Roberts, he left the *Rising Sun* at 12.20am with a fellow-lodger called Clarke. They got home at 12.45am, were let in by their landlady, and slept there all night.

Concerning the post card signed "Alice", Bertram Shaw, in evidence, said that when he was getting his belongings together in readiness for moving to different rooms at number 29, he found the post card in a drawer of the chest, under the drawer's newspaper lining.

* * * * *

The prosecution claimed Wood had known Emily Dimmock since the spring of 1906. Wood said he had never seen her at all until Friday September 6th. Sir Charles Matthews called a number of witnesses who claimed to have seen Wood with Dimmock before the murder.

Mrs. Emily Lawrence, the wife of a printer, said she saw Wood and Dimmock in a pub in Gray's Inn Road called the *Pindar of Wakefield*.

Mrs. Lawrence had been a prostitute at one time. She said that in September 1906 she went to the *Pindar* with Dimmock where they met Wood. Emily said she would not introduce him by name because he lived with his parents and he did not like to be seen talking to women. Mrs. Lawrence said she noticed Wood and Emily in the *Rising Sun* on Friday September 6th, and again on Monday the 9th. On the Monday they left the pub together, saying they were off to the Holborn Empire. It looked, said Mrs. Lawrence, as if Emily did not really want to go with Wood. It seemed that somehow she felt obliged to. Emily told her Wood was a bad character. When she saw him on the Monday, she said, "There's that so-and-so rogue." Later that night, in the *Rising Sun,* Wood and Dimmock told Mrs. Lawrence they had not gone to the Empire after all. Instead, they had been sitting in a pub on the corner of the Hampstead and Euston Roads, called the *Adam and Eve*. Mrs. Lawrence picked out Wood in a line-up at Kentish Town police station. When she touched him on the shoulder to identify him, Wood said to her, "Good morning." Mrs. Lawrence's evidence was confirmed by her companion on the nights concerned, a woman called Florence Smith, also known as Emily Stewart, of Arlington Road, Camden Town.

Gladys Warren, a servant, of Union Street, Newington, said she knew Emily Dimmock. Emily had stayed with her for a week in a house on Judd Street after being thrown out of her lodgings. Warren said she saw Wood and Dimmock in the *Rising Sun* in the April and the June of 1906. Warren complained that her employer had sacked her when he found out she was to be a witness in the case. This treatment was deplored by Justice Grantham. He said it was deplorable that she should be sacked for doing her public duty, but the judge made no reference to the stigma which had become attached to Warren's moral character. A servant with her background would not have been welcome in any respectable person's home. William Lineham, who was working as a lavatory attendant in the Strand, testified that he had seen Wood and Dimmock together in the *Rising Sun* "four or five times between June 1906 and January 1907".

Evidence was given by an unsavoury character called John Crabtree. He had recently been discharged from prison after serving a two-year sentence for keeping two brothels. Crabtree said Robert Wood visited Dimmock in May 1906 at his establishment at 1 Bidborough Street, and in June 1906 at 13 Manchester Street. Crabtree admitted he did not pick out Wood at first, but, after some encouragement by the police to pick someone out, he did identify Wood. "I thought at first the police had taken me for murder," said Crabtree.

* * * * *

For about three years, Wood had been friendly with a woman named Ruby Young. He had been known to refer to her as his fiancee, and sometimes as his "sweetheart". It was through Ruby that Wood was arrested. In her evidence, Ruby Young said that on Friday September 20th, in the week following the murder, she received a telegram from Robert Wood. It said, "Meet me at 6.30. Phit-Easi's, tonight, Bob." The message referred to a well-known footwear shop in Southampton Row. Ruby met Wood as arranged. They went into a Lyons tea shop. While they were in the cafe, Wood asked her if she would say, if asked, that she always went out with him on Mondays and Wednesdays. To ensure that Ruby did not forget this request, Wood wrote, on a small card, "Mons and Weds" and gave it to her. On the following Monday, the 23rd, she got a post card from Wood, making another date with her at the Phit-Easi, for that evening at 6.30pm. That night they went to the Prince of Wales theatre. Before they parted that night, Wood again reminded Ruby of her promise. He said to her, "Mondays and Wednesdays, don't forget."

Ruby Young said she next saw Bob Wood on the following Sunday evening. He called on her at her Earls Court flat between 8 and 9pm. That morning, Ruby had, as usual, looked at the *News of the World*. It had given her quite a nasty surprise. Printed in the newspaper was a picture of the post card sent to "Phyllis" and signed "Alice". The police were seeking the writer of the card. Ruby realized the writer was her friend, Bob Wood. She cut the picture out of the paper, wrote a letter to Wood, and put them into an envelope. She left it, ready for posting, on a table in her room.

Although he had not been exactly faithful to her, Wood had always been kind and generous. After all, she was not exactly an angel herself. Sometimes she thought she would like to marry him, perhaps, one day. Now she was very worried indeed. When Wood arrived at her flat that evening, she became really afraid.

Wood said, "Ruby, I'm in trouble." "Yes, I know," she replied. Showing him the cutting, she said, "This is your handwriting." Wood read the letter she had written and threw it into the fire. He kept the cutting between his fingers.

"Have patience and I will tell you all," he said. He asked her to say she was with him on Wednesday the 11th. In return, Ruby asked Wood where he really was on the night of the killing. Wood would not give her a proper answer. He simply said he could not prove where he had been at the time of the murder.

Eventually, Ruby Young agreed to provide Wood with a false alibi for September 11th. Later on Sunday the 29th, she walked with him to the tube station. She rode with him as far as Piccadilly Circus. Wood went on to Holborn. In evidence, Ruby described the conversation she had with Wood on the train journey. He said to her, "If your name gets besmirched in any way, I will marry you if I get free." Ruby told him she had no wish to marry him. In trying to persuade her, Wood said, "Your word and mine would stand against the world."

Later in the week, on Friday October 4th, Ruby Young got in touch with the Weekly Dispatch. By arrangement, she met a reporter from that paper in a Regent Street restaurant. Ruby told him she knew who had written the post card. The reporter telephoned the police. They met Detective-Inspector Neil outside Piccadilly station. Arrangements were then made for Ruby to go to Gray's Inn Road and meet Wood as he came out of his studio. Ruby was then to walk with Wood along the street, where police officers would be waiting to arrest him. At 6.30pm on Friday, Ruby met Wood from work. All was going according to plan. As the couple walked towards Holborn, Wood drew Ruby's attention to a man standing against a shop front. He said, "I believe he is a detective." "Take no notice," said Ruby. Wood, however, was right. A cab drew up to the kerb and Wood was guided into it. As Wood climbed into the cab, he turned to Ruby and said to her, "Goodbye dear, don't worry. If England wants me, she must have me. Don't cry, but be true." "Leave that to me," replied Ruby Young. With that, Wood was driven off to Highgate police station.

* * * * *

Why should Robert Wood, as the writer of the "Alice" post card, have been the prime suspect for Emily's murder? The answer lay in the two documents Roberts said Emily Dimmock showed him on the morning of Wednesday September 11th. According to Roberts, the post card, and a letter of assignation for 8.30 that night at the *Eagle* tavern, were both in the same handwriting. Emily is said to have burned the letter in the fire grate, but the police had rescued a charred fragment of the letter and found that it was indeed a request for Emily to meet the writer at the *Eagle* on the night of her death. Moreover, Emily's post card album was found open in her room. Cards were strewn on the floor, as if her killer had been searching for a particular card, presumably his own, to deflect suspicion away from himself. The police, therefore, believed that Wood had met Emily at the *Eagle*, as arranged by the charred letter, gone back to her flat with her, and then, possibly between 4 and 6am in the morning, killed her and fled.

When, through the efforts of Ruby Young, Wood was in safe custody at Highgate police station, he was persuaded to make a signed statement. Wood's version of events was that he had first met Emily in the *Rising Sun* on Friday September 6th, never having come across her before at any time.

She asked him if he had a penny for the gramophone. While they were chatting, a post card seller came around the pub. Emily asked Wood to buy her one. Wood said the cards were poor and that he had a more artistic one in his pocket. Emily told him she had a large collection of cards at home. Wood promised to post the card to her. Next day, Saturday 7th, Wood met Emily at the top of College Street, near Camden Town railway station. They went into the *Eagle*, on the corner of College Street. Wood said they chatted for a while and then went their separate ways. Emily, whom he knew as "Phyllis", reminded him to send her the post card. Having posted the card, he saw Emily a third time, on Monday the 9th, at the *Rising Sun*. According to Wood, Emily told him she had fixed up to meet later "a fellow she did not like". They left the pub and strolled together as far as St. Pancras Church. Here, they came upon a group of four "horsey men"(cab drivers) on a corner by the church. Emily, said Wood, knew one of the men and talked to him for a few moments. At this, said Wood, he shook hands with her and said goodnight. Wood said that this was the last time he ever saw her. In his police statement, Wood said he did not see Emily at all on the 11th of September.

What did Wood at first say about his whereabouts on the night of the murder? Ruby Young said Wood had told her to pretend she was with him that night, although this was untrue. Predictably, in his police statement, Wood said he was with Ruby, "On Wednesday I walked up to Holborn with Ruby Young, my sweetheart, who had called for me. We had tea in Lyons till about 8.15pm. We strolled about the West End. We said goodnight and got home at about midnight." Wood stated that he first heard about the murder on September 13th, from a man called Moss who worked in the same studio. Wood said, "I did not pay much attention to it as I did not recognize the name 'Dimmock'. Moss read the paper and noticed the name 'Phyllis'." Wood said that on the following Sunday he saw, on newspaper placards, photographs of a girl in a sailor suit. At first, said Wood, he did not recognize her. Later he knew who she was, "From what I read, I knew it must have been the girl I met, I decided to have nothing to do with the matter."

Unsure as to what he should do, Wood went to see his younger brother Charles. On the Sunday of the publication of the card, Charles Wood read the *News of the World* and, later in the day, spoke to Robert about it. Wood admitted he had written the card and asked Charles for his advice. Robert, however, denied any part in the murder. At the inquest, Charles Wood described what happened next. He said Robert told him he first met the woman on the night of September 6th. There had been a second, chance meeting, and one on Monday night, the 9th, arranged by sending the post card. As he was walking home on the evening of his brother Robert's visit, Charles Wood formulated an idea of what he could do to help his brother get out of the quandary. The plan was to send a letter, addressed to himself, to a Poste Restante address for later collection, disclaiming any responsibility for Emily's death, stating that his brother did write the post card, but saying Robert did not want to contact the police. The reason for his silence was that the subsequent publicity would ruin his father's already poor health. He was ashamed to have associated with a woman like Dimmock. In the hope that Robert might have his cake and eat it too, a document was drawn up by Charles Wood. It was witnessed and signed by his wife Bessie and by Robert himself. Charles then addressed the sealed letter to himself, "Charles Wood, Poste Restante, St. Martin's-le-Grand". As it turned out, Charles never did claim the letter. The police found it waiting for collection at the post office.

When Robert Wood heard from the police that they believed he wrote a letter to Emily, making an appointment at the *Eagle* on the night of her death, and wrote "Alice" on the earlier post card as well, he said, "I never wrote anything to her except the post card."

Referring to the letter waiting for collection at St. Martin's post office, Wood told the police, "I want you to get it, to show I did not conceal the matter." Wood repeated this plea several times. He was also alleged to have said, "I only met the girl by accident on the Friday night. I know practically nothing about the matter. If one has a good name, you do not care to be mixed up in matters of this sort."

There was someone else close to Robert Wood who saw the post card displayed in a newspaper and recognised the writing on it. This was John Tinkham, a foreman at the glass works in Gray's Inn Road, to which Wood's work studio was attached. In evidence, Tinkham said he saw a picture of the card in the *Daily Mirror* on Saturday September 28th. That morning, at work, Tinkham tackled Wood about it. "You wrote that post card, didn't you, Bob?" "That's quite right," replied Wood. "I wrote it, and I'll explain why I wrote it."

Wood asked Tinkham to keep the secret to himself, because his father was ill. "Jack," said Wood, "will you, as a personal favour to me, keep this information to yourself? My father is ill, and if he knew I was connected with this, the blow would knock him over." Tinkham promised to say nothing. The following Monday, said Tinkham, Wood told him he had spoken to his brother Charles and a letter had been sent to the police. "He told me the information was in the hands of the authorities," said Tinkham.

We now come to evidence which, if believed by the jury to be truthful, would have a severely destructive effect on Wood's chances of escaping a trip to the gallows. The witness giving this evidence was a man called Robert Henry McCowan.

* * * * *

Early in the morning of Thursday September 12th, at the time Emily Dimmock was believed to have been killed, McCowan left his home at Chalk Farm and set out to look for work. McCowan was then working as a "car-man", hired out on a casual basis to unload wagons and coaches. It was, said McCowan, 4.40am. He was walking along St. Paul's Road, heading towards the home of his work-mate, a man called Coleman. They were going to find work loading bread vans at a bakery. As he walked, McCowan heard, from behind him, the sound of footsteps. Looking round, he saw a man coming out through the gateway of a house, later identified as 29 St. Paul's Road. He heard the "click" of the gate latch. Turning round occasionally, McCowan watched a man walking behind and away from him, in the direction from which McCowan himself had just come. According to McCowan, the man wore a bowler hat and a dark-coloured, short, loose overcoat. His collar was turned up against the early morning chill. McCowan noticed the peculiar way the man walked. He continually jerked his right shoulder. His left hand was kept down at his side. As McCowan waited for his friend Coleman to arrive, he looked at the lurching figure about half a dozen times as it receded from him along the curve of St. Paul's Road, towards Kings Road. At first, McCowan thought Coleman was playing a trick on him, pretending to be a man with a strange walk. When Coleman turned up, McCowan told him what he had seen – the man, he was later to tell police, had "a swaggering gait".

Evidence of identification is notoriously unreliable. McCowan did not see the man's face. It was, said McCowan, a thick, muggy morning, and not yet quite daylight. (Greenwich Mean Time operated throughout the year in those days.) There was, he said, an electric lamp nearby. On October 7th, a group of men, including Robert Wood, was instructed to walk in a parade around the police station yard. McCowan picked out Wood as the man with the swaggering gait. However, McCowan had at first told the police that the man he saw was about 5ft 8in tall, stiffly built, with broad shoulders. Wood was taller than this, and was slimly built. At first McCowan said the man's overcoat reached below his knees. only later did he say the coat was short.

Cross-examined by Marshall Hall, McCowan said he reported his sighting to the police at the Somers Town police station on Saturday morning, September 14th. He voiced this complaint, that of an innocent bystander: "I have been caused great annoyance since giving evidence, I might have committed the murder myself for all the trouble I have had. Letters have been sent to me, threatening to cut my throat. In future, if I actually saw with my own eyes a man getting his throat cut in the street, I do not think I would give evidence again."

Having arranged a false alibi with Ruby Young, Wood took further steps to obscure his actions on the night of the murder. After his meeting with Ruby on September 20th, Wood got in touch with his friend Joseph Lambert. Lambert, who worked in Westall's bookshop at 106 Charing Cross Road, knew Wood had been in Emily's company a few hours before she was killed. In evidence, he said he had known Wood for two years. Lambert said that on the 11th of September, he was in the *Eagle* at about 9pm. He saw Wood and Dimmock chatting together. Wood introduced her as 'Phyllis'. Her hair was in curlers. (The curlers were confirmed by a barmaid at the *Eagle* called Lilian Raven.) Emily said to Lambert, "I hope you will excuse my dress. I have just run out." While Wood bought drinks, Emily said, "He's a nice boy." She said Wood had some business to attend to in the district. After ten minutes with them, Lambert left the *Eagle*. Before he went, he gave Wood the telephone number of the bookshop.

On Friday the 20th, while he was working in the shop, Lambert got a telephone call from Wood. Wood asked Lambert if he had heard about "the Camden Town affair". He told Wood he should come over and they could talk it over. A few minutes later, Wood rang again, and asked Lambert what time he finished at the shop. Lambert told him 8pm. Wood said he would come between 7 and 8pm. At 7.15pm, Wood arrived at the bookshop. He asked Lambert to cover up for him about their encounter in the *Eagle*. Wood said, "If Mr. Moss says anything to you about the affair, tell him we met and had a drink, but leave the girl out of it." "That will be all right," replied Lambert. Wood then added, "So far as you are concerned, you know nothing about it at all."

* * * * *

The first suspect for the crime was Bert Shaw, but it was soon clear that he was away in Sheffield at the time of the killing. He could not possibly have committed the crime. The next suspect was Roberts. He had spent the previous three nights with Dimmock at St. Paul's Road. However, he had successfully convinced the police that he was not there on the night of the 11th. Several witnesses swore that Roberts was in the *Rising Sun* until well after midnight on the Wednesday. When cross-examined by Hall, the defence counsel asked Roberts, "Are you prepared to say you were not in Emily Dimmock's company that night?" "Yes," replied Roberts. "I can give the name of a man who knows what time I went home that night."

A remark passed in an undertone between Matthews and Hall, to which Hall replied, "Most certainly I do not accuse him of the murder!"

A third suspect was a man known as "Scotch Bob". For some time it was thought that he could have killed Emily. A great deal was heard about this man at the October inquest. A woman called May Campbell had known Emily Dimmock for two years. Emily told May that a man called "Scotch Bob" had threatened to "do her in" because he thought she had given him a disease. Campbell said she met Emily on the night of the murder. Emily, said Campbell, told her a letter had arrived from Scotch Bob, asking Emily to meet him that evening outside Camden Town station. Emily told Campbell that she was afraid to meet him, but said, "I am bound to meet him or it will be the worse for me." Campbell said she saw Emily again at 9pm, and again just after 10pm, on the street corner near the *Rising Sun*. On the second occasion, Emily was trembling. Campbell asked her if she had found a friend for the evening. Looking round, May saw the man she knew as Scotch Bob. He was wearing a bowler hat and a short overcoat. He and Emily walked away, towards Camden Town. According to Campbell, she saw them again at about 11pm, near the music hall in the Euston Road.

Scotch Bob was also mentioned by John Crabtree. He said that in 1906, at Crabtree's brothel in Bidborough Street, Phyllis was often visited by a man who quarrelled with her and beat her. The man, whom he knew as "Scotch Bob", had threatened to cut Emily's throat. One day, said Crabtree, at his other house in Manchester Street, Scotch Bob produced a razor and threatened to "do" for him and for Phyllis as well. Crabtree stated that he, at first, believed Scotch Bob had killed Phyllis and he had expected to see him in the police identity parade.

The police eventually located Scotch Bob and eliminated him from their inquiries. His real name was Alexander Mackie. At the time of the murder he was working and living-in as a kitchen porter at a hotel in Portpatrick, Wigtownshire. He was away in Scotland from September 1906 to December 1907, working at the hotel. On the Monday before the trial, Mackie returned to London and booked into a temperance hostel. Mackie gave testimony confirming he was in Scotland when Emily was killed.

The Crown had built up a formidable body of circumstantial evidence against Wood, evidence which included Wood's efforts to conceal his involvement with the dead woman. Wood's policy after the murder was clearly to throw dust in the eyes of the police and keep his own movements under a cloud. The fact that he was possibly seen leaving the scene of the crime in the early hours did nothing to improve his chances of being acquitted.

* * * * *

When Edward Marshall Hall opened the case for the defence, he first sought to establish a credible alibi for Wood. Alibi defences are often difficult to construct, because the dates of various events are, understandably, prone to error and confusion. Events which a witness truly believes he experienced on a particular day are often found to have occurred at some other time in the past. Moreover, it might not go well with the jury that Wood tried unsuccessfully to concoct an alibi with the help of Ruby Young.

Hall's first witness was Wood's father, George Wood. He said he had been twice-married and had fathered twenty children. Robert Wood was living in his father's house at the time of the murder, in Frederick Street, off Gray's Inn Road. Robert slept in the ground floor front room. Mr. Wood and his stepson James slept in the back room. There were folding doors between the two rooms. This made it easy to hear from the back any movement in the front. Mr. Wood said that at about midnight on September 11th, while he and James were in their beds, Robert came into the back room, stepped across the floor, took the alarm clock from the mantelpiece, said a few words to James, and went to his own room.

In cross-examination, Mr. Wood admitted it was possible to go from the street door to the front room and back again without passing the back room. He also admitted that Robert often came home late and he would not see or hear him. Almost every night, Robert came and took the alarm clock. Mr. Wood knew it was the night of September 11th because that evening he spilled a bottle of lotion on to the carpet.

James Wood told the court how, on the 11th, he came home at 11.20pm and saw a pool of water where the lotion had been spilled. He went to bed at about 11.50pm. At about 12.20am, Robert came in and spoke to him. Next morning, James made breakfast and Robert left for work as usual.

Corroborating evidence for Robert Wood's arrival home on the 11th was provided by Joseph Rogers. An old man, Rogers was a jeweller who lived in the basement directly beneath the Wood family. At midnight, Rogers was out in the front garden at Frederick Street, gathering worms as bait for a fishing trip the following day. Rogers said he saw Wood go into the house at about midnight. Later he heard Wood moving around in his room and the sound of his door being locked.

Marshall Hall, in an attempt to cast doubt on McCowan's alleged sighting of Wood in the early morning of September 12th, called to the witness box Mr. William Brown, an official with the St. Pancras electric lighting department. Brown swore that on the morning of the 12th, the street lights in St. Paul's Road were automatically switched off by 4.40am at the latest. If this were so, it contradicted McCowan's evidence that the lights were shining when he saw the man he claimed was Wood. In addition, the weather for the morning of the 12th was recorded as being dry, yet McCowan had said it was "a muggy morning with drizzle". Perhaps McCowan had got the day wrong. Marshall Hall claimed McCowan had been confused as to which day he actually saw the man with the funny walk.

On the Sunday before the trial, the defence had discovered that another man was in St. Paul's Road on the morning of the 12th. This was William Westcott, a ticket collector at King's Cross tube station. He lived at 26 St. Paul's Road, on the side opposite number 29 and some 250 yards away. Westcott testified that on the morning of the 12th, as he was leaving home at 4.55am, he saw a man walking down the passage two doors from number 26, going towards Brewery Road. Westcott was a boxer. He always used to deliberately put a swing in his walk, especially in the mornings. Westcott said he followed the maxim "a swing of the arm is good for the chest". Cross-examined by Sir Charles Matthews, Westcott said he himself never passed number 29 when he was going to work. Francis Barney, who lived in the same house as Westcott, testified that Westcott had "a jerk of the shoulders and a peculiar twitching movement" when he walked quickly.

The defence produced two witnesses who swore that, in the early hours of September 12th, they saw Emily Dimmock with a man who bore no resemblance to Robert Wood. Henry Sharples, a bookmaker of Wicklow Street, said he saw Dimmock with a man in the Euston Road at about 12.15am. He was similar to a man Sharples had seen her with in the *Rising Sun* on the previous Sunday. The man, said Sharples, was wearing a blue suit and a bowler hat. Fred Harvey, a music seller, of Parkfield Street, Islington, was with Sharples. He said he saw Dimmock after midnight in the Euston Road with "a well-built man". Harvey raised his hat to her, but she did not acknowledge him. In cross-examination, neither Sharples nor Harvey could remember what Dimmock was wearing, even though they recalled the man's appearance.

The final witness for the defence was Robert Wood himself. By giving evidence at his own trial, Wood was breaking relatively new ground. The Criminal Evidence Act of 1898 had allowed a defendant to go into the witness box. However, as yet, no person on a murder charge had given evidence and been acquitted.

* * * * *

Mr. Hall's first question to Wood was, "Did you kill Emily Dimmock?" "It is ridiculous," replied Wood. "You must answer straight," said Hall. "I will only ask you straight questions. Did you kill her?" "No, I did not." "Do you emphatically deny Crabtree's evidence?" "Yes." "Were you ever in a house of his?" "No. I hope God will destroy me this moment if I have entered a house of his or ever knew him." "How did you come to know Emily Dimmock?" asked Hall. "It was the 6th of September in the *Rising Sun*, under the glare of the light. I will leave that to the jury. No doubt many of the jury will know what goes on in public houses."

Hall steered Wood through his version of events. Wood said that he last saw Emily on the evening of the 11th. He said he parted company with her outside the *Eagle* at about 11.30pm.

Concerning the letter to Emily, fragments of which were recovered from her fire grate, Wood admitted it was in his writing, but said he "could not account for it". He suggested that the partly-burned paper might have contained "little sketches I was doing in the public house bar".

There was a good deal of wrangling between prosecution and defence as to what was actually written on the charred paper. Wood said he had no idea what the writing was. The judge came down on the side of the defence when he said, "I am afraid the jury will be able to make no more of it than the accused." Whether or not it was an assignation with Emily at the *Eagle* on September 11th, it was for the jury alone to decide.

In cross-examination, Sir Charles Matthews reminded Wood that a number of people had testified that he knew Emily Dimmock before September 6th. Wood replied, "This is all mistaken evidence, incorrect and concocted, undoubtedly." Of his telling Mrs. Lawrence and Mrs. Smith about aiming to go to the Holborn Empire on September 9th with Emily, Wood declared, "I should say it was a concoction."

Wood said he wrote "many things" in Emily's presence, "chiefly sketches and amusing phrases. She had many things I had written. She looked through my letters and papers which I used to take out of my pocket when pulling out my sketch book at the bar. Girls like that are very bold," said Wood. "When I pulled out my sketch book, everything fell out. She was very forward. It may have been written there."

Wood denied he had ever been at 29 St. Paul's Road with Dimmock. He did not, he said, know the building. Matthews asked Wood, "Have you ever had sexual intercourse with Dimmock?" To this, Wood replied, "It is only to you, Sir Charles, that I would answer that question at all. I should be indignant with the average man." "But I still put the question to you." "Then most distinctly, I did not," said Wood. "Did she tell you she had an album?" "She may have done so," said Wood. "I paid no attention to it." "Did you yourself ever see that album?" "No," said Wood. "I have never been in the house, consequently I could not. She had no album in the *Rising Sun*."

"Is your memory good?" asked Matthews. "Probably Brixton has had some effect," was Wood's reply. Wood said that he found out that Ruby Young was working as a prostitute "some little time after meeting her". And yet, as Wood admitted to Matthews, "The relationship was intimate the whole time." "You asked Ruby Young to arrange an alibi, didn't you?" "I asked her to do me a little kindness," said Wood. Wood admitted saying to Ruby, "Your word and mine would stand against the whole world."

* * * * *

After Wood had completed his evidence, Marshall Hall made his final remarks to the jury. Hall began by suggesting that Wood had no motive for killing Emily, neither did he plan to kill her. Hall failed to mention the possibility that she had been killed in the heat of the moment, perhaps after some kind of dispute. Hall said,

"If Wood had intended to kill Dimmock, why did he introduce her to Lambert in the *Eagle*? If he saw Lambert by chance, would he not have changed his plans?"

It was clear that Wood had seriously incriminated himself by lying about his whereabouts on the 11th. Not only had Wood lied, but he had gone out of his way to persuade others, notably Moss, Tinkham, Lambert and Ruby Young, to tell lies on his behalf. Wood, at first, said he never saw Emily on the 11th. Then he changed his mind, when compelled to do so, by saying he did see her, by chance, in the *Eagle*, but did not go with her to St. Paul's Road that night. Hall said Wood formulated a cover-up to preserve his good name and reputation. The false alibi with Ruby Young was devised "more to meet any charge of immorality than to rebut any charge of murder". Hall said of Wood, "He is a kindly and affectionate man, but he is also a person of overweening personal vanity, a vanity that is inordinate. This will give you the keynote in this strange and mysterious case."

Sharples and Harvey had spoken of seeing Emily in the Euston Road with a man, but not Wood, after midnight on September 11th. Hall, who had called them as witnesses for the defence, complained that the Crown knew full well of their existence but did not call them in the prosecution case. Sir Charles Matthews objected, saying to the judge, "I will not allow that to go. I strongly protest against that statement, my lord. I offered to call these two witnesses if Mr. Marshall Hall wanted it." Hall would not retract the remark, but, after words from the judge, he did withdraw it.

The Crown alleged that Wood searched in Emily's album to find his own incriminating post card. The Crown claimed that because the card was hidden in the chest of drawers, Wood failed to locate it. Hall's suggestion was that the real murderer did find the card in the album, and hid it in the lining of the drawer in an attempt to throw suspicion upon Wood. Hall put it this way, "Is it not equally as conceivable as the Crown's theory that the murderer, whoever he is, put the post card where it was ultimately found, in order to implicate Wood?"

Hall disregarded the likelihood that the murderer would have had very little time to devise such a plan after he had cut Emily's throat, unless of course, he had planned to kill her beforehand. Hall hinted that Roberts might have been involved in framing Wood.

It was the prosecution's trump card that Wood was allegedly seen coming out of 29 St. Paul's Road at about 4.45am on the morning of the 12th by Robert McCowan, who later identified Wood by his peculiar walk. Hall claimed that McCowan's testimony was "the only iota of evidence" against Wood. He said, "I submit that on the evidence of McCowan as to the walk of the person he saw in St. Paul's Road on the morning in question, the testimony is not sufficient upon which to destroy a poor suffering animal, let alone a human being."

Warming to the theme, Hall told the jury, "If any of you have some poor suffering animal to kill, I do not think you would kill it on that sort of evidence. The prosecution here are in a dilemma – either to believe McCowan or the officials of the electricity supply department. (The reaction of the public gallery to this choice is not recorded, but official records of any kind assumed, in 1907, something of the nature of holy writ, at least in the eyes of barristers-at-law.)

Hall said McCowan was mistaken as to whom he saw that morning. As Hall made this claim, he took the opportunity to criticise McCowan's character. "I think," said Hall to the jury, "you will be thoroughly satisfied that McCowan had made an honest mistake, but a callous mistake, the mistake of a callous and careless witness."

Concerning the exact timing of the alleged sighting, Hall said, "Even the clocks are to be put to one side in order to convict this man of murder."

Marshall Hall referred to Ruby Young's statement that Wood walked with an unusual gait. He said, "I can only suggest it was invented by her in a spirit of revenge for some question which had to be asked in the case, namely, a suggestion made to her in the Police Court that her calling was a prostitute – which, in fact, it was." Hall dismissed Ruby's statement as "a gross and vindictive lie".

There was no mistaking Wood's apparent serenity and composure, both when giving evidence in the witness box and throughout all the court proceedings. Of Wood's manner, Hall said, "The calm and unruffled demeanour of Robert Wood after the murder is based upon a calm and unruffled conscience." Hall went on to make an unfair comparison between the reliability of two witnesses. "The old gentleman in the basement (Rogers) is one of the most honest witnesses called before a jury, just as Crabtree is one of the finest specimens of the opposite."

The culmination of Hall's speech was a final appeal to the jury. He said, "If you are satisfied beyond all reasonable doubt that the man standing there, on the night of 11th September, murdered Emily Dimmock, although it breaks your heart to do so, find him guilty and send him to the scaffold. But if, under the guidance of a greater power than any earthly power, making up your minds for yourselves on the evidence – if you feel you cannot honestly say you are satisfied that the prosecution have proved this man to be guilty – if, after giving effect to everything said by counsel for the prosecution and by the learned judge, you feel, on the evidence laid before you, that you cannot honestly and conscientiously say beyond all reasonable doubt that the prosecution have proved their case, then I say it will be your duty, as well your pleasure, to say, as you are bound to say, that Robert Wood is not guilty of the murder of Emily Elizabeth Dimmock."

* * * * *

It was now the turn of Crown counsel, Sir Charles Matthews, to make his final speech for the prosecution. It has become traditional that when prosecuting in a murder case, the Crown counsel does not resort to an impassioned plea that the jury convict a defendant, nor prosecute the case to the absolute limit, as might be done when a barrister is arguing in a civil case, such as defamation or libel. This tradition contrasts sharply with the prevailing situation in the United States. To this extent, Sir Charles Matthews was at a disadvantage. Hall was, in the tradition of the Victorian advocates, oratorical and emotional in his appeals to the jury on behalf of his client. In addition, Marshall Hall was, physically, a very imposing and powerful figure in the court-room, a tall man with a strong, persuasive vocal delivery when he addressed a jury. Matthews, in contrast, was a short, rather squat man with a harsh and jarring voice, not a person greatly gifted in the art of oratory. A Crown counsel is not expected to browbeat the jury into a guilty verdict; rather he should allow the evidence against the accused to speak for itself. Matthews was, therefore, less well-equipped than Hall for the task in hand.

Matthews said the absence of motive, or an unknown motive, was unimportant when assessing Wood's innocence or guilt. The concoction of an alibi by Wood was most serious. Matthews said Wood's father and his brother had, "Honestly persuaded themselves that they knew every detail of what occurred at Frederick Street on the night of September 11th, even down to the locking of the accused's door." They were, suggested Matthews, wrong in allocating the date of September 11th to their evidence. Referring to Wood's coolness and good humour, Matthews ascribed it not to Wood's clear conscience, but to "a cold-blooded and extraordinarily heartless reaction to the murder he had committed." Matthews probably should have made no reference to Wood's manner and appearance in court, if only because it was, as far as the facts of the evidence were concerned, quite irrelevant in law. Of Wood, Sir Charles said,

"You have in the accused a man who is a peculiar man, a man cool and collected, an extraordinary man whose nerve is such that when from day to day, the newspapers were publishing accounts of the murder and he was spoken to about it by his foreman (Moss), he preserved his calmness and cheerfulness. It was a cold-blooded murder, and the accused is a singular, a very singular, man – unnaturally, dreadfully singular – a man with nerves so extraordinary that nothing can move him, nothing, absolutely nothing."

Matthews went on this tack at length:

"When he found that the woman, whom he had been with only a few short hours after he met her in a tavern, had been murdered, he did not blench. There was no change in his demeanour, not a flicker of an eyelid. When the newspapers took up the tale, sparing no detail, did he tremble? Not a scrap. When he discovered after a talk with the witness Moss that, as Wood put it, 'one more unfortunate has gone to her death', that one was Dimmock, he showed no sign." At this point Matthews seemed to be arguing against himself.

Hall had said earlier that the police and the prosecution had followed a process of "exclusion and selection" of evidence, accepting evidence leading to Wood's guilt and sifting out any evidence in his favour. Instead of ending his speech with force, Matthews chose to make a defence of the police. This was well outside his brief, and, as a closing point, petty and trivial. He said to the jury. "I ask you not to act upon suspicion, but only on evidence. I do not think the police have been quite generously treated. I am content that, from beginning to end, they have done nothing which entitled them to be treated other than fairly."

* * * * *

In his summing-up, Mr. Justice Grantham began by coming down against Wood. The Judge said,

> "The accused had lied and endeavoured to suborn a witness. Throughout the history of the case, he has lied and been untruthful. With what object? With only the object of getting other persons to screen himself. His conduct had made the case against him doubly strong."

The judge then changed tack completely, guiding the jury in the direction of acquittal. Mr. Justice Grantham said,

> "Although it is undoubtedly my duty to do all I can to further the interests of justice, so that criminals are brought to justice and properly convicted, it is also my duty to inform you, to tell the jury, that, however strongly animosity may go against him, you must not find a verdict of guilty against the accused unless no loophole is left by which he can escape.
>
> "In my judgement, strong as the suspicion in this case undoubtedly is, I do not think the prosecution had brought the case home near enough to the accused – with the exception of McCowan. The evidence of McCowan, if implicitly relied upon, would justify you in finding him guilty; but that evidence is considerably controverted."

The judge ended his remarks to the jury like this:

> "Unless the effect of the evidence is so conclusive, so much against the accused as to warrant a conviction, so that there can be no doubt to anyone's mind, you should give him the benefit of the doubt and say that you do not think he is guilty. You are not bound to act on my views at all, but it behoves us to be most careful before we find a man guilty of such a charge. It is, of course, a matter for you, and for you alone. I think I have spoken plainly."

* * * * *

Ruby Young had spoken of how Wood had, with her assistance, concocted an alibi for the evening of September 11th. This alibi did not apply to the time of Emily's death – between 4am and 6am on the 12th – only to the period 6.30pm to 10.30pm on the 11th. However, Wood at first told the police that he never saw Emily at all on the 11th. It was only later that he went back on this and put forward the second alibi of being with Ruby Young. The fact that both alibis were false was very strong evidence against Wood.

The defence had suggested that Roberts invented the letter of assignation at the *Eagle* for the evening of the 11th. Hall claimed that Roberts had done this to divert suspicion away from himself, perhaps towards Bert Shaw, but Roberts did not invent the letter. Fragments existed which the Crown interpreted as a message arranging for Wood to meet Emily at the *Eagle*. After all, Roberts did not know that any fragments existed. The similarity of the handwriting on the post card and the letter pointed a finger at Wood. Clearly the murderer had searched for a post card immediately after his act. The actual wording on the charred fragments, according to the Crown, was as follows,

> "ill...you...ar...of...the....e....Town....Wednes....if....rest... excuse.....good....fond...Mon....from.....the..."

Roberts's version of the message on the letter, which the prosecution said was the correct one, was,

"Will you meet me at the bar of the Eagle at Camden Town 8.30 tonight Wednesday – Bert."

The reader may see a similarity. However, it is worth remembering that the trial jury had to work with the original message, written on several pieces of blackened notepaper.

Wood had tried to interfere with a number of witnesses to conceal his friendship with Dimmock. The defence claimed Wood was frightened only of being known as a man who spent time with a prostitute. The loophole in this line of defence is that Ruby Young was known to have worked as a prostitute. Why therefore should Wood have tried to pretend he saw her every Monday and Wednesday? In truth, Wood's character, which the defence claimed was refined and good, was not truly relevant to his guilt or innocence of murder.

Two witnesses testified to seeing Emily with Wood in the *Eagle* on the 11th. Emily was wearing curling pins in her hair. It was as if she had popped out of her flat and intended returning there soon, and perhaps for the night, with Wood. Her unkempt appearance, for which she apologised to Lambert, strongly suggested she was not going about her usual business that evening. When Lambert met Emily and Wood, it was past 9pm, a time when Emily would normally have been properly dressed to ply her trade.

McCowan's sighting of a man, whom he later identified as Robert Wood, in the early morning of the 12th, apparently coming out of 29 St. Paul's Road, weighed heavily against Wood. The defence claimed the man McCowan actually saw was Westcott. If McCowan did see Westcott, then Westcott might have been able to recognise McCowan, but he was unable to identify him. Another factor against Wood was that McCowan had come forward voluntarily to tell the police about seeing a man, whereas Westcott had to be sought out by the defence. In addition, McCowan said the man he saw was wearing a bowler hat. Westcott usually wore a cap. The defence claimed that Wood was an immoral liar but not a murderer. However, the suppression of evidence by a defendant is very prejudicial, implying as it does a desire to evade justice and a sense of guilt.

If the jury actually considered these matters, they spent little time over it. Having heard the judge sum up in favour of Wood, the jury retired at 7.43pm on the final day. At 8pm they were coming back into court. More often than not, the quick return of a jury heralds a guilty verdict, but not on this occasion. Wood was found not guilty. When the pandemonium had subsided, Marshall Hall said to the judge,

"I have to ask your lordship that the accused may be discharged." "Yes, certainly," replied Mr. Justice Grantham, thereby restoring to Robert Wood his freedom, and absolving him of any fear of the gallows.

Now that Wood had been cleared of any part of Emily Dimmock's death, the villain of the piece was the person who had, at first, agreed to help him and had then informed the police – Ruby Young. To avoid the violence of the crowd, Ruby dressed up as a charwoman and left the court building by a side entrance.

Chapter 8

The Greenwood Case

On July 2nd 1896, Harold Greenwood, a 22-year-old solicitor's clerk, married Mabel Bowater. For about two years of their marriage, Harold and Mabel lived in London. In 1898, Harold obtained an articled position with a firm of solicitors in the village of Kidwelly, some twelve miles from Carmarthen. When he qualified as a solicitor, Harold Greenwood went into partnership in a firm called Johnson and Stead in Llanelly. He commuted daily to and from Kidwelly. Greenwood eventually set up his own solicitor's practice in Frederick Street, Llanelly. He specialized in property deals.

By the summer of 1919, Harold and Mabel Greenwood were living in a three-storey mansion called Rumsey House. The family consisted of Harold and Mabel and their four children – Irene (21), Eileen (17), Ivor (15) and Kenneth (10). There were also three women servants in the household – the cook, Margaret Morris, Gwyneira Powell, and Hannah Maggie Williams. Ivor and Eileen Greenwood were usually away at boarding school, returning to Rumsey House for the holidays.

In the little village of Kidwelly, Harold Greenwood had a reputation of being a ladies' man. There is no doubt that although Greenwood was very popular with women and enjoyed their company, he did not get along with men. This was chiefly because of his outspokenness and distinct lack of tact in delicate situations. These two qualities served to make Greenwood something of a controversial character in the district. He was generally regarded as a troublemaker.

Mabel Greenwood, at 47, was a semi-invalid. She was subject to fainting attacks. These were attributed to a weak heart. In the spring of 1919, Mabel Greenwood complained of heart pain and internal pain. She became unable to sleep on her left side. If she tried to do so, she felt as if she were suffocating. The Greenwood family doctor, Thomas Robert Griffiths, began to treat Mabel for an internal growth in her womb. She herself believed she had cancer. In May 1919, she told her husband she did not expect to live very much longer.

News of Mrs. Greenwood's medical condition spread quickly

around the village. Unlike her husband, Mabel was well-liked, a popular member of St. Mary's church in Kidwelly. She was a religious person, unlike Harold, who rarely went with her to church. As the gossip about Mabel spread, a Miss Gwyneth David let it be known that Mrs. Greenwood was not really ill at all, rather that she was suffering a nervous collapse brought on by Harold's cruel behaviour towards her.

Harold Greenwood was incensed by Gwyneth David's accusations. On Thursday, June 5th 1919, at his office at 1 Frederick Street, Llanelly, Greenwood wrote the following letter to Miss David:

> "Dear Miss David, I am indeed very much surprised to hear that you told Miss Alice Jones yesterday that Mrs. Greenwood was not ill at all, and that her brother had not been to see her. Why and what is your object in telling these deliberate lies? Your only object, that I can see, is that you, for some unknown desire, wish to break my friendship with the Jones family, which I feel happy to say, is more than your flippant tongue can achieve. I must ask you in future to leave me and mine alone, unless you can speak the truth concerning them – but I must call for an explanation of the innuendo you suggest by making the false statements you have. Yours truly, H. Greenwood."

On the Sunday after Greenwood wrote this letter to Miss David – June 8th, Mabel went to St. Mary's church on her own. On Monday the 9th, she had tea with a neighbour in the grounds of Carmarthen Castle during an eisteddfod. On Wednesday the 11th, Mabel and Harold went out in their car. On the 12th she attended a meeting of a historical society at Kidwelly town hall. On Friday the 13th Mabel was measured for a new dress. Ill or not, Mrs. Greenwood had a busy week.

The next two days were to prove controversial. The events of June 14th and 15th at Rumsey House, Kidwelly, have become, in part, enshrouded in mystery. They form a riddle which, to an outside observer, remains a real enigma. Our story now turns to that fateful weekend.

* * * * *

On the Saturday morning, Mrs. Greenwood paid a visit to Martha Morris, one of her former servants who still worked at Rumsey House as a daily help. Mrs. Morris noticed that Mrs. Greenwood was not her usual self. She did not look at all well. She seemed to have lost some weight recently and complained of diarrhoea. After leaving Mrs.

Morris, Mrs. Greenwood attended a meeting at Ferryside tennis club. She was accompanied by the vicar of St. Mary's, the Reverend David Ambrose Jones. She seemed to be unwell, but was quite cheerful. After her trip to Ferryside, she returned home to Kidwelly by train. Her daughter, Irene, who had come back on the same train from Carmarthen, walked home with her from the station. On the way, Mrs. Greenwood called in at the Phoenix Stores and bought a bottle of burgundy.

On the Saturday evening, the Greenwoods had two visitors – Martha Morris and a Miss Phillips. When Mrs. Morris arrived, she found Mabel and Miss Phillips sitting on the veranda. Mrs. Morris thought Mabel looked very poorly. In contrast, Miss Phillips remembered her as being "quite bright, usually well". She said, "Her complexion was a lovely shade of pink, which was quite unusual with her." Mrs. Greenwood went to bed at 10.15pm. Harold remembered that she was very restless during the night. Several times she got up to see young Kenneth, who was sleeping soundly.

On the Sunday morning, the Greenwoods breakfasted at 10am on boiled eggs, bread and butter, and coffee. The cook, Margaret Morris, remembered her mistress coming into the kitchen once that morning, looking very ill. Harold Greenwood was outdoors most of the morning, working in the garden and on his motor car. Lunch was served at 1pm. The four Greenwoods ate hot roast beef with vegetables, followed by gooseberry tart and custard. The servants ate the same fare shortly afterwards. With her meal, Mabel Greenwood drank some burgundy wine.

After lunch, Mrs. Greenwood went to lie down. Later in the afternoon, she sat out on the lawn, reading a book. At about 4pm, Irene Greenwood arrived back at Rumsey House after a driving lesson. At 4.30pm, tea was served in the drawing room. Between 6.30 and 7pm in the evening, Mrs. Greenwood complained of sickness and of suffocating pains in her chest. Harold gave her some brandy, but this caused her to vomit. He and Irene helped Mrs. Greenwood to bed.

At about 7pm, Mrs. Greenwood walked the short distance between Rumsey House and the house opposite, the home of Dr. Griffiths. When the doctor arrived at Rumsey House he found Mrs. Greenwood sitting on a couch, vomiting. She said the gooseberry tart had disagreed with her, "as it always did". Dr. Griffiths put Mabel to bed and gave her brandy and soda water. While Irene was helping her mother to undress, Mrs. Greenwood was seized with another fit of vomiting, and with diarrhoea. With his patient safely in bed, the doctor and Harold Greenwood played a round of clock golf on the lawn.

At about 7.30, Dr. Griffiths looked in on Mrs. Greenwood again. When he got back to his own house, the doctor made up a bottle of bismuth mixture and sent it over with his maid. Soon afterwards, Miss Phillips arrived. Harold said to her, "The wife is very ill; run upstairs." Seeing Mabel's condition, Mrs. Phillips went to get the district nurse, a Mrs. Jones. She asked the nurse to come at once, because, she said, "Mrs. Greenwood is very bad with her heart."

By the time Nurse Jones got to Rumsey House it was 8pm. Mrs. Greenwood had by now collapsed. Her body temperature had fallen considerably. Nurse Jones said that the doctor should be called in, but Miss Phillips explained that he had already given her medicine. At about 9pm, Nurse Jones returned home to put her own child to bed. Miss Phillips and Irene Greenwood were left in charge of Mrs. Greenwood in the bedroom.

Nurse Jones came back at 10 o'clock. Mrs. Greenwood lay in a daze, occasionally waking up to be sick. The nurse gave her brandy, soda and milk every quarter of an hour, but Mabel could keep nothing down. Her diarrhoea continued virtually incessantly. Nurse Jones's experience told her that Mrs. Greenwood was extremely ill. Mr. Greenwood and Irene showed little concern. When Mrs. Greenwood's condition began to worsen, Nurse Jones told Greenwood to get Dr. Griffiths again.

After 10pm, as Mabel got worse, Nurse Jones, yet again sent Harold for the doctor. After what seemed like an eternity, Irene went over to the doctor's house to see what might be causing the delay. When Irene got there, she found her father chatting to Mary, the doctor's daughter, at her front door.

Dr. Griffiths was to make four visits to Rumsey House that night. At no time did he express any alarm about Mabel. Harold Greenwood kept asking his wife how she felt, to which she kept replying, "Very bad." Irene, who had to go to her work in a bank the next morning, went to bed at 11pm. While Greenwood was seeing Miss Phillips off the premises, he met Dr. Griffiths at the gate. When the doctor enquired about Mabel, Greenwood told him she was "easier". Nurse Jones did not think so, however. As far as she was concerned, her patient was still poorly.

At about 1am, Dr. Griffiths prepared two pills for Mabel. Harold brought them across with him from doctor's house. Soon afterwards, Mabel asked Nurse Jones if she was dying. Mabel said she did really wish she could have lived to bring up her children. The nurse could later hear her praying. Mabel said that she wanted her sister to look after the children when she had gone.

Immediately after taking the doctor's pills and talking about death with Nurse Jones, Mabel lapsed into a coma. Just before 3am, Harold went again to Dr. Griffiths. Mabel seemed now on the point of death. Again there was delay. Greenwood returned to say he could not rouse the doctor. Nurse Jones went over, rang the bell, and wakened Dr. Griffiths almost at once. At 3.30am on the morning of Monday June 16th, Mabel Greenwood passed away. Dr. Griffiths issued a death certificate, citing the cause of death as "valvular disease of the heart".

* * * * *

From the outset, an element of uncertainty and suspicion surrounded the reason for Mabel Greenwood's death. Nurse Jones asked Mr. Greenwood what Dr. Griffiths had written on the certificate. She did not receive a clear reply. Mr. Greenwood simply told her that Mabel had died of heart failure. It seems that Dr. Griffiths had made no reference to Mabel's vomiting and diarrhoea. Nurse Jones believed that this had been the primary cause of the cardiac arrest. Later in the morning of June 16th, Nurse Jones called on the vicar and mentioned her concern about the matter. The Reverend Jones said that he would take it up with Mr. Greenwood before the funeral.

That same morning, at 10am, Harold Greenwood motored away to Llanelly. He paid a visit to the offices of the *Llanelly Mercury* and told his friend Llewellyn Jones about his wife's death. It seems that when Mr. Greenwood got to Llanelly, he realized he had forgotten to take with him the keys to the safe of his office there. He now had no money on him. He borrowed twenty pounds from Llewellyn's sister, Miss Gladys Jones, visited an undertaker, and then accompanied Gladys to various Llanelly shops where he bought mourning clothes. Later that day, Greenwood went with the vicar to Kidwelly church-yard and chose a site for Mabel's grave. As promised to Nurse Jones, the vicar asked Greenwood about the cause of Mabel's death. Greenwood simply said it was due to heart failure. He elaborated no further. There was no mention of sickness or diarrhoea. The Reverend Jones asked if he might have a look at the death certificate. Greenwood said he had left it at home and would show it to the vicar later. He never did. This failure served only to increase the vicar's misgivings, already aroused by his conversation with Nurse Jones.

Mabel was interred in St. Mary's church-yard on Thursday, June 19th 1919. Out of the first inkling of doubt and suspicion from Nurse Jones, there spread a web of gossip and rumour. Mabel Greenwood had been a popular part of Kidwelly life, unlike her husband, who had gained a reputation for being over-fond of the company of unmarried women. Mabel had had a private income of her own. This helped to fund the Greenwoods' comfortable lifestyle. Her life was not insured. None of her money passed to Harold. Mabel did not leave a will. Her money, under the terms of her late father's bequest, passed to her four children in equal shares.

It was well known locally that Harold Greenwood was accustomed to spending a great deal of his time at the home of the family of Mr. William B. Jones, part-owner of the *Llanelly Mercury*. He enjoyed the company of his son and daughter, Llewellyn and Gladys Jones. Harold had been friendly with the Jones family since he had first come to the area in 1898. He had known Gladys since her childhood. The atmosphere of speculation and rumour surrounding Mabel Greenwood's death was still apparent when, within a month of her funeral, it was announced that Harold had proposed marriage to Gladys Jones and been accepted.

The news of Harold's impending marriage to Gladys Jones, coming so quickly after Mabel's untimely death, hit Kidwelly like a bolt from the blue. The flames of still-smouldering rumour were instantly refuelled. The news came as quite a blow to Dr. Griffiths's daughter, Mary. It seems that Mary Griffiths was extremely fond of Greenwood, and had gained the impression that her feelings towards him were reciprocated.

Following close upon the heels of Greenwood's engagement, there emerged into public knowledge an extraordinary conversation, said by Mary Griffiths to have taken place between her and Greenwood on the night of Mrs. Greenwood's death. Greenwood himself denied that it ever took place. When Greenwood arrived at Dr. Griffiths's house to summon him to Mabel's assistance, Mary Griffiths asked Greenwood if it was one of Mrs. Greenwood's "usual heart attacks". According to Mary, Harold was in "his usual high spirits". He confided to her that Mabel was very ill and might not recover. As

Greenwood was leaving, Mary mentioned that she was going on holiday. Incongruously, Greenwood is then said to have told Mary that he had recently visited a fortune teller, who had told him that his next trip away from home would be a honeymoon. In view of later developments, Greenwood's unusual remark proved to be uncannily accurate.

On September 24th 1919, less than four months after Mabel Greenwood's demise, Harold informed the Llanelly registrar of his intention to marry Gladys Jones at the Bryn Chapel on October 1st. Two days later, only five days before the wedding, Greenwood wrote a rather personal and affectionate letter to Mary Griffiths. It read:

> "My dearest Mary – I have been trying hard to get you this last fortnight, but no luck; always someone going in or you were out. Now, I want you to read this letter most carefully, and to send me over a reply tonight.
>
> There are very many rumours about, but between you and me this letter reveals the true position. Well, it is only right that you should know that Miss Bowater and Miss Phillips between them have turned my children against you very bitterly – why I don't know. It is only right that you should know this, as you are the one I love most in this world, and I would be the last one to make you unhappy. Under these circumstances, are you prepared to face the music? I am going to do something quickly, as I must get rid of Miss Bowater (Mabel's sister) at once, as I am simply fed up. Let me have something from you tonight – Yours as ever, Harold."

As arranged, Harold Greenwood married Gladys Jones on October 1st. His daughter Irene was told about it only two days before the ceremony. Greenwood, as Mary Griffiths alleged he had predicted, did take a honeymoon trip after all. Soon after his return to Rumsey House with his new bride, on Friday October 24th, while working in his office, he received a visit from the Llanelly police. There was a second visit the following Friday.

* * * * *

The police investigation into the circumstances surrounding the death of Mabel Greenwood continued over the winter months. Police activity surfaced into public view some six months later. On April 6th 1920, Mabel's remains were exhumed from Kidwelly churchyard. That same morning, an autopsy was performed by Dr. Alexander Dick of Llanelly. The body organs were analysed by a Home Office chemist called Webster. There was no evidence of any disease of the heart, valvular or otherwise. However, all the organs examined by Mr. Webster were found to contain arsenic.

There was now enough evidence upon which to directly suspect Harold Greenwood of feeding his wife poison. The affair had now spread beyond the domain of village gossip. It was, thanks to the efforts of various newspapers, of interest to the whole nation. It overshadowed the news of the troubles in Ireland on English breakfast tables. On Saturday April 17th, the day after the post-mortem, Greenwood was interviewed by a reporter from the *Daily Mail*. He claimed to have been singled out as a scapegoat for his wife's death. The newspaper statement read:

> "I am the victim of village gossip, of village scandal. If you know Welsh village life you will know what that means. It all started from the fact that four months after my wife's death I married again. That started the gossip. It is only fair to me to say that my first wife had suffered in health for at least two years before her death. Not only was her heart bad, but she also suffered from an internal disease which caused her intense depression. It was, however, from the heart attack that she died on June 16th. No-one, not even the doctor, thought that the attack would be fatal."

It is noteworthy that the police had not put Greenwood under arrest. On May 12th he confided again in the *Daily Mail*. This time, he said he could not understand how arsenic had been found in Mabel's body; but he said also that he would not have been surprised had poison of some kind been discovered, owing to Mabel's habit of, "Constantly taking medicines of every kind." Greenwood discounted suicide.

An inquest into Mrs. Greenwood's death opened on June 15th 1920. After hearing evidence, the inquest jury returned a verdict of wilful murder against Harold Greenwood. Shortly after the coroner had started to sum up, Sergeant Hodge Lewis and Constable W.J. Thomas left the court, changed into plain clothes, charged Greenwood on suspicion, and took him to a cell in the police station. Immediately after the inquest, Greenwood was seen by Chief Inspector Haigh of Scotland Yard. When Greenwood was charged with murder, he said, "All right." A moment later, Greenwood said, "What was the actual verdict?" When told, he said, "Oh dear." Amidst hisses and cheers, Greenwood was driven away to Llanelly. it was exactly a year since his wife's death. Next morning, he appeared before the

Llanelly magistrates and was remanded in custody. After a three-day committal hearing beginning on July 1st, Greenwood was ordered to stand trial at Carmarthen Assizes.

* * * * *

The trial of Harold Greenwood opened at the Guildhall in Carmarthen on Tuesday, November 2nd 1920. The tiny court-room was packed each day. Accommodation in the town was at a premium. Much of the available space had been booked weeks in advance. Arrangements were made to escort the jury as they walked to and from their lodgings in the Central Hotel. Greenwood, who had been incarcerated in Carmarthen Jail for eighteen weeks, received a hostile welcome as his carriage went up the steep hill to the Guildhall.

The trial judge was Mr. Justice Shearman. Sir Edward Marley Samson K.C. led for the Crown, Sir Edward Marshall Hall for the defence. As the jury was being sworn in, Greenwood objected to three potential jurors and they were replaced. Not one of the jurors was from Kidwelly.

In his opening remarks, Sir Marley Samson outlined the events of June 15th and 16th 1919. Samson emphasized that in February and April of 1919, Greenwood bought tins of "Eureka" weed-killer. The powder contained sixty per cent of arsenic. The weed-killer easily dissolved in water, producing a red-coloured solution. The poison was, therefore, unnoticed if dissolved in red wine. The Crown alleged that Greenwood administered arsenic to his wife in the table wine she drank at lunch on Saturday June 15th.

To prove the presence of arsenic in Mrs. Greenwood's body, the Crown called Mr. Webster, the chemical analyst who examined samples from the body organs. Webster testified that the body contained just over a quarter of a grain of arsenic. He found no other poison. Webster had mixed some "Eureka" weed-killer in port wine and found no change in colour or taste. A similar result was obtained with tea. The defence claimed that Mrs. Greenwood did not die from arsenic at all, but from the effect of morphia tablets, given to her by Dr. Griffiths. In cross-examination by Marshall Hall, Mr. Webster agreed that any morphia that might have entered the body would, after ten months in the ground, have become undetectable, owing to chemical changes. Significantly, Mr. Webster admitted that the amount of arsenic in the body was quite small at a quarter of a grain.

He agreed that the minimum fatal dose was usually considered to be about two grains.

A witness for the Crown, Dr. Willcox, said Mrs. Greenwood died from heart failure due to prolonged vomiting and diarrhoea, due to the ingestion of arsenic. The doctor said that if death occurred at 3.30am on June 16th, the arsenic would have been taken before 6.30pm on the 15th. He said the arsenic was taken in solution, probably between 12.30 and 6pm. A dose of at least two grains was swallowed within twenty-four hours of death.

The burgundy wine, which the Crown alleged Greenwood had dosed with arsenic weed-killer, was put on the lunch table by the maid, 18-year-old Hannah Maggie Williams. When Miss Williams came to give evidence, she was clearly terrified by the whole situation in which she found herself. In reply to Sir Marley Samson, she said that when laying the table for lunch on the 15th of June, she put the bottle of wine in front of Mrs. Greenwood's seat. She said she put the wine on the table again for supper and never saw the bottle again. Hannah said she did not know who removed the supper things from the table that evening. Miss Williams also described how, before lunch, she went to get the silver basket for the cutlery. It was kept in a small room called "the china pantry". When she was about to go into the pantry, she was unable to get in. She said that Mr. Greenwood was "washing up" in the pantry, a thing he never did. She had to wait about a quarter of an hour before Greenwood eventually left the pantry and went into the dining room. She found the wine, a partly-filled bottle, in the dining room cupboard. Miss Williams also said that she poured the wine into Mrs. Greenwood's glass during the meal. Mr. Greenwood, she said, drank whisky and soda. Miss Irene drank water. In the afternoon, Hannah laid the supper table. She put out some whisky and wine, but, she said, the bottle of wine used at lunch had, by now, disappeared. She was unable to find it and so she put out a fresh bottle. She said she looked for the old bottle again on the Monday, but again she could not find it.

In his cross-examination, Sir Edward Marshall Hall had little difficulty in tying the hapless Hannah Williams completely in knots. On several occasions Miss Williams contradicted the evidence she had given in evidence-in-chief. It was apparent that the tiny Welsh servant girl was, through fear and trepidation, able to remember hardly anything. She had at first testified that only Mrs. Greenwood drank wine with lunch. Now she said that she put two wine glasses out on the lunch table. Marshall Hall suggested one of these was for Irene Greenwood to use. Hannah, though, said that "Miss Irene" never drank wine with her meals. Although she was trying her best to remember the events she described, and probably also the evidence which she had earlier rehearsed, Hannah Williams was shown to be quite unreliable as a witness.

If the prosecution had little success with Hannah Williams, the performance of Dr. Griffiths, the Greenwood family doctor, who attended Mabel during her brief illness and signed her death certificate, was nothing short of a disaster. During his cross-examination of Dr. Griffiths, Marshall Hall continually played to the gallery. During the course of the Greenwood trial, Hall, whose style throughout his career was, at the best of times, theatrical and histrionic, was constantly admonished by Mr. Justice Shearman for bullying the prosecution witnesses. His frequent exchanges with the judge were decidedly heated. Hall's manner was violent and intimidating at every contested point or contrary opinion. On numerous occasions, Hall referred to the fact that his client faced the death penalty were he to be found guilty.

Dr. Griffiths, in cross-examination, was asked by Hall why he gave Mrs. Greenwood, a woman whom he believed to have a weak heart, two half-grain tablets of morphia, a dose that might well have killed her, and which the defence said actually did kill her. At the committal hearing the previous July, Dr. Griffiths had testified that when he saw Mrs. Greenwood's pain and vomiting, he prescribed "bismuth and two morphia pills". In reply to Hall at the trial, Greenwood now changed his mind about the composition of the pills. Now he said the pills contained not a half-grain of morphia, but "half a grain of opium and 1/40th grain of morphia". This complete change of mind, pointed out by Hall, undoubtedly created a very bad impression on the jury.

Marshall Hall had more in store for Dr. Griffiths. The doctor's evidence was becoming hesitant and he started to be contradictory in his answers.

In court, Hall displayed two bottles. One contained bismuth solution, the other contained Fowler's solution, a medicine containing arsenic. Hall then suggested to Dr. Griffiths that he had made "a colossal blunder" by giving to Mrs. Greenwood the arsenic Fowler's solution instead of the bismuth. After all, did they not stand side by side on a medicine rack in the doctor's surgery? Clearly taken aback by Hall's suggestion, Dr. Griffiths said that the medicine he gave to Mrs. Greenwood would have been recorded in his prescription book. Unfortunately, Dr. Griffiths had recently retired and was unable to locate the book. By the time Hall finished with the doctor, he could have had very little credibility with the jury. Throughout the evidence of the prosecution witnesses, Harold Greenwood remained cool and serene, calm and collected, sometimes smiling, occasionally laughing and sometimes looking extremely bored.

There was evidence which pointed to delaying tactics by Greenwood in hindering Dr. Griffiths's access to his wife. On one occasion, Irene had to bring Greenwood back to the house after he had been away at Dr. Griffiths's for the best part of an hour. At 1am, Nurse Jones told Greenwood to go for the doctor. He came back after about ten minutes and said, "I could not get him." Nurse Jones said she went across herself and got the doctor immediately. Dr. Griffiths said he did not remember this 1am visit. At 3am, the nurse sent Greenwood again. Greenwood returned and this time said he had rung the bell but could not rouse the doctor. Nurse Jones went over and got him at once. Mabel was, by now, at death's door. She passed away, said Nurse Jones, at about 3.20am. Miss Phillips testified that as she was leaving Rumsey House at 11pm, Dr. Griffiths came strolling past the gate. The doctor asked Greenwood, "How is she?" Greenwood replied, "Easier." This did not fit in with Mabel's condition, which was by then deteriorating rapidly. The prosecution said that these incidents arose out of Greenwood's desire to reduce and delay his wife's chances of recovery.

* * * * *

Why should Greenwood want to dispose of his wife? The prosecution evidence on motive was weak. There was no evidence of any improper behaviour between Greenwood and Gladys Jones before Mabel's death. At the time of Greenwood's marriage proposal to Gladys, Miss Jones was already engaged to a soldier called Frank Russell. She wrote to his base at Bombay to break the four-year engagement. Russell wrote back from a London hospital, upbraiding Gladys for her faithlessness.

The prosecution alleged that arsenic was put into the dinner wine. A search of Rumsey House, its stables and outbuildings, revealed only three small bottles of horse liniment, labelled "Poison". With the exception of weed-killer, no purchase of poison could be traced to Greenwood.

There was evidence that Gladys Jones and Greenwood may have planned to marry after Mabel had passed away. Mrs. Groves, the cleaner and caretaker for Greenwood's office in Llanelly, testified that on Monday June 16th, only a few hours after Mabel's death, she saw a letter to Greenwood from Gladys Jones. It contained, said Mrs. Groves, the words, "It will be nice when I am your wife." This letter was posted on the night of Saturday June 14th, before Mabel's illness had begun.

For the defence, Marshall Hall called Lt.-Col Dr. Toogood, a toxicologist working for the local council, to give his view as to the cause of Mabel's death. The prosecution's view was that arsenic was responsible. Dr. Toogood said death, in his opinion, was due to morphine. This, he said, followed acute gastroenteritis set up by swallowing gooseberry skins from the lunch dessert. Cross-examined by Samson, Toogood said he was not an analytical chemist and was, therefore, not qualified to challenge the quantity of arsenic found in the body by the Crown's expert, Mr. Webster.

Dr. Williams of Swansea said the discovery of a quarter-grain of arsenic in the body did not prove conclusively that arsenic had caused death. The witness agreed with Dr. Toogood the morphine had been responsible.

Greenwood's legal advisers were at first reluctant to put him into the witness box. There was no obligation upon Greenwood to give evidence anyway. It was believed that he might be far too talkative in the box. He might, therefore, say far more than he need say and thereby do more harm to his case than good, particularly when cross-examined by Sir Marley Samson. However, Greenwood's relaxed attitude during the earlier part of his trial persuaded his solicitor and Marshall Hall that by giving evidence on his own behalf, Greenwood would probably increase his chances of acquittal.

When first arrested, Greenwood made a statement to Superintendent Jones. He was later to deny that the version of the statement produced by the prosecution at the trial was a true record of what he actually said. Greenwood allegedly stated that Mrs. Greenwood drank no wine with her lunch. He said she drank whisky and soda. She ate hardly anything at all, and then went to lie down. At 5.30pm, said Greenwood, Mabel was walking slowly up the garden with Irene and then sat out on the lawn.

Greenwood said at about 6 o'clock he and Mabel were walking back to the house, when she complained to him about a "suffocating pain in her heart". Greenwood got her some brandy, whereupon she was sick. At 6.30pm, said Greenwood, Mabel did look better. At 6.45pm, Greenwood went over to fetch Dr. Griffiths. He came over to find Mabel lying on a couch, sick and in pain. According to Greenwood, Mabel said her illness was due to the gooseberry tart she had eaten at lunch. The doctor gave her a few sips of brandy and soda and she went to bed. Greenwood did not mention diarrhoea at that time.

Miss Phillips claimed that it was she who sent for Nurse Jones. Greenwood said it was he who sent for the nurse. He told Supt. Jones that he thought the two morphia tablets prescribed by Dr. Griffiths had killed Mabel. However, the vicar testified that on the day of the exhumation, Greenwood said to him, "I wonder how the whole thing arose? I wonder if is she took anything herself? She was often depressed and kept looking at water." There was no mention of morphia then.

At the outset of Marshall Hall's examination, Greenwood gave his answers in a voice hardly raised above a whisper. As Hall's questioning proceeded, Greenwood's voice rose to a more normal level. He remained outwardly cool and unruffled. Greenwood said, "I was married to Mabel Bowater 23 years ago. There are four children of the marriage, all of whom are alive." "On what terms did you live with your wife?" asked Marshall Hall. "Very happy," said Greenwood. "Had your wife any private means?" "Yes. I don't know exactly how much, but about £900 a year." "Your wife died on 16th June 1919, and were you present?" "Yes." "You have since married Miss Jones. Had Miss Jones any money or other means?" "None whatever."

Hall then asked Greenwood, "Now, Harold Greenwood, did you directly or indirectly administer, or cause to be administered to your wife, any arsenic at any time in your life?" "I have not," replied Greenwood. "Had you anything to do with your wife's death?" "Nothing whatever." "After your wife's death, what happened to her private means?" "They went to her children."

The judge then asked, "Did they go under her will?" "No, through her people."

Hall then asked, "You have been in prison for four and a half months, and are now ready to answer any questions my learned friend may ask you in relation to this case?" "Yes," said Greenwood. Hall sat down.

In cross-examination, Sir Marley Samson began, "Do you consider that you were showing you affection for your late wife by marrying again so soon?" Greenwood replied, "I felt so hopelessly out of it – it was not like a home." Greenwood said he had never personally bought any wine from Phoenix Stores. His wife's health, he said, had been failing for nine months. They had not had sex in the last two years. Greenwood said he had known Gladys Jones for the past twenty years.

"When did you become fond of her?" asked Samson. "I did not become fond of her until 12th July." "It really dawned on you all of a sudden?" queried Samson. "All of a sudden," said Greenwood. "I suggest that you were seeing Miss Jones frequently during the last year of your wife's life?" "No." "And that she was staying at your house and had been there often?" "She was staying at my house when she was invited by my daughter."

Greenwood said he proposed marriage to Miss Jones on July 12th. She asked for a fortnight to consider it and then accepted. When Sir Marley Samson showed him a bottle of burgundy, Greenwood said, "I have never brought into the house a bottle of wine like the one produced. My wife usually bought it. I usually uncorked it."

Hannah Maggie Williams had testified that just before lunch on Sunday June 15th, Greenwood had spent a long time, at least a quarter of an hour, in the china pantry. The prosecution was claiming that Greenwood used this time to poison the wine. Hannah had also said that Greenwood never usually went into the china pantry at all. Questioned about this by Samson, Greenwood said, "I went there every day." "But did you go that Sunday?" asked Samson. "No doubt I would go," replied Greenwood.

Here the judge intervened and asked, "If you did, you say it was a natural thing?" "Yes."

Samson continued, "I suggest that you went to the china pantry that particular Sunday and were there a quarter of an hour, and then you were in the dining room for about five minutes?" "Pure imagination," said Greenwood. "On that particular Sunday I did not go in to wash my hands until the gong sounded for lunch." "What did your wife have to drink that Sunday?" "Either burgundy or whisky. She often had whisky and soda with lunch on Sunday."

Concerning the alleged statement about going on honeymoon, Samson asked Greenwood, "You have heard about the conversation with Miss Griffiths, and you say it is untrue?" "She invented it all," said Greenwood.

To the judge, Greenwood denied twice that it was true.

Greenwood said that when Mary Griffiths found out about his engagement to Gladys Jones, she burst into tears. She asked him, he said, to write her out a marriage proposal, so that she could formally refuse it and thereby save her face. The phrase in his letter, "face the music", meant, said Greenwood, that Miss Griffiths should say "yes".

Questioned about the pills prescribed for Mrs. Greenwood, Harold said Dr. Griffiths gave them to him, wrapped in a piece of paper. According to Greenwood, the doctor said to him, quite clearly, "Here are two morphia tablets." Greenwood claimed that Nurse Jones had said she thought the pills had killed Mabel. He at first thought that Supt. Jones had come to see him about the two pills.

Concerning the statement written down and attributed to him, Greenwood said, "That is not my statement at all." Greenwood said sections of the actual statement had been removed and other words had been added, He claimed that some of the pages of the Superintendent's notebook had been torn out since the time of the committal hearing. Jones, said Greenwood, had received the notebook back after the hearing and had altered it.

Asked about his possession of weed-killer, Greenwood told the court that it was kept in the store next to the potting shed. It was all used up, he said, on the day it was bought. He opened the weed-killer in the garage with jobbing gardener Ben Williams. It was poured out into a big can and then diluted with three times its volume of water. Ben and he then sprayed it on the paths. Williams threw the remaining weed-killer away. Greenwood saw him throw it into the river with its original "Eureka" tin. The weed-killer, said Greenwood, was a dark red colour. He said that path-spraying was always done after the proper gardener, Gould, had gone away on the Saturday.

Greenwood said it was not only he who believed that morphia pills killed his wife. He said Nurse Jones believed it too. After the death, said Greenwood, he told Dr. Griffiths he had made a mistake by giving Mabel morphia. The doctor was complaining that Nurse Jones was gossiping her opinion around the village. To answer Greenwood's claim, Dr. Griffiths and Nurse Jones were recalled to the witness box. Dr. Griffiths denied that this alleged conversation with Greenwood about morphia had ever taken place. Nurse Jones said she never said to Greenwood, "Damn those pills." She did not think she had ever discussed the pills with Greenwood.

Marshall Hall asked Nurse Jones, "The accused says, 'Nurse Jones asked me not to tell anyone about the pills.' Is that true?" "No," replied Nurse Jones. "And that the pills killed his wife. Is that true?" "No." "And did you not say to Greenwood that one or two pills were too strong?" "I did not." "No discussion about the pills at all?" "No."

Harold Greenwood had done well in the witness box. The prosecution claimed that Mrs. Greenwood had been poisoned by the wine she drank with her lunch. Hannah Williams said only Mrs. Greenwood drank any of the wine. The defence had a final witness. This was young Irene Greenwood. She was questioned by junior defence counsel, Trevor Hunter.

* * * * *

Irene Greenwood said she also drank burgundy at lunch, as well as her mother. It was, she said, of the Beaune variety, and drunk, she said, out of a red tumbler. Not only that, but Irene testified that she also drank some more of the wine at the evening meal. In saying this, Irene contradicted Miss Phillips, who had said there was no wine on the table at all. Miss Phillips had said, "If there had been any I would have had some." Clearly, if the jury believed Irene Greenwood drank some of the wine, the prosecution's case would be in fragments. Irene supported her father's evidence that it was he and not Miss Phillips who first sent for Nurse Jones. Mr. Hunter asked her, "Do you remember Nurse Jones coming?" "Yes," she replied. "Do you know how it was that she came?" "Miss Phillips fetched her." "Do you know why?" "Because Daddy and I asked Mama whether she would have Nurse Jones, and she said yes." "What state was your father in when your poor mother died?" asked Hunter. "He was crying," said Irene. "He seemed to be very much upset."

In cross-examination, Sir Marley Samson was unable to shift Irene Greenwood from her evidence that she too drank from the wine bottle that the prosecution alleged had killed her mother. Irene said she was told by her father that the morphine pills had killed her mother. From two weeks after her father's marriage, she had been living with an aunt. Irene said both Mary Griffiths and Gladys Jones stayed for two consecutive weekends at Rumsey House when her mother was away, and without her mother's knowledge.

By the close of the case for the defence, Sir Edward Marshall Hall and Trevor Hunter had rendered more feeble the already weak case against Harold Greenwood. An admission had been made by analyst Webster that the amount of arsenic found in the body was far less than the generally accepted fatal amount. In his cross-examination of the servant girl Hannah Williams, Marshall Hall had rendered her evidence – of Greenwood lurking in the china pantry poisoning the wine – virtually worthless. Mrs. Greenwood's doctor, Dr. Griffiths, who had originally said he prescribed her two morphia pills, had at the last moment changed his mind to two opium pills. There was even a possibility that the doctor may have accidentally given Mrs. Greenwood arsenic Fowler's solution instead of bismuth solution. Finally, in putting Irene Greenwood into the box, the defence had destroyed the Crown's theory that Mrs. Greenwood was killed by poisoned wine. It would have been small wonder that, as Marshall Hall got to his feet to make his final address to the jury, he would have been even more confident than usual of securing his client's acquittal.

* * * * *

In his closing speech to the jury, Marshall Hall mentioned Greenwood's visit to the china pantry before lunch on Sunday June 15th. Hannah Maggie Williams, who testified that the visit lasted for at least a quarter of an hour and was a most unusual event, was described by Hall as "a poor little frightened thing". She had, indeed, appeared to have been quite terrified in the witness box. Her fear was not eased by the severity of Hall's cross-examination which, in view of the penalty Greenwood might pay were he to be found guilty, was justified. Hall asked the jury, "Do you believe it credible that Greenwood would have, out on the table, a bottle of poisoned wine for his wife, at a time when two of the children were waiting for a meal? It was a most natural thing that he should use the china pantry when he wanted to wash his hands instead of going to the bathroom upstairs. I don't know if it has been the misfortune of you to be in a house where there has been a death the night before. At any rate, I don't think you will attach any importance to the fact that no-one knows what became of the bottle."

Hall said that a poisoner would have kept his actions more secret. He said, "If Greenwood were a poisoner, he would want the secrecy that all poisoners want, yet he has a hospital nurse in the bedroom, and he had Miss Phillips, the local gossip, in the bedroom too. Do you think, if he wanted to poison his wife, he would have those people there?"

Concerning Greenwood's alleged obstructive tactics to delay Dr. Griffiths seeing to his wife, Marshall Hall said, "He thought the bell rang in the doctor's bedroom as a night bell ought to, but it turned out it rang somewhere else, that it was an ordinary kind of night bell. It was just the kind of bell that the doctor would have." About the clock golf, which the Crown alleged was another delaying tactic and a ploy by Greenwood, Hall said, "It was an act of forethought. Had the doctor left the house and gone across to the surgery, someone might have called and taken him miles away." Hall suggested three different substances in which the arsenic could have been taken by Mrs. Greenwood. He claimed that this was the first case in which such a small quantity of arsenic had been put forward as constituting a fatal dose. Hall said, "Glucose could have been poisoned by arsenic, as were seventy people in Manchester, poisoned by glucose in the beer they drank." Dr. Toogood had testified that Mrs. Greenwood died of morphia poisoning. Hall said, "If you believe that, then the case of the prosecution fails." He then put this question to the jury, "Did Dr. Griffiths give Fowler's solution instead of bismuth? When Mrs. Greenwood took the medicine, the nurse tasted it herself and said it caught her throat."

Pointing out that there was no written record available from Dr. Griffiths's book as to what medicine was actually prescribed, Hall said, "The mistake was to give her two pills of morphia at once, to complete the work done by the 8pm dose of Fowler's solution."

Hall criticized the delay in bringing a charge against Greenwood, "Why did the police wait from October to April to exhume the body? At Kidwelly, the accused has done an unpardonable thing. He has broken the custom and married within twelve months of his first wife's death, therefore, there must be something wrong. So within three weeks the police were on the hunt for evidence."

Why should Greenwood have used arsenic? Hall said, "If Mrs. Greenwood was unlikely to live long, why poison her, and with arsenic, which as a solicitor he would know to be retained by the body. There were many other poisons available."

At the end of his speech, Hall referred to Shakespeare's 'Othello'. It was the scene where Othello enters Desdemona's bedroom, contemplating either killing her or putting out her night light. Hall said, quoting the bard, "'If I quench thee, thou flaming minister, I can again they flaming light restore, should I repent me. But once put out thy light, thou cunningest pattern of excellent nature, I know not where is that Promethean heat, that I can they light relume.' Are you, by your verdict, going to put out that light? Gentlemen of the jury, I demand at your hands the life and liberty of Harold Greenwood."

* * * * *

Sir Marley Samson, in his final address, emphasized the claim that two grains of arsenic entered the body. Some of it was carried away by vomiting and purging. He said the idea that Fowler's solution was given accidentally could be dismissed because Nurse Jones tasted the medicine herself and had felt no aftereffects.

At the outset of the case, the Crown had said that the arsenic was in the wine. Once Irene Greenwood had sworn that she drank that wine too, the Crown's theory was completely dissolved. In a last minute effort to find a credible vehicle for the arsenic, Samson said, "My learned friend has suggested that it not open to me to put to you that the arsenic had been put into anything but the wine. I dissent from that view. Mrs. Greenwood had on that day taken wine, medicine, tea and brandy. There was a straw flask containing brandy by Mrs. Greenwood's place at supper. (Irene Greenwood had testified to this.) There was a fatal dose found in the body; it could not have been taken accidentally. Only Greenwood had the opportunity, the means and the motive to have administered the poison, between 1.30 and 6 o'clock on that particular Sunday."

Concluding his speech, Sir Marley Samson told the jury, "I have no desire, even if I had the ability, to imitate the brilliance of my learned friend. I can only hope in this solemn matter that Almighty God, in whose hands are all our destinies, will guide you to a conclusion that is both just and right."

* * * * *

On Tuesday, November 9th 1920, the judge, Mr. Justice Shearman, gave his summing-up. The twelve-man jury retired at 1.20pm. They returned two and a half hours later. Their foreman, Mr. E. Willis Jones, wanted to read out a detailed written verdict which the jury had compiled, but Mr. Justice Shearman disallowed this. The paper with the detailed verdict was handed to the judge.

After a not guilty verdict had been announced, most people in the

Carmarthen Guildhall were puzzled and disappointed. There was criticism of the Crown authorities for putting a man on trial for his life on such apparently slender grounds. However, many local folk believed that Greenwood killed his wife. He was shunned and ignored by the villagers of Kidwelly and forced to leave the district. He attempted to commit suicide, but failed. In March 1922, Greenwood successfully sued a company who exhibited his likeness in their waxworks. Greenwood adopted the name "Pilkington".

The jury's written verdict at Greenwood's trial was made public in 1930. This is what it said:

"We are satisfied on the evidence in this case that a dangerous dose of arsenic was administered to Mabel Greenwood on Sunday, 15th June 1919, but we are not satisfied that this was the immediate cause of death. The evidence before us is insufficient, and does not conclusively satisfy us as to how, and by whom, the arsenic was administered. We therefore return a verdict of not guilty."

Harold Greenwood died on January 17th 1929 at the age of 54, a ruined and broken man.

Chapter 9

Simon Dale

During the afternoon of Sunday September 13th 1987, Simon Dale, a 68-year-old retired architect, was found battered to death in the kitchen of his home at Heath House, a twenty-five room Queen Anne mansion at Hopton Heath in the former county of Herefordshire. Nearly five months later, on Wednesday January 6th 1988, Susan de Stempel, 53, the wife of a German baron, together with two of her children – 26-year-old Marcus Wilberforce and his sister Sophia Wilberforce, aged 15 – appeared in the dock at Hereford Magistrates Court charged with the murder of Mr. Dale. He was the children's father. On the same day, the baroness's husband, Baron Michael de Stempel, 58, a London economist, was jointly charged, with the other three, of conspiring to defraud the baroness's aunt, Lady Illingworth, and her estate, between 1983 and 1987.

* * * * *

The Baroness de Stempel was born Susan Cecilia May Wilberforce on May 6th 1934 at the home of her mother in Queens Gate, London. Her father was William Wilberforce. He was a descendant of the Victorian anti-slavery campaigner of the same name. Susan's father, who was lord of the manor at Markington Hall near Harrogate, was killed in action in Tunisia on her ninth birthday. Susan was then a boarder at St. Mary's convent in Ascot. At the age of 15, Susan Wilberforce was sent to a school in Paris. A year later, her mother remarried. In 1953, the year of the coronation of Queen Elizabeth II, she had a season as a debutante, living at the home of her aunt 'Puss', Lady Illingworth, her late father's elder sister. Her aunt was then living at 44 Grosvenor Square, the last remaining private house in the square.

Simon Dale married Susan Wilberforce on September 11th 1957 at St. James's Church at Clerkenwell Green. He was 38, she was fifteen years his junior. They bought a flat in Old Brompton Road. Their first child, Alexander, was born there in July 1958. The following year, the Dales bought a large mansion at Hopton Heath called Heath House. Their second child, Ilgerus Sebastian, was born in December

1959. The Dales moved into Heath House at Christmas that year, occupying one of the flats on the top floor of the country mansion. It was Susan and Simon's intention to renovate Heath House and thereby increase its value. To this end, builders worked on the house for years. The cost of the improvements was paid out of Susan's money. It was her money too that had paid for Heath House itself.

The Dales had three more children, making five in all. These were Marcus (born in 1961), Simon (1964) and Sophia (1972). As time passed, Simon Dale's eyesight began to diminish. Doctors told him that the deterioration of his vision was irreversible and permanent. As Dale's visual power declined, so did the number of commissions he received as an architect. After 1964, the marriage deteriorated also. Simon would cut himself off in his study for weeks on end. There were episodes of physical violence between him and his wife. In 1972, Susan filed for divorce. Since Heath House belonged to Susan and her money had paid for it, she stayed on in the house for a further year. Eventually, Susan moved out with the children and went to live with her mother. After the death of her mother, Susan moved into a small flat at Ross-on-Wye.

In 1977, Susan Dale moved into Forresters Hall Cottage at Docklow, a hamlet about five miles east of Leominster, on the road to Worcester, and just a short drive from Heath House.

Before she met Simon Dale, Susan had been friendly with Michael de Stempel. She met him again in 1982 and in September 1984, at St. Helier, Jersey, she became his wife, assuming the title 'Baroness'. The title had been in the de Stempel family since the 1300s and was conferred by the Holy Roman Empire. In December 1984, she began annulment proceedings against the baron, on the grounds of non-consummation.

By the late 1980s, Simon Dale was almost completely blind. When, in September 1973, Susan moved out of Heath House, Simon had stayed on. Although his divorce settlement with Susan stipulated that the house should be sold and the proceeds divided, Dale had obstinately stayed put in Heath House. He used to tell people, "I'm not moving yet because the divorce settlement is not yet absolute." This was far from the truth. Legally, Dale should have moved out of Heath House years earlier. Simon's reluctance to leave the house was a real bone of contention between Susan and her ex-husband.

Simon Dale had some unconventional ideas about Heath House

itself. He believed that the house had at one time been the centre of a pagan cult, destroyed in the seventh century, and linked with Camelot, the legendary court of King Arthur. He also believed that the ancient ruins of Camelot itself were lying beneath the cellars of the house. Dale had the idea of turning the place into an archaeological centre for excavation and study, with the house as its focal point. In 1983, Dale persuaded the Hereford and Worcester County Council to carry out an exploratory dig in the walled garden. Nothing of any archaeological interest was found.

Dale gradually became convinced that there was an official campaign of conspiracy against him and his plans for Heath House. He persisted in pestering the local council and scientific bodies to take his historical theories seriously, but to little effect. Simon used to make regular visits to the public library at Shrewsbury, where he researched and wrote a manuscript on Arthurian legends, as well as a complicated treatise on the science of vision.

In 1987, Simon Dale was still firmly installed in residence at Heath House, much to the displeasure and ever-present irritation of Susan de Stempel, his ex-wife. She wanted to sell the house but, with Dale still entrenched there after some fourteen years, it was still impossible for her to put it on the market. With Susan becoming increasingly incensed by Dale's stubbornness, relations between the two of them began to take on the character of an undeclared war. This state of affairs did not go unnoticed by outsiders. Susan looked upon the house as her own property, to which she could come and go as she wished. Simon still regarded it as his home where his friends could visit him. He tolerated Susan's frequent intrusions. She attended to the garden and to the continuing renovation and redecoration of the house on a virtually permanent basis. She would arrive at Heath House, uninvited and unwelcome, whenever she had a mind to do so.

Dale told his friends that Susan was eavesdropping on his telephone conversations, intercepting his mail, and occasionally challenging his visitors. He said she would enter the house through the windows. She was, he said, not averse to helping herself to anything in the house she believed she was entitled to take. Her children, Marcus and Sophia, often accompanied Susan on her visits.

* * * * *

In March 1987, County Council archaeologist, Adrian Tindall, went to Heath House to see Dale. As he was driving away, he was surprised to see a woman leaping out of the undergrowth at the side of the drive. She stood in front of Tindall's path and flagged him down. It was Susan. The council official was immediately put on the receiving end of a very one-sided conversation. Susan told Tindall she knew who he was because she had been reading Simon's letters. She said Simon was a dangerous man who had, on several occasions, tried to kill her. Not only that, he had poisons in the house, and had dug a grave for her in the garden. This did not fit with Tindall's impression of Dale, whom he believed to be an almost blind semi-invalid of advancing years. Susan, however, said she was terrified of her ex-husband. What is more, she gave Tindall the impression that she really was frightened. She certainly looked frightened. Susan told Tindall that when she visited Heath House she always carried something to defend herself. Susan pointed to an object looped over her arm. It looked to Tindall like a metal walking stick. On closer examination, he could see it was a crowbar.

Mr. Tindall's experience with Susan was by no means unique. Many of Simon Dale's visitors were, at one time or another, victims of Susan's attentions. She would either walk into the house and interrupt their visits to Simon, or accost them in the grounds and inflict on them an harangue on the subject of Dale's violence and his other shortcomings.

One of Dale's friends, Veronica Bowater, seems to have been, as far as Susan de Stempel was concerned, the least popular of Simon's visitors. On many occasions, objects were placed in the driveway to obstruct her path. Once, Susan covered the drive with logs and bricks. Marcus kept watch, bobbing up and down behind a hedge. In order to get away from the house, Mrs. Bowater was forced to drive across a lawn. As she was driving away, Susan appeared on the scene, screaming something and treating Mrs. Bowater's car radiator to several hefty, sharp kicks. One of Mrs. Bowater's more memorable encounters was, when arriving at Heath House, being confronted by Susan, eyes blazing, making for her with a lighted blowtorch in her hand.

"Hello, Mrs. Wilberforce," said Veronica, rather lamely. This greeting did not go down at all well with Susan. "I am the Baroness de Stempel," she said. "I suppose you have brought your friends to visit my house, have you?" Mumbling pleasantries, Veronica and her colleagues hurried into the relative safety of the house.

In July 1987, Simon Dale tried to persuade a man named John Miller to invest money in his scheme for converting Heath House into a conference centre. The fact that he was no longer legally entitled to even live there did not seem to worry Dale one iota. Mr. Miller, who later withdrew from the project, was leaving the house one day when, like others before him, he found the driveway blocked. This time, the offending obstruction was a wheelbarrow. Susan emerged from a bush, accompanied by Marcus. Mr. Miller, like Mr. Tindall, was informed by Susan that Simon had physically mistreated her and wanted to be rid of her. What etched itself on Miller's memory was that Susan and Marcus looked very frightened.

While Susan appeared to outsiders to be scared of Simon, he confided in his friends that he was being ill-treated by her. Dale, who sometimes had bruises on his face, said that Susan put obstacles in the house itself, hoping that Simon's defective vision would cause him to stumble and injure himself. Things in the house, said Dale, would either go missing or would be moved from place to place. He had also heard someone, whom he assumed was Susan, following him around the house.

* * * * *

We now turn to the events of a key date in the story of Simon Dale – Friday September 11th – the third anniversary of Susan's short-lived marriage to Baron de Stempel. That morning, Simon got up at about 9am. He had to visit his osteopath at Leominster. At 10am, Geoffrey Bowater picked Dale up at the top of the drive. After the appointment, Dale set off with Mr. Bowater on the return journey to Hopton Heath. On the way back, the car broke down. Bowater took it to a garage in Leintwardine and Dale was stranded without transport, only a mile or two from home.

As a way out of his difficulty, Dale went into a call-box and telephoned Jo Corfield. She had been helping him out with typing and secretarial work. She picked Dale up at the garage and drove him home. They reached Heath House at about 1.30pm. Simon lunched on bread, cheese and tomatoes, after which he and Jo spent the afternoon working on the manuscript of one of Simon's books. Mrs. Corfield left at about 5.15pm. Before she went, she arranged with Dale to return on the Monday. Simon said he would walk up to the village, call on a friend who lived near the station and buy from him some more tomatoes and some green beans. As Jo left Heath House, she saw two of Susan de Stempel's children: Marcus was busy cleaning a car windscreen, Sophia was pushing a wheelbarrow.

Later that Friday evening, at about 7pm, Simon was visited by Susan Evans and Ben Scott. They arrived at Heath House in Mrs. Evans's van. Susan Evans had worked for Simon as a proof reader in 1986 and had kept in touch. Sometimes she cooked him a Sunday lunch. Ben Scott, in his early seventies, had, like two of Mrs. Evans's sons, an interest in Arthurian legends.

The front of Heath House was framed by a stone archway spanning the drive. When Susan and Ben arrived, they could not drive under the arch. Their path was blocked by a large water butt. As on previous occasions, Susan de Stempel, or her children, were the cause of the obstruction. When the van stopped, Susan drove into view, put her head right up against the windscreen, and said, "Who are you, then? Are you the famous visitors? Let me tell you this – I'm the ex-wife. I suppose he's told you I'm mad, but I am no madder than him. What do you want to go there for? The upstairs rooms are full of fleas, and the kitchen is filthy. He'll be out at the end of the month, you know."

Mrs. Evans and Mr. Scott were, by now, well-accustomed to Susan de Stempel's attitude to Dale's visitors. She used to tell them the house was hers and that Dale had no right to invite people in. She was always appearing when people were there, trying to put them off visiting Dale again. This time, Dale apologized for his ex-wife's behaviour and gave his two guests a glass of sherry which, he assured them, would calm them down.

At about 8.45p.m., Mrs. Evans and Mr. Scott said their farewells to Simon Dale. It was now dark and raining. As they pulled out of the drive, they saw Susan de Stempel, framed in the headlights, standing there, staring at them. Ben Scott was later to recall that, as he was getting into the van outside Heath House that rainy night, he could see the bright gleam of an electric light, shining through the surrounding gloom, from a window of the little cottage adjoining the main house.

* * * * *

On the following Sunday, September 13th, Giselle Ward, who, like Jo Corfield, had been working as a secretary on Simon Dale's books, set off from her home at Kempton in Shropshire and drove across the Hereford border to Heath House. Dale had promised to phone Mrs. Ward to fix a time for her to come to see him on Sunday, but he had not done so. Unable to get a reply to her repeated telephone calls, Mrs. Ward had decided to see Dale anyway, hoping that by the time she reached Heath House, he would be available and perhaps want her to do some work. As Mrs. Ward drove to Hopton Heath, she could not help wondering if Simon was all right. She was concerned that he was living alone, almost completely blind, in that huge house. On arriving at Heath House, Mrs. Ward was unable to get Simon to come to the door. Her intuition told her that all was not as it should be. She telephoned for the police.

When access was gained to the house, Simon Dale was found lying dead in his kitchen. The smoke and heat inside the kitchen was choking and intense. The oven of the cooker was still in operation, as was one of the burners on the cooker hob. On top of it was a melted saucepan. Inside the cooker were the charred remains of a meal. Smoke poured from the oven. There were scorch marks on the ceiling from the burning hob. On a nearby work surface were some partly-skinned green beans. Beside them were five sherry glasses. One glass still had some sherry in it.

Simon Dale lay on his back with his eyes screwed up and his mouth open. His hands were on his chest; his finger clutched at his sweater. A pool of blood had flowed and spread from his head for a distance of over three feet. The pool had dried on the blue-and-white tiled floor of the kitchen. On a table was more blood. A broken basin lay on the floor nearby. In the connecting lobby, just outside the kitchen, blood was spattered across a white door.

Dale had injuries to his throat and neck. It looked as if he had been killed by an intruder as he was preparing his supper. Some kind of blunt instrument had been used. It was felt that Dale had probably been killed late in the evening of Friday the 11th. The groceries he bought that day at 5p.m. were left untouched. He seemed to have been struck on the head while he was standing just in front of the kitchen door. This door gave access to the outside of the house. Dale was seemingly pushed into the room from the door and then had collided with a heavy table, moving it slightly. After falling backwards, he would have struck the floor with his head. Death was caused by Dale choking in his own blood after his larynx had been fractured by a severe blow. There were five head wounds.

The fact that no fire had broken out in the kitchen was little short of miraculous. Detective-Inspector Matthews went to Forresters Hall to break the news to the baroness. Sophia answered the door. Susan was in the front room. Matthews told her, "I'm afraid there is a problem at Heath House." Before he could say any more, Susan interrupted him, saying in a rather offhand manner, "What's he done now, burnt the place down?"

The police believed that someone Dale knew must have gone into the house. A row had probably ensued and the visitor had struck Dale and killed him. There was nothing stolen from the house and Dale's wallet was undisturbed in his pocket. It contained about twenty-five pounds. There was the possibility that the killer was an intruder unknown to Dale. This seemed less probable, because it was well known that Dale was very careful to open the door only to people he knew. Nevertheless, the police announced that they were trying to trace an unknown male hitch-hiker seen in the neighbourhood on the day of the killing.

Meanwhile, the police were building up a picture of the background of the case. The baroness and her children were interviewed. Detective Inspector Matthews, with Constables Andrew McVicar and Robin Longmore, paid a visit to Susan de Stempel's cottage at Foresters Hall. Inside the cottage, they found a whole host of valuable furnishings and artefacts. On the floors, Persian rugs were piled on top of each other. There was valuable antique furniture. Oil paintings hung on the walls. The lighting was arranged upon elaborate chandeliers. It was clear that the baroness was a woman of considerable wealth.

One of Susan de Stempel's most distinct characteristics was her air of authority and self-assertion. As well as impressing those around her with her confident manner and powerful force of personality, Susan seemed to have no fear of dealing with figures of apparent authority and power. Other, more timid mortals might have acted more deferentially, but this, as the police soon discovered, was not the baroness's way. Knowing the history of ill-feeling between Susan and her ex-husband, she was immediately pencilled-in as a candidate for having killed him. Susan clearly had a strong motive for disposing of Dale, standing as he was, for years, in the way of her selling Heath House. There were plenty of people who knew that Susan and Simon's relationship was not simply hostile, but one of almost total war. If Susan was to be eliminated from police inquiries, she would first have to undergo an especially thorough investigation. Det. Inspector Matthews and his two constables were well aware of this situation when they first visited Forresters Hall Cottage.

"Heath House is mine," declared the baroness. "It was paid for out of a trust fund. You see, my husband came into the marriage with no money." She then complained about her poverty. Her complaint was not reflected in the apparent wealth and prosperity of her home surroundings at Forresters Hall. On the face of it, Susan did not seem to be poor. Outside the rented cottage were three vehicles – two brand new Peugeots and a Mercedes van. Nevertheless, Susan told Inspector Matthews, "My ex-husband has been squatting in my house for the last fourteen years. He has consistently refused to move out so I can sell it. My family and I have been forced to live on the breadline."

It gradually became plain that the policemen had not visited the baroness simply out of courtesy. As Inspector Matthew began to probe into Susan's relationship with the dead Simon, her manner and attitude became more dismissive. As if bringing the discussion to a close, she said, "Of course I wanted him out of that house, but I had no reason to murder him, if that is what you are trying to suggest. He was about to be moved out legally through the courts. Now, will that be all?"

Inspector Matthews tactfully withdrew. As he was leaving the cottage, he asked Susan if he might have a look inside the cars and the van parked outside. Inside one of the cars he found a poker. After examining it, Matthews said to Susan, "It's been wiped clean?"

"Of course it's clean," she said. "Why would I carry a dirty poker around?"

The police invited the baroness and her children to the police station. It was hoped they could be persuaded to answer questions and make formal statements. The police wanted to know where Susan and the children had been on the night of the killing. They believed it had happened on Friday September 11th. At Bishop's Castle police station, Susan de Stempel said that she and three of her children had been working at Heath House on the Friday afternoon. She said her daughter Sophia left for Docklow early, at 7p.m. Herself and Marcus, she said, stayed until 7.55p.m. and then went home.

Susan said that on the following day, Saturday the 12th – when presumably Simon Dale was already dead in his smoke-filled kitchen – she visited Heath House twice. Usually, whenever Susan and her children went to the house, they used as their base the adjoining

Heath House Cottage. There was then no absolute necessity for them to enter Dale's quarters at all, especially if they were working in the grounds. Susan told the police how, on her first visit to Heath House on the Saturday, she went with her son, Simon junior. He delivered a bench and left. She went into the walled garden to check the beehives. To prevent the hives blowing in the wind, Marcus had been putting bricks on top of them. She was going to saw up some trees for logs. Unfortunately, the chainsaw would not work, so she went back to Docklow. In the late afternoon, she said, she returned to Heath House with Simon junior. They took some ladders she had forgotten to take earlier. Susan put a brick on another hive. She did not, she said, go into the house at all that day.

On the Wednesday after the killing, young Sophia Wilberforce told the police she believed someone whom her father knew must have gone to Heath House, argued with him, and killed him. This was what the police already believed. When it was put to Sophia that her mother could have done it, she said, "Not my mother. Oh no, never my mother." Nevertheless, Susan de Stempel had not yet been eliminated from police inquiries. When a crowbar was found in a cupboard at Heath House Cottage, police opinion began to turn, from mere suspicion of the baroness, towards a search for evidence which might have to stand up against her in court.

* * * * *

Susan de Stempel's late father's sister was affectionately known as 'Aunt Puss'. She was Lady Margaret Illingworth, wife of the late Lord Illingworth of Denton, formerly Albert Illingworth. He served as a cabinet minister in Lloyd George's government, and was Postmaster-General in 1920. Lady Illingworth died in 1986. She spent her final days in a nursing home. Her body was cremated at Hereford at a cost of £380. After a year, the bill was still unpaid. Police visited the home where Lady Margaret died. The staff said that her family had wanted nothing more to do with her because, they said, she was an alcoholic. In fact, Lady Illingworth was suffering from senile dementia. Further inquiries revealed that at the time of her death, Lady Margaret seemingly had no money apart from her state pension. Her lack of money was, to say the least, surprising. Her husband had been extremely wealthy. Lady Margaret had for years been accustomed to live the life of a rich woman with ample funds.

An investigation was begun into Aunt Puss's finances, in an effort to discover how she had come to die in relative poverty. Her last will was made in 1984, two years before her death. Susan de Stempel was the sole beneficiary. Lady Illingworth's previous will, drawn up in 1975, made no mention at all of her niece Susan. Further inquiries revealed that during the final year of her life, massive withdrawals had been made from her bank accounts on a regular basis. The bulk of these withdrawals had been made from cash-dispensing machines using a bank card – a system which did not require Lady Margaret's signature of authorization. Moreover, her house and its contents had been sold – a process which would have realized a great deal of money. No trace of it could be found. It also came to light that a deposit of gold ingots in a private bank vault had vanished. The value of the gold bullion was estimated at no less than ten million pounds.

At 7.30am on Monday December 7th 1987, Susan de Stempel and two of her children were arrested on suspicion of conspiracy to defraud Lady Illingworth. Baron de Stempel was arrested in London on the fraud charge. Susan, Sophia and Marcus faced a second charge – of conspiring to murder Simon Dale.

On January 27th, the murder charges against Marcus and Sophia were dropped. The fraud charges against all four, including the baron, were allowed to stand. It was now alleged that Susan de Stempel planned and executed her husband's murder on her own. At the end of a committal hearing at Hereford Magistrates Court on April 6th, the baroness was sent for trial at Worcester Crown Court. She was granted legal aid.

* * * * *

The trial of Susan de Stempel for murder started at Worcester on Wednesday July 19th, 1989. By now, Susan had been in custody for over eighteen months while preparations for the trial were made. The delay in bringing the baroness to trial showed the extent to which the judicial process had been slowed down by the 1980s. A twelve-month wait for a prisoner on remand was by now commonplace.

Defence counsel at Susan's trial was Anthony Alridge Q.C. Leading for the Crown was Anthony Palmer Q.C. The judge was Mr. Justice Owen. The jury comprised eight men and four women. In his opening statement, Mr. Palmer described to the jury how, two years after her marriage to Dale, the baroness used her own money to buy Heath House. It was to be sold. Susan would then receive half of the proceeds immediately. The balance of the proceeds were then to be withheld, pending her application for maintenance.

Simon, of course, refused to leave Heath House. Mr. Palmer said, "Simon Dale was determined to stay in occupation, hoping he would be entitled to as much as fifty per cent from the sale."

After Susan's brief marriage to Baron Michael, said Palmer, Susan "set about with renewed vigour to sell Heath House, staying in Heath Cottage next door." It was clear, "said Mr. Palmer," that Dale was murdered on the evening of Friday September 11th, after he had put toad-in-the-hole into the oven." Mr. Palmer alleged that Susan had attacked Simon "as he unlocked his door to let her in on a day, as was her habit, she spent many hours tidying the garden." Two months after the killing, the keys of Heath House were handed over to her.

All the evidence against Susan was circumstantial. However, Mr. Palmer said to the jury, "The accused had every motive for wanting to see Dale off the face of the earth. She had a hatred for him that had built up over the years and festered." Of the murder, Mr. Palmer said, "This killing was the culmination, the end, the high point of a long history of bitter discord between this woman and her husband."

There had been talk before the trial about a hitch-hiker in the district at the time of the killing. An unidentified red Cavalier car was also seen parked and empty, late at night, in a lane near Heath House. However, the prosecution claimed that Dale would not have let a stranger into the house. Lynne Williams, his cleaner for two years, gave evidence that Dale was very security-conscious. He would never, she said, let anyone in he didn't know.

The Crown alleged that Susan killed Simon by striking him on the head and throat with a crowbar. Archaeologist Adrian Tindall described his encounter with Susan outside the house. He said she was holding in her hand "a crowbar or jemmy". A medical witness, Dr. Acland, said that the crowbar found at Heath House Cottage and exhibited in court, was likely to have caused Dale's wounds. However, when cross-examined by Mr. Alridge, Dr. Acland conceded that it was impossible to draw any firm conclusion about the size, shape, or weight of the instrument used by Dale's assailant. Dr. Acland admitted that he could not say the fatal weapon was definitely the crowbar.

* * * * *

On the second day of the trial, the court adjourned from Number One courtroom and reassembled in the old law library upstairs. A fifteen-minute police videotape was then shown on a large television screen, showing the murder scene with Dale's body still in place. As the tape was played, Susan de Stempel watched, impassive and unruffled.

Friday was given over to the forensic evidence. Testimony was heard from Home Office scientist Dr. Norman Weston. He presented to the jury the results of a detailed examination of Simon Dale's kitchen. Dr. Weston's evidence did little or nothing to improve the Crown's case. Dr. Weston said the blows to Dale's head, and the single blow to his throat, had occurred over a period of time. His view was that Dale had first received a heavy blow across the throat, pivoted towards the kitchen door, and fallen backwards, so that his head struck the floor with some force. There could, said Dr. Weston, have been a struggle near the refrigerator. Bloodstains were present on a plant stand, chair legs, a skirting board, and the back of a door. Turquoise carpet fibres were found in the kitchen. When cross-examined by Mr. Alridge, Dr. Weston confessed that neither the turquoise fibres, nor red fibres found on the frame and jamb of the door, matched anything belonging to Dale or to Susan. No blood was found on Susan's shoes or on her gumboots. Mr. Alridge put this question to Dr. Weston:

"The upshot of all this is that you could find absolutely nothing to connect the baroness with the scene of the crime?"

"I found no positive connection," said Dr. Weston.

* * * * *

Monday July 24th was devoted to evidence from the police. In cross-examination, Detective-Inspector Derek Matthews admitted that at one stage in the inquiry, the police had been looking for a man, perhaps a hitch-hiker, seen twice on the road outside Heath House on the night of the murder. The man had long hair and wore an anorak. In spite of public appeals, this man had not been traced. Detective-Constable Michael O'Keefe testified about alleged statements made to the police by the baroness. He said that Susan described how, once during the summer 1987, she had seen a young woman banging on the door of Heath House, shouting "Let me in, you bastard!" The woman, whom Susan assumed was looking for Simon, got no answer and left.

The picture painted of Simon Dale by Susan's statements to O'Keefe did not fit in with the views of his friends. They found Dale a cheerful, kindly and generous man, if a little eccentric. Susan's comments implied that Dale had the nature of a violent lunatic. Susan claimed that after the young woman left Dale's door, Susan saw Dale through a window. He was, she said, "wearing lipstick, tatty trousers and ladies' high-heeled shoes. He was making faces at himself in a mirror, imitating the woman." Susan also told O'Keefe she had seen Dale wearing high-heeled shoes on numerous occasions. He had, she said, asked her to put ladies' face cream on him. She said he had been interested in unnatural sex. When she refused, he said she was inhibited. Susan said that Dale's mood swings, after the birth of Marcus, led her to fear him.

Susan made the remarkable allegation that Dale threatened to kill her. She claimed that Dale told her he had dug a grave for her, under a yew tree in the garden of Heath House. In a second allegation, Susan said Dale intended to kill her and throw her body down a lead mine, between Bishop's Castle and Shrewsbury. She had given the map reference of the mine to her solicitor so that it could be located and searched in the event of her disappearance. Dale, she said, became "increasingly sullen and violent" during their marriage. He became "obsessed with the working of the human eye and wrote letters on the subject to surgeons and hospitals." His attitude, she said, was "belligerent and arrogant." Susan said she feared for herself and for her children. She told O'Keefe that on the night of the murder, she was at home watching television.

* * * * *

On the fifth day of the trial, Tuesday July 25th, Mr. Alridge opened the defence case. He said the picture of the baroness as "a raving loon", determined to kill Dale, would be dispelled. He announced that she would be going into the witness box and would deny the murder. Mr. Alridge told the jury, "I anticipate I will be able to submit that she is not guilty of the crime."

Mr. Alrdige said that when Dale refused to move out of Heath House, Susan had "left the situation of the house to drift." She had children to bring up, making money for a legal action against Dale difficult to find. After her divorce from the baron in 1986, Susan renewed her interest in trying to sell the house. Mr. Alridge referred to solicitors' letters about the attempt to get Heath House valued and sold. In a letter to her solicitor on September 9th 1987, only two days before Dale's death, Susan referred to Dale as 'his highness sitting in his deckchair." The letter urged the solicitor to 'gird his loins' for action against Dale. Clearly, claimed Mr. Alridge, Susan was doing all she could to legally remove Dale from the house. Mr. Alridge reminded the jury that Susan had returned to the house the day after Dale was believed to have been killed. The defence council said, "Somebody with murder on their mind would hardly go round advertising their presence." There remained, he said, unanswered questions about the hitch-hiker and the red car. After pointing out that on the evening of the killing, Susan went home to Forresters Hall and watched *Miss Marple* on TV, in an attempt to lighten the proceedings, Mr. Alridge said, "Perhaps the baroness could do with Miss Marple's assistance now."

On the sixth day of her trial, Susan de Stempel entered the witness box. She wore a blue floral-patterned skirt, a high-necked white blouse and a light-blue jacket. In response to Mr. Alridge's first few questions, the baroness spoke very quietly. Mr. Justice Owen directed her to sit next to him, in a position from which the jury could hear her more distinctly. When her voice grew louder, she was moved back into the witness box. Susan told the jury how Simon had got into the habit of using physical violence towards her. She said he had damaged her back. He had, she said, struck her so often at the base of her spine that she now had a permanent injury. They had no social life because Simon would shut himself away for days on end. Simon was, said Susan, quite adamant that he would not move out of Heath House. She said, "I wanted the house to be sold very much, but I was thwarted by Simon. He would make excuses to break agreements with people coming to view the house. This went on for years. He used to say it was his house and that I had nothing to do with it. That was why I told his visitors not to go into the house."

Susan described how Simon had "a deep obsession" that Heath House was the seat of King Arthur. He wanted to turn the house into a national centre for archaeology, the biggest site in the country. Susan and some of her children started going to the house to renovate it, in the hope that Simon would eventually leave and it could be sold. Before March 1986, when she and the children began to work on the house, nothing whatever had been done to it. On Susan's first visits, Simon used to let her in through the front door. Later, he became "nasty" and refused her entry. She said she used to get in through the cloakroom window.

"He was abusive," said Susan. "He told me to get out all the time. I was frightened of him."

Mr. Alridge mentioned a visit from the police on the Sunday night after the discovery of Simon's body. This visit led to the police allegation that Susan showed no reaction when she heard Simon was dead. The reason, they said, for Susan's coolness, was that she, having killed him herself, already knew he was dead. Susan said, "I used to be sat in a chair for ten minutes. When I was six I had to sit absolutely still and not bat an eyelid. I was always brought up not to show emotion." She said she did not ask how Simon died because, "I assumed that if they wanted to tell me, they would do so. The police adopted such an extraordinarily furtive manner that I thought there was no point in asking anybody anything."

At the end of his examination, Mr. Alridge asked the baroness, "Were you the person who went into the lobby and struck Simon Dale with a weapon, causing his death?"

"No, I was not," she said firmly. "That is utter nonsense. I saw Simon Dale walk through the rocking-horse room in the house, continue along the glass passageway, check the front door, and walk across the hall. That was the last time I saw him. My son and I then went back to the cottage, collected some things, and drove back home to Docklow."

* * * * *

A memorable aspect of Susan de Stempel's trial for murder was the way she responded to Mr. Palmer's questions during cross-examination. Her strength of character in dealing with the Crown counsel was remarkable. Not only did the baroness answer Palmer with confidence, she made it quite clear that she did not take kindly to having her honesty put into question, least of all by a barrister like Mr. Palmer. Susan put herself forward as Palmer's intellectual equal and, as the questioning proceeded, she adopted an attitude of superiority over him. She refused to be browbeaten. She dismissed Palmer's suggestions of guilt as if she were reproving an erring servant or some other kind of underling. Susan de Stempel's performance was a remarkable tour-de-force. It could not have failed to have strongly impressed itself on the minds of the jury. The cross-examination began on the Wednesday afternoon. It was not over until the lunch adjournment on the Thursday.

Mr. Palmer began by referring to Susan's dispute with Simon. He asked her, "The object was to watch his every move and try to outwit him? There was a war of wills between you, was there not?"

"Yes," replied Susan. "I think you are right on that."

"Would you agree that you were both obsessed characters?"

"No," she replied.

"You had an obsession he was going to stay there as long as he could?"

"No, I was not obsessed by it. I was just fed up with the situation."

"Would you regard yourself as a strong-willed woman?"

"Yes."

"There was not a glimmer of love between you by 1983?"

"Yes."

"He had treated you and your children badly?"

"Yes."

"The love had gone out of the marriage by 1962?"

"Yes, earlier than that," she said.

"Do you think he was mad?" asked Palmer.

"Yes."

"Since when?"

"About a year and a half before I started the divorce proceedings."

Again and again, Palmer suggested that Susan had been angry with Simon on the night of his death. Eventually, the baroness said to Palmer,

"Bollocks, Mr. Palmer, that's absolute nonsense."

Palmer continued to push. Again he suggested Susan was angry that Dale would not vacate Heath House. She replied,

"It was just a great nuisance and a waste of my energy, but I was not bitter."

"You hated him, didn't you?"

"No, I did not. I was exasperated by him, but I did not hate him. I did not feel anything particularly."

Mr. Palmer said: "The evidence is that on Friday night you were angry?"

Susan replied, "I suggest the evidence is wrong. That is the truth."

Still Mr. Palmer persisted. Susan replied,

"I wish you would get it into your head, Mr. Palmer, that I was not angry." Referring to the police videotape, shown at the trial, of Dale's body at the scene of the crime, Palmer asked Susan why she appeared to display no reaction while watching it. In a faint voice, she said, "I was going to be sick." Palmer said Simon's death had removed his irritation from Susan. She said, "It has been nothing but a problem ever since."

The baroness admitted she disliked Simon's friends. She said, "There was this woman, Mrs. Bowater. She was the bane of my life. She used to insist on taking visitors around my house when it was in the most appalling state. I am all for visitors going round a house when it is clean and tidy, but not when it is a complete slum. I think it sets an awfully bad example of how people live."

Mr. Palmer turned his attention to the events of September 11th. This date happened to be the anniversary of her marriage to the baron. Palmer said, "I do not suggest you planned to kill Mr. Dale over any length of time. I am suggesting that on Friday September 11th, things were so building up in your mind that you went to have a confrontation with him and that is when you killed him. You were very pent up indeed, weren't you?"

"No," she replied. "At no time that day was I pent up."

"You were sad when your marriage to the Baron ended. You loved him very much, didn't you?"

In a whisper, Susan replied, "Yes."

"On September 11th 1987, no doubt you thought back to marriage with the Baron, exactly three years before?"

"No. I didn't realise it was my wedding anniversary."

Pressing on, Palmer continued the accusation, "You realized that with two people each regarding the other as mad, one was going to be injured by the other. That was why you carried this jemmy, wasn't it?"

"No, it was not. He was more and more determined never to get out. I regarded him as becoming more and more mad than I had regarded him in the past."

Explaining why she hung back at Heath Cottage until Dale's visitors had left, Susan said, "On the Friday night, I was waiting for the visitors to go, but not so I would know that Simon Dale was alone. I was waiting for them to go so I could walk through the arch without interrupting their conversation. Marcus and I stayed out there. We were just going for a little walk to admire the work we had done on the house."

Mr. Palmer said, "There was no reason for you to be there, save to watch Mr. Dale, to make sure he was alone in the house. Marcus went across to feed a colony of bees; do you remember that?"

"No," replied Susan. "I don't remember it."

At the close of the Wednesday session, Mr. Palmer asked Susan, "You went there on Saturday, because you knew Simon Dale was dead, didn't you?"

"No, I didn't."

"You were walking with impunity past the house, and to the walled garden, breaking the habit of several months?"

"He would not have known I was there."

"You twice went to that house when he lay dead on the Saturday morning?"

"Yes, but I think you forget I am a woman. This is a case against a woman, brought by men."

* * * * *

It was on the Thursday morning that Mr. Palmer really began to come out second best in his cross-examination of Baroness de Stempel. He suggested that after Susan's first police interview on the Monday, she discussed with Marcus and Sophia what they had told the police. She had then changed her statement accordingly. As a result, claimed Mr. Palmer, there were inconsistencies about the route she walked in the garden on the Saturday, when she put the brick on the beehive. Susan would have none of this. She said to the prosecuting counsel,

"There seems to be no inconsistency, no matter how much you twist it. Now stop it, Mr. Palmer!"

"Will you please confine yourself to the question?"

"When I was interviewed, my children were interviewed at the same time and were taken off to different parts of the country. When we got back in the morning, we did not speak to each other because we were just too tired."

"You added these facts between Monday and Wednesday, didn't you?"

"So what?" she said.

"I suggest you went back to the house to see what had been found out and to take the case opener back?"

The baroness said, "You can suggest that until you are blue in the face, but it is not true."

This reply seemed to rattle Palmer slightly. He said, "You are very cunning and clever at being able to say what suits you, aren't you?"

"No."

"What you blurted out, about Dale burning down the house, was a self-conscious thought about the oven and the cooker. You thought the house had caught fire, didn't you?"

"I had no such thought," she replied.

"It would have taken you only a moment to get the jemmy and go round to Dale's kitchen door for a verbal confrontation. You realized the leopard would never change his spots and he would never leave?"

Susan said, "It doesn't make sense for me to have killed him. The courts were going to get him out cleanly and legally. I believed it for the first time in fifteen years."

"Having watched the visitors go and seeing him lock up, you used that weapon on him, didn't you?"

"No, I didn't. As far as I can remember, I was with Marcus the whole time after the visitors left."

"Has Marcus anything to hide about this matter?"

"Certainly not. He was given a grilling for hours on end. If he had anything to hide, the police would have discovered it. I know perfectly well none of my children would have hidden anything if I had done it. They would not have approved of that. They were grilled for hours and hours. Never once did they incriminate me."

She went on, "This was a crime I had nothing to do with, and I didn't even have a motive. There was no point in killing him when the courts were going to get him out. I agree I had the opportunity and the weapon, but there are millions of jemmies in the world. Why should I have killed him? Think of all the hassle I have had since. It would have been much easier to have left the courts to deal with him. I was amazed when they arrested me because I knew I had not done it."

* * * * *

It was the prosecution's claim that Susan killed Simon, either to remove him from her house, or out of frustration at being unable, after many long years, to evict him. The defence argument was that legal proceedings to remove Dale were about to bear fruit. Susan would therefore have no good reason for killing him. Evidence was heard from Susan's solicitors, a Mr. Sax of Gray's Inn Road, London. He said that Susan wanted Dale removed from her house, "painlessly, cheaply, and above all, speedily." Mr. Sax said she wrote to him in February 1985 about her attempts to get Dale out of Heath House. In her letter, she said she was living in poverty, "starved, almost destitute, disillusioned." Mr. Sax, in evidence, said he had represented

Susan since 1973. He never had another client who had written the way she had done. Mr. Sax said, "In a very sorry matter, her wit was her gleam of hope." He believed that "the end was in sight" for Susan's legal proceedings at the time Simon was killed.

In his final remarks to the jury, Mr. Palmer said that on the Friday night, Susan waited for Simon's visitors to go. She then got the crowbar and went round to confront him. Mr. Palmer said,

"This was not a premeditated murder. It happened like a domestic killing. There was a build-up and then an explosion. There was a loveless marriage, a settlement Simon Dale would not stick to, and a valuable house. This was the background for total war. She agreed with me that this was war, and in war, someone is likely to get injured and killed. She knew the leopard would never change its spots. There was no other visitor that night. The only visitor Dale received was his ex-wife. After Dale's killing, she was back in possession of her own house."

Answering for the defence, Mr. Alridge stressed that there was insufficient evidence against Susan to warrant a conviction. He said,

"If you have an ex-wife, whose husband has been killed, and she has been advertising to all and sundry her animosity towards him, a wife who stands to gain from his death, it is all too easy to look no further."

The mysterious hitch-hiker had never been located. There was, said Mr. Alridge, "no reason to suggest that, simply because Dale opened his door, the caller was someone he knew." The jemmy, said Alridge, was not the only kind of object that could have caused Dale's wounds.

Mr. Alridge rightly pointed out that most of the evidence was given to the police by the baroness herself. There was just no scientific nor forensic evidence to connect Susan with the crime. Mr. Alridge said,

"Only one trace of blood and her story would have been exposed." He reminded the jury that she had been, "Grilled by the police and cross-examined at length by Mr. Palmer. Not once has she given herself away."

Mr. Justice Owen began to deliver his summing-up on the second Monday of the trial. He completed it the next morning. The judge told the jury,

"She did not always hate her husband, but there had been no love between them for twenty-five years. She says she thought he was mad. How much further it went, you will have to judge. Although Simon Dale had thwarted her wishes for fourteen years, there was a procedure, which might or might not have been successful, to lead to the eviction of Dale from that House. It must have ultimately been successful because nobody can go on defying the law for ever."

Did the baroness, after continual provocation from Dale, lose her self-control and attack him? The judge said,

"You will have to consider if Dale's conduct would have caused a reasonable person to lose control. You have heard that Dale was an awkward man who was violent towards the baroness and her children."

Perhaps, because of his interest in the legends of King Arthur and his belief in the house as a site of archaeological interest, the jury, said the judge, might consider Dale a "crank".

* * * * *

When Mr. Justice Owen resumed his summing-up on the Tuesday morning, he said, "The prosecution case is that the baroness knew it was the anniversary of her wedding to the baron, whom she still loved. When she considered Simon Dale, who was still living in the house, it was too much for her. They say it had a significance in her mind that was far deeper. It is a suggestion, but I say to you that suggestions are not evidence. You have to ask what her true feeling were at the time, for Simon Dale. She says she did not hate him and you have to bear in mind whether that is a true answer."

The judge drew the jury's attention to three points in the prosecution case. The first was that Dr. Acland had said that, in his opinion, the crowbar was likely to have caused Dale's fatal wounds. The doctor also said that from the limited severity of the wounds it seemed to him that a woman had been yielding the crowbar. The third point was the suggestion by the prosecution that there was blood on Susan's clothes at first and she burned them to destroy the incriminating evidence. It was known that a chimney flue at her cottage at Docklow was cleaned out and swept soon after the killing. The prosecution said this was done to clear away any possible traces of the clothing she had burned in the fire.

Mr. Justice Owen said the jury might think it would be wrong to attach significance to the baroness's use of the word "bollocks" while under cross-examination. He said, "Words which our grandfathers would not have used are today used in mixed company."

* * * * *

In mid-afternoon on August 1st 1989, after deliberating for nearly four hours, the jury returned a verdict of not guilty of murder and not guilty of manslaughter. Susan de Stempel displayed little emotion when the verdicts were announced. She simply stared blankly ahead. The court-room, however, erupted. The baroness's children, Marcus and Sophia, who were in the public gallery, reacted with unrestrained joy. There were shouts of delight and a good deal of applause. Someone threw a small posy of flowers into the dock form the public gallery. The baroness stooped and picked it up. She was escorted to the rear of the building where her children were waiting for her.

Susan de Stempel did not regain her freedom that day. As she stepped from the dock, acquitted of killing Simon Dale, Inspector Michael Cowley took her by the arm. He reminded her that she was still under arrest, for, amongst other things, forging Lady Illingworth's will.

On April 21 1990, Susan, with Marcus, Sophia, and the Baron de Stempel, stood in the dock at Birmingham Crown Court, convicted and awaiting sentence for forgery and theft. Susan had pleaded guilty to five theft and two forgery charges. Marcus, Sophia and the baron had pleaded not guilty to the charges against them. The judge told the baron, "Stripped of your airs and flowery language, you are undoubtedly a conman." The baroness was sentenced to seven years imprisonment. Marcus was sentenced to 18 months, Sophia 30 months and de Stempel four years.

Over two years later, in August 1992, a High Court injunction granted the return to Lady Illingworth's estate of a large number of her possessions. Assets of the baroness and her family, to the value of twelve million pounds, were frozen. Ten million of this was said to represent the value of gold bars, allegedly missing from Lady Illingworth's private bank deposit.

Chapter 10

The Shirley Valentine Affair

It was September 1991. Carolyn Taylor had just had a very bad year. Within the previous twelve months, Mrs. Taylor had suffered several bereavements. She had lost her mother, her best friend, her favourite horse and, in December 1990, she lost her husband Harry. After a long illness, Mr. Taylor had died of cancer. Carolyn was left with three children and a large £750,000 detached mansion on an isolated estate at South Holmwood, near Dorking in Surrey. The house was called *Taresmocks*.

That September, the painful memories of the previous months had at last begun to ease a little for Carolyn Taylor. She flew away, with her 25-year-old daughter, Samantha, for a holiday in Corsica. Like the heroine of Willy Russell's play *Shirley Valentine*, 53-year-old Carolyn Taylor was to find romance with an islander in the Mediterranean summer sunshine.

Driving along one day in Corsica, Carolyn and Samantha spotted a restaurant by a beach. Mother and daughter decided to stop for a drink. After a few minutes, Carolyn's attention settled on a man sitting at a nearby table. He was looking at her and smiling. The man had just landed his aircraft on the beach in front of the restaurant. His name was Gaeton Beissy. He flew pleasure trips for tourists in his two-seater plane, up and down the beach and out over the warm blue sea. When Carolyn's eyes locked into his eyes, she found herself falling under his spell.

From that day on, Carolyn and the 54-year-old Beissy were together every day. It was as if Carolyn had been given a new lease of life by meeting Beissy. On a post card home to a friend, she wrote, "I have met this wonderful man with sexy blue eyes." The couple had, almost instantly, and irrevocably, fallen in love with each other.

Carolyn's late husband, Harry Taylor, was a self-made millionaire, a fashion and property tycoon. After his death, *Taresmocks* became Carolyn's house. As well as the house, she owned a number of horses, several dogs, and a Jaguar convertible. In contrast, Gaeton Beissy was not a man of means, He lived in a bedsit over the restaurant where he and Carolyn first met. His sole asset was his aircraft, flying to and fro each day above the island when anyone wanted to hire him.

When the holiday was over, Carolyn and Samantha returned to Surrey. However, Carolyn continued to keep in touch with Beissy. She spoke to him on the telephone each day. After a fortnight or so, Carolyn flew out to Toulouse to meet his family. She stayed there for a week. Soon afterwards, at about the end of October 1991, Beissy came to England. He was supposed to stay with Carolyn at *Taresmocks* for a fortnight. In fact, he stayed on permanently. It was only when Beissy arrived at Carolyn's home that it dawned on him that she was a rich woman. Until them he had known nothing of her wealth.

Carolyn and Beissy were not alone at *Taresmocks*. Carolyn's younger son Mark also lived in the house. Samantha lived with a boyfriend in a bungalow in the grounds of the main house. Gaeton Beissy settled into a domestic routine. He cooked, baked bread, cleaned the house, and mended the kitchen cabinets. Carolyn was eager to introduce him to her friends, but because Beissy had great difficulty understanding English, whenever he and Carolyn mixed socially, they were at a considerable disadvantage. When friends came to visit Carolyn, the evenings were rather stilted and dull affairs. Although Carolyn was not a very social person, she and Beissy both gave and were received at a number of dinner parties. These, however, soon fizzled out.

As time passed, Beissy began to be steadily more possessive of Carolyn. It got to the stage where he would hardly let her out of his sight. If she said she was going out to visit someone, Beissy would hide and sulk, sitting silently for what seemed an age. It was as if he resented Carolyn having to be apart from him, even for a few hours. The only way she could shake him out of a sulking fit was to make a great fuss of him and be more pleasant to him than usual. Perhaps it was just Beissy's possessive nature that made him behave that way. Possibly he felt lost and alone when she was away from him. Beissy's ignorance of English may have added to his sense of isolation. Whatever the reason, Beissy's clinging behaviour gradually became more pronounced and, as time went on, took on a more aggressive character.

* * * * *

A large portion of Carolyn Taylor's life revolved around her horses.

One day each week, she used to go to Goodwood. Once, when Carolyn arrived back at *Taresmocks* from one of her Goodwood trips, Beissy ran up to her car, grabbed hold of her, and marched her into the house.

There was no doubt that Gaeton Beissy was devoted to Carolyn Taylor. During his time at her house, he treated her like a queen. In the summer of 1992, Carolyn fell off a horse and broke a leg. While she was recovering at home, Beissy was kindness itself to her. He nursed her and cooked for her. He even carried her into her bath and washed her hair. Although Carolyn was at first flattered and pleased by the attention she was receiving from Beissy, she found herself becoming smothered and stifled by his constant acts of kindness. In truth, she was not used to such treatment from a man. Certainly her late husband had not fussed over her so much. The situation began to worry her, and the worry did not go away.

It seems that Beissy believed that when Carolyn had sold *Taresmocks*, as he knew she intended to do, then the two of them would settle in a cottage somewhere, to live together in private bliss. This was not Carolyn's intention at all, however. She was looking for a property big enough to house both herself and her immediate family. Samantha was by now expecting a baby. Carolyn wanted Samantha, her boyfriend and the baby to live with her, as well as Mark and her older son Craig. When Beissy found out about Carolyn's plans for a family house he was shocked and upset. He possibly began to feel that Carolyn was not really as interested in him as she had once been. He possibly began to feel even more insecure than he usually did.

Matters came to a head in the middle of July 1992. After a contentious and disagreeable weekend, Carolyn and Beissy slept in separate rooms on the night of Monday the 13th. They stayed in separate quarters the following night too. Before Carolyn went to bed on the Tuesday, the 14th, she told Samantha, "Sam, I don't know what to do with this man. He wants everyone else to just disappear."

Events which took place on the morning of Wednesday July 15th would later be a matter of dispute between prosecution and the defence. According to Mark and Samantha Taylor, an argument between their mother and Gaeton Beissy resulted in Mrs. Taylor being stabbed to death by the Frenchman. Beissy was later to deny responsibility for Carolyn's death. He would say that Mark Taylor killed his own mother. Inquiries, led by Detective-Inspector John Erskine, resulted in Beissy being charged with Carolyn Taylor's murder. He appeared before magistrates at Dorking on Monday, July 20th 1992. On Monday, February 8th 1993, Beissy faced trial by jury at the Old Bailey.

* * * * *

Beissy, assisted by a French interpreter, pleaded not guilty to the murder charge. He also entered a not guilty plea to a charge of attempting to murder Mark Taylor. The events leading up to the killing, based on information provided by the Taylor children, were presented to the jury by prosecuting counsel, Mr. Boal. He alleged that at about 6.30am on the morning of July 15th 1992, Mark Taylor was awoken by the sound of his mother screaming. He rushed out of his bedroom and went downstairs to investigate. There, he found his mother in an hysterical state. She was naked and covered in blood. She had been punched in the face by Beissy.

In evidence, Mark Taylor testified that his mother said to him, "Look what he has done! He has hit me with his fists. What am I going to do?" Mark said he washed her face and brought her a T-shirt to put on. Mark wanted to call the doctor, but Carolyn was against it. However, Mark insisted, and telephoned. The lady doctor's husband answered and went to wake his wife. The time, according to the doctor's husband, was 6.40am. The events in the kitchen at *Taresmocks* in the next five minutes were destined to instil uncertainty and confusion in the minds of the jury.

According to the prosecution, and in the words of Mr. Boal, "What happened, in the event, was dreadfully and fatefully simple." It was alleged that Beissy, who had by now entered the kitchen, lunged at Carolyn with a knife he had been hiding behind his back. The knife went through her heart, causing a seven-inch wound. A second stab went through her stomach. According to Mark Taylor, Beissy looked at him and said, "Your mother has been sleeping around."

Mark Taylor said that as he was on the telephone to the doctor, Beissy made a lunge at him with the knife. He missed. Escaping through a window, Mark said he ran to Samantha's bungalow and telephoned the police from there. The 999 call was logged at 6.45am.

Gaeton Beissy had a very different story to tell. In evidence, he gave his own version of how Carolyn had been killed. Beissy said Mark Taylor stabbed her to death. Through an interpreter, Beissy said that on the morning of the killing, he and Mrs. Taylor were woken at 6am by Mark Taylor. Beissy said Carolyn told him to leave the bedroom while she talked to Mark. Later, said Beissy, he found mother and son in the kitchen. Mark was on the telephone to the doctor. Questioned by his defence counsel, Rosina Hare Q.C., Beissy said, "Her face seemed to have been battered by punches. She was trying to push Mark back. There was a knife by the telephone. Mark picked the knife up. At the same time, Carolyn screamed. She turned herself around and held on to the breakfast bar. She took two steps towards me. I held her behind her head and had my other hand round her body. Then I helped her to collapse."

The jury were presented with two versions of Carolyn's death. The prosecution said that while Mark was on the phone to the doctor, Beissy came into the kitchen and stabbed Carolyn. Mark then fled to get help. The defence contended that Mark put the phone down, picked up a knife, tried to attack Beissy, but stabbed his mother instead. He then fled through the window.

The lady doctor said that when, after a few minutes, she came to the phone, she could overhear a woman's voice. The woman wailed, "Look what you've done!"

For Beissy, Rosina Hare insisted that Mark stabbed his mother during an argument over his father's legacy. She claimed it was Carolyn herself saying, "Look what you've done," to Mark, after he stabbed her. For the prosecution, Samantha Taylor said it was she who wailed out these words, to Beissy, when she walked into the kitchen and saw her mother lying bleeding on the floor. It was she whom the lady doctor overheard through the telephone.

A few minutes after they received Mark's call from Samantha's bungalow, the police arrived at *Taresmocks*. Mark Taylor was taken away for questioning. When the police arrived, Beissy was nowhere to be found. A hunt for him was set in motion. A police helicopter was used to help locate the missing Frenchman.

Later that morning, soon after 10am, Beissy was found. He was in a nearby field, lying at the foot of a tree. He was in an alcoholic stupor. Beside Beissy were two near-empty bottles. One contained some port and the other some whisky. A large-bladed, bloodstained kitchen knife was also near his unconscious form. He was removed to hospital to receive treatment for alcohol poisoning.

When interviewed by police, Beissy chose not to answer their questions. He simply said that he was "very sad". According to prosecuting counsel Boal, three days later, while in custody, Beissy tried to kill himself, cutting his wrists and arms with glass from a pair of his spectacles. At the trial, Mr. Boal told the jury, "The Crown suggests he did that because he knew he had killed his lover." Beissy's counsel, Rosina Hare, defended him by accusing Mark Taylor of the murder. In cross-examination, Hare put it to Taylor that he had indeed killed his mother and falsely accused her lover. Taylor, a self-employed mechanic, denied the accusations. Hare suggested that Mark killed Carolyn as she tried to stop him attacking Beissy, the man he believed was, by marrying his mother, going to deprive him of his father's legacy.

Mark Taylor said, "Gaeton loved her very dearly. He was very considerate towards her. My own personal understanding was that he was very possessive of her." Taylor said his inheritance was of no interest to him. He admitted that he resented his mother's giving Beissy his father's signet ring but, he said, "My principal concern in the relationship was my mother's happiness and welfare." Taylor also said he was unaware he would be unable to inherit any of his father's estate until his thirty-fifth birthday.

After a nine-day trial, the jury were unable to reach a verdict. A retrial was ordered. Less than two months later, a second trial of Gaeton Beissy was held at the Old Bailey. After hearing evidence for two weeks, and after deliberating a verdict for nearly ten hours, the jury at the second trial told the judge that they too were unable to agree on a verdict.

Having now been tried twice, and having been in custody for almost a year, Beissy was discharged from police custody.

After the second trial, the judge, Robert Lymbery, said the sooner Beissy left the country the better, for his own benefit. Beissy's solicitor, Richard Dymont, said of his client, "He is very satisfied with British justice." When Beissy heard he was to be given his freedom, he wiped tears from his eyes and said, "I am still the loser because I no longer have the woman I love."

Surrey police announced that they would not be looking to charge anyone else with the crime. As far as they were concerned, the case was closed.

It had been alleged that Gaeton Beissy killed Carolyn Taylor "out of old fashioned jealousy". Beissy said Mark Taylor had tried to kill him, but had accidentally killed Carolyn instead. At neither trial was any evidence given to support the theory that Beissy had a violent disposition, apart, of course, from the alleged events of July 15th 1992. After Beissy's release, it came to light that, in 1989, his ex-wife Helene Barbaglia, at St. Livrade-sur-Lotte, reported Beissy to the authorities for assault and battery. Although Beissy was questioned over the accusations, no charges were levelled against him. The police considered it a private domestic matter.

Beissy returned to France. A few days later, after the second trial, Samantha Taylor said to a reporter, "It is just a feeling of nothingness, an empty space. It remains a story without an end." The course of justice had failed to produce a clear decision on Beissy's innocence or guilt.

Also of Interest:

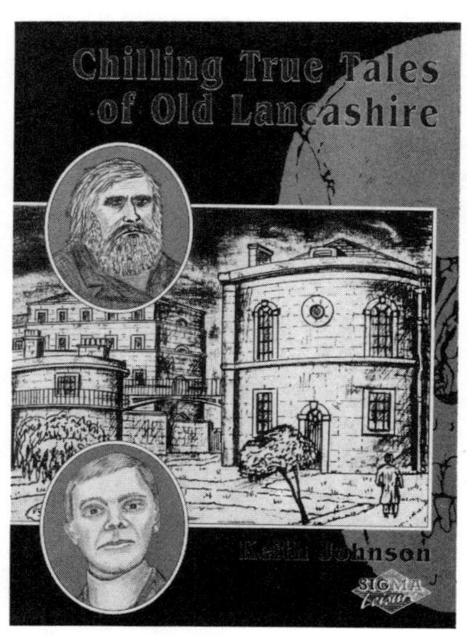

CHILLING TRUE TALES OF OLD LANCASHIRE

Keith Johnson's collection of tales give a fascinating insight into the county's past. This is a journey back to the days of toil, torment, trouble and tragedy. When the workhouse loomed large, the cotton trade flourished and coal held a place of honour; widows and orphans begged for bread and drunkenness led to degradation. Here are the pick of the headline-making stories of murder, mystery, mayhem and mortality. Judge for yourself the trials and tribulations of a bygone age. *£6.95*

CHILLING TRUE TALES OF OLD LONDON

This collection of stories from historian Keith Johnson gives a fascinating insight into London's past when villainy and vice abounded. The capital city had capital crimes to match. No one was safe from the evil doer. Justice was severe and the law in its harshness terrified all who fell foul of it. "Chilling True Tales of Old London" affords the opportunity to relive the anguish and the anxiety behind the newspaper headlines of nineteenth century London. *£6.95*

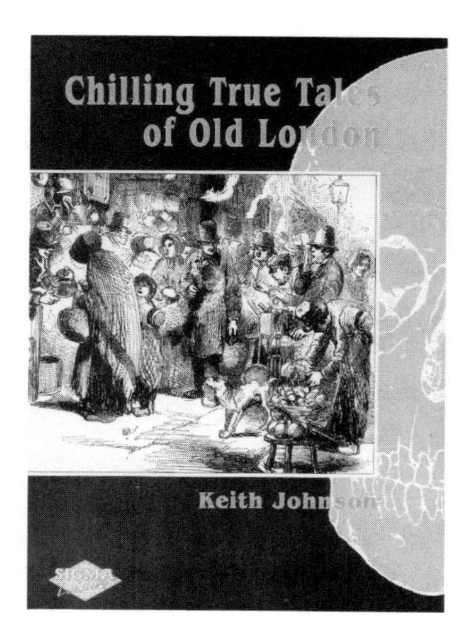

LADY POISONERS

DAVID BECKETT

LADY POISONERS

"If I were your wife, I would put poison in your coffee," said Nancy Astor. "If I were your husband, I'd drink it," said Winston Churchill. David Beckett is a well-established crime writer and this book is his follow-up to "The Ones That Got Away?" It explores the many and varied ways that lady poisoners have killed, or attempted to kill, their victims. A dozen of the most infamous cases from all over the country are examined, spanning almost a century of crime. *(Autumn 1997)* *£6.95*

GREAT BRITISH SCANDALS

The eleven stories in this book contain their full measure of bribery, sex, corruption and injustice! Classic scandals of yester-year are recalled in lurid detail as all is exposed to public view. Stories include the Prince of Wales Baccarat Scandal, Colonel Baker's misbehaviour in a railway carriage and the 'Honours for Sale' racket. The Prostitutes' Padre rubs shoulders with Oscar Wilde and Queen Victoria's friendship with John Brown is put under David Beckett's microscope.

(Autumn 1997) *£6.95*